The Heritage of American Catholicism

A TWENTY-EIGHT-VOLUME SERIES DOCUMENTING THE HISTORY
OF AMERICA'S LARGEST RELIGIOUS DENOMINATION

EDITED BY

Timothy Walch

ASSOCIATE EDITOR
U.S. Catholic Historian

A Garland Series

Thomas W. Turner, Howard University Student

Black Catholic Protest and the Federated Colored Catholics 1917-1933

THREE PERSPECTIVES ON RACIAL JUSTICE

MARILYN WENZKE NICKELS

Garland Publishing, Inc.
New York & London
1988

Copyright © 1988 by Marilyn Wenzke Nickels
All rights reserved

The plates are reproduced from photographs in the Thomas W. Turner Collection at the Moorland-Spingarn Research Center of Howard University, Washington D. C. The author is grateful to the Moorland-Spingarn Research Center, and Ms. Lois Broadus, who donated the collection, for permission to publish these pictures.

Library of Congress Cataloging-in-Publication Data

Nickels, Marilyn Wenzke.
  Black Catholic protest and the Federated Colored Catholics, 1917-1933.
  (The Heritage of American Catholicism)
  Originally presented as the author's thesis (Ph. D.--Catholic University of America, 1975).
  Bibliography: p.
  1. Federated Colored Catholics of the United States--History. 2. Afro-American Catholics--History--20th century. 3. Turner, Thomas Wyatt. 4. Markoe, William Morgan. 5. LaFarge, John, 1880-1963. I. Title. II. Series.
BX1407.N4N5 1988   282'.73'08996073   88-9811
ISBN 0-8240-4098-8 (alk. paper)

Design by Mary Beth Brennan

Printed on acid-free, 250-year-life paper
Manufactured in the United States of America

BLACK CATHOLIC PROTEST AND THE FEDERATED COLORED CATHOLICS, 1917-1933

TABLE OF CONTENTS

PREFACE TO THE GARLAND EDITION iv

Chapter
I. INTRODUCTION 1

II. THOMAS WYATT TURNER 19

    Early Religious Concerns 25
    Committee Beginnings 31
    Federated Colored Catholics 42
    Markoe and the *Chronicle* 61
    The Controversy 96

III. WILLIAM MORGAN MARKOE 136

    Articles in *America* 140
    Catechetical Work in St. Louis 155
    Pastor of St. Elizabeth's 169
    Editor for the Federation 175
    Campaign for Interracialism 189
    National Catholic Interracial Federation 201

IV. JOHN LAFARGE 210

    Innsbruck 213
    "The Manner is Ordinary" 214
    Southern Maryland 216
    Ridge Schools 220
    The Cardinal Gibbons Institute 226
    America and the Federation 236
    Interracialism and the Controversy 266
    The Aftermath 281

V. CONCLUSION 286

    I. The Problem 286
        A. Turner 286
        B. Markoe 289
        C. LaFarge 293

II.	The Catholic Church	294
	A. Turner	296
	B. Markoe	298
	C. LaFarge	300
III.	The Federation	302
	A. Turner	304
	B. Markoe	308
	C. LaFarge	310
IV.	Summary	312
BIBLIOGRAPHY		315

PREFACE TO THE GARLAND EDITION

In his unpublished memoirs, Thomas Wyatt Turner, the subject of this book, recalls his visits as a Howard University student to the home of the great abolitionist Frederick Douglass. Turner made those visits during the last year of Douglass' life. "His 'Open House' occasions in Anacostia, to which our instructor in history would take groups of us on certain Sundays, made his passing a sort of personal loss to many Howard students," Turner remarks. This passage has particular meaning for me, since I currently serve as the historian for the Frederick Douglass Home. Beyond that, however, I have always been impressed by the continuity which this experience represents, the young student sitting at the feet of the aging abolitionist. Some eighty years later, I repeated that process. I sat at the feet of Dr. Turner, who was even older at the time than Douglass had been.

I first met Turner in 1973, when he was ninety-six years old. Over the next five years I sat at his feet, listening to history from one of its makers. Part of that story is contained in this book, along with that of two other men who profoundly influenced it.

When this study was completed more than a decade ago, scholarship in the field of Afro-American Catholic history was in its infancy. A few master's theses, doctoral dissertations and brief overviews were all that

were available. The Josephite priest, John T. Gillard, had attempted two
books on the subject, <u>The Catholic Church and the American Negro</u> (1929)
and <u>Colored Catholics in the United States</u> (1941), both of which had been
severely criticized for their paternalism and racism. Many of the other
works explored what had been done to and for black Catholics in the United
States, rather than the story of their own lives and achievements. One
major exception was an article, in retrospect a landmark publication,
entitled, "The Negro Catholic Congresses, 1889-1894," by David Spalding,
which appeared in the <u>Catholic Historical Review</u> in October of 1969. In
this work Spalding explored the efforts of a group of black Catholics at
the close of the nineteenth century to obtain equality in their
predominantly white church. The article was important not only because it
explored the work of black Catholics themselves, but because it destroyed
common stereotypes about the kind of individual who would remain a member
of such a church. It made clear that a sizable number of black Catholics
were not only outraged by the discrimination they were experiencing in the
Church, but were vocal in demanding an end to such inequality.

  My concern when I began this study, therefore, was not only to
explore the world of black Catholics from their own perspective, but their
response to their unique position as a minority within a minority; i.e., a
minority within the American Catholic Church and a minority within the
Afro-American community. During the course of my work ten years ago (as
is reflected in the concluding pages of this study) the role of black
Catholics within the American church was undergoing dramatic change.
Following the death of Dr. Martin Luther King, Jr. in 1968, black priests
and eventually religious sisters and laity began asking renewed questions

about racism in their church institutions. As a direct consequence of this questioning, significant changes have occurred since this study was first completed in 1975. The number of black bishops has risen from three to eleven. Most dioceses have established an office of black Catholics or of minority concerns. Recently the black bishops themselves called the first National Black Catholic Congress (significantly named) in modern times. It was held at the Catholic University of America in Washington, D.C. from May 21-24, 1987. Approximately 1500 delegates representing 107 dioceses attended. These delegates spoke on behalf of approximately 1.3 million black Catholics in the United States.

This scene is in sharp contrast to the annual meetings of the Federated Colored Catholics, who are the subject of this study. At the last of their annual meetings, held in New York City in 1932, approximately 4000 delegates attended at least the opening Mass, but a much smaller number attended the actual sessions. They represented a black Catholic population estimated at no more than 250,000. What is more telling, however, is that there were no black bishops and only two black priests in the entire country. The hierarchy present, then, was entirely white, with the exception of one black priest who was able to attend.

Clearly, then, black Catholics have grown in numbers and influence in the last several decades, with much of that achievement experienced quite recently. What is even more notable to me as an historian, however, is the increased awareness among black Catholics of their rich and varied heritage. Much of the credit for this growing self-awareness must be attributed to a few individuals who have invested a lifetime in effecting this change.

The Rev. Peter Hogan, S.S.J., archivist of the Josephite Fathers in Baltimore, Maryland has devoted a full professional career to establishing the finest collection of Afro-American Catholic materials available anywhere. A sizable number of the current black Catholic bishops have personally committed themselves to learn and to promote education in black Catholic history. The Rev. Clarence Rivers of Cincinnati, Ohio has contributed his considerable talent over many years to a revolution in Catholic liturgy, rooted deeply in the Afro-American experience. Only in recent years has it been acknowledged that his work in sacred music has profoundly changed the course of liturgical celebration not only in the black but also in the white Catholic community.

The culmination of all these efforts, however, is the inclusion of material on black Catholics in larger works on the Afro-American religious experience, such as in Albert Raboteau's recent work, <u>Slave Religion</u>. In this vein, perhaps a milestone will be reached when the Rev. Cyprian Davis, O.S.B. completes his forthcoming volume in black Catholic history, to be published as part of a series in Afro-American religion, under the direction of C. Eric Lincoln.

I began this preface with a story about continuity. Perhaps I should end it with a recent one. In an article in <u>America</u> magazine about the recent National Black Catholic Congress, the Rev. Edward K. Braxton recalled a story told at the Congress by Bishop Joseph Francis, S.V.D. of Newark, New Jersey. Bishop Francis was ordained as one of the newer black bishops shortly before Thomas Wyatt Turner died. Bishop Francis had the privilege of meeting Turner, who was by then in his hundredth year. The bishop asked Turner to pray for him. The old man replied that he had been praying for the black bishop since before he was born. And so he had. The rest of this book tells the story of those prayers.

Every preface ends with expressions of gratitude. My own is no exception. My first is to the gentleman without whom there would be no story, Thomas Wyatt Turner. The second is to his niece, Lois E. Broadus, who opened her home and her heart for countless hours of interviews with her uncle, but above all, recognized more than anyone that this frail elderly man had been a giant in his time. Her dedication to his memory has kept his legacy alive. Fr. Peter Hogan, whom I mentioned earlier, has contributed more than anyone will ever know to every stage of this work, believing as he always has that documents are valuable only if someone keeps them alive in each generation.

Finally, I have two major debts which can never be repaid. To my family--my husband, Ken, who has been there literally through research, writing, rewriting, always with the deepest respect for this work; my son Robert ("R.J."), whose considerable expertise in computer science made this current manuscript possible; and my son John, whose middle name, Thomas, is a reminder of Thomas Wyatt Turner and who has exercised patience and enormous generosity as we have all worked on this project together. The second debt is to the black Catholic community everywhere. Countless individuals and organizations have responded with enthusiasm and enormous interest over the years as they have heard portions of this story. They have shared their insights, their love and their appreciation. Their response has confirmed my belief in the importance of this story.

In conclusion, I wish to apologize for any shortcomings in this text. When Garland offered to publish this study, I knew there would be little time for revisions in a work completed some twelve years ago. I believed, however, that the material was so valuable that it should be made accessible to others. I hope that the effort will be a beginning, not an end.

Marilyn W. Nickels
August 15, 1987

CHAPTER I

INTRODUCTION

Black protest movements within the American Catholic Church are not new phenomena. Although black Catholics have always been a minority within a minority, they made their voices heard in the majority white institution as early as 1889 in an assembly known as the Catholic Afro-American Congress.[1] The study of events such as these, however, has hardly kept pace with the history of their development. It is rare for white Catholics to be aware of the existence of their black fellow

---

[1]Five Catholic Afro-American Congresses were held between 1889 and 1894, under the leadership of Daniel A. Rudd of Cincinnati. Rudd had founded a black newspaper in 1884 entitled the Ohio State Tribune. In 1886 he made the journal a strictly Catholic Weekly, changing the name to the American Catholic Tribune. The few remaining copies available are in the files of the American Catholic Historical Society of Philadelphia. The Congresses published a souvenir booklet after the first three conventions called Three Catholic Afro-American Congresses (Cincinnati: American Catholic Tribune, 1893). Brother David Spalding traced the history of the movement in an article, "The Negro Catholic Congresses, 1889-1894," offering several reasons for the waning of the Congresses: objections on the part of the clergy to the growing militancy of the delegates, the general conservatism of the Church at the turn of the century, particularly toward lay movements, political conservatism in the country at large, and finally, the lessening influence of Rudd himself, who had aroused disapproval from clergy and delegates alike. Spalding ends with an interesting statement: "Further study may establish a clear continuity between the congresses and the Union (St. Peter Claver's Union, which the congress had become) and such twentieth-century organizations as the Federated Colored Catholics and the Knights of St. Peter Claver, to which they bear marked similarity in makeup, purpose, and spirit." See David Spalding, "The Negro Catholic Congresses, 1889-1894," Catholic Historical Review 55 (October 1969): 337-57.

churchmen, and rarer still to read of their efforts for equality in the earlier pages of American Catholic history.

The purpose of this study is to analyze historically the origin and development of one such movement, the Federated Colored Catholics, and especially a clash of views on racial justice which split the organization into factions as it developed. Each of the principals in this controversy--Dr. Thomas W. Turner, a black layman and founder of the Federated Colored Catholics, and two prominent white Jesuits, Rev. William M. Markoe and Rev. John LaFarge--viewed the issue of racial justice from his own special experience. It is my intention to establish the three perspectives.

In delineating each man's view, I shall present the events, in chronological order, out of which arose his grasp of the race question. After describing these views separately, I will attempt to relate them to one another in an analysis of the controversy itself. A brief history of the Federated Colored Catholics may serve as a framework for understanding the persons and events involved.

The Federation originated as a spontaneous response to the experience of racial discrimination. In this sense, it began as a grassroots effort spearheaded by small group of concerned individuals.

In 1917 Dr. Thomas Wyatt Turner, a professor of biology at Howard University, Washington, D.C. and a member of St. Augustine's Catholic Church, invited a few black Catholic friends to his home for a meeting.[2] The subject for discussion was the place of blacks in the Catholic Church. Out of several such meetings grew the "Committee Against the Extension of Race Prejudice in the Church." Its members wrote letters to the hierarchy about discriminatory practices in the Church, the lack of proper educational facilities for black children or opportunities for their higher education, and the urgent need of a black priesthood. The Catholic press publicized these pleas in favorable editorials and articles of the period.[3]

By 1919, the committee had grown to twenty-five members, was known as the "Committee for the Advancement of Colored Catholics," and had divided into subcommittees, some of which visited members of the hierarchy in person. In 1923 a call was issued for delegates to a meeting in Washington, D.C. on December 30, at which time a temporary organization was developed. A year later a permanent organization was established, founded with a brief temporary constitution.[4]

In 1925, encouraged by the favorable response of the hierarchy to letters and visits, and the support of Bishop Emmett Walsh of

---

[2] H. M. Smith, "An Outline of the History of the F.C.C. of U.S.," Chronicle, December 1929, pp. 3-5. This brief article is one of the few published records of the Federation's beginnings. Much of the history to follow is based upon this source, and several unpublished ones. Several black organizations were founded about this time; e.g., the N.A.A.C.P. (of which Dr. Turner was a charter member) in 1909 and the Association for the Study of Negro Life and History (now Afro-American Life and History) in 1915.

[3] Ibid., p. 3.

[4] Thomas W. Turner, "The Federation of Colored Catholics in the United States," (manuscript, Hampton, Virginia, 1963-64), pt. 2, chap. 10, p. 11. This unpublished source was poorly paginated, at least in the copy available to me; thus, the lengthy reference to section and chapter.

Charleston, South Carolina, secretary of the National Catholic Welfare Conference, the committee decided to "reorganize and expand on a nation-wide scale."[5] The first annual convention of what was to be called the Federated Colored Catholics of the United States was held at St. Augustine Church and the N.C.W.C. headquarters in Washington, D.C. on December 6 and 7, 1925. The program included speakers from Hampton, Virginia,[6] Washington, D.C., Philadelphia, Baltimore, and Chicago. Various agencies serving black Catholics were also represented. Archbishop Michael Curley of Baltimore had agreed to serve as Spiritual Director of the organization,[7] officers were elected, including Dr. Turner as President, and a committee appointed to prepare a permanent constitution. During these first sessions the delegates resolved to support the Cardinal Gibbons Institute, a national Catholic secondary school for black students recently opened in Southern Maryland. It was a focal point of Federation support for many years, largely through the influence of Fr. John LaFarge, who had spent several years ministering to the black Catholics of that area. He was a strong and early advocate also of the Federation, joining in some of the meetings which led to its foundation.[8]

---

[5]Ibid.

[6]Dr. Turner by this time had left Howard University for a position on the faculty of Hampton Institute in Virginia.

[7]At this time the Archdiocese of Baltimore included the District of Columbia and five counties in neighboring Maryland. The position of Spiritual Director in Catholic societies was often, as in this instance, little more than an honorary title, which indicated hierarchical approval of the organization in question.

[8]John LaFarge (1880-1963) labored for fifteen years (1911-26) among black Catholics in Southern Maryland (with a brief period away

At the second annual convention held in Washington, D.C. in December 1926, Senator David I. Walsh of Massachusetts delivered the major address. He called upon the members of the Federation to reflect upon the importance of their work:

> You are Catholic men and women and your presence here indicates you are leaders in the Catholic world and its activities. I want to congratulate you on assuming the duties of leadership, and banding together that your strength, your solidarity and religious fervor may be made known.
>
> I wonder if you have stopped to think what it means to be leaders, spokesmen, pleaders, fighters. Your work, that of relating the church to the Negro problem, is a great honor and privilege.

Fr. Norman Duckette, a black priest stationed in Flint, Michigan and a former parishioner of St. Augustine's, celebrated the opening Mass. Through the influence of Fr. Alonzo Olds, pastor of St. Augustine's, a small committee of the Federation met with the Apostolic Delegate, the Most Rev. P. Fumasoni-Biondi, on the second day of the convention. It reported:

> The Delegate was most cordial and democratic in his reception of the committee and showed a wide knowledge of the difficulties and problems with which the colored people are confronted. He, also,

---

for study). During those early years he met Dr. Turner, with whom he worked closely in the founding of Cardinal Gibbons Institute and the Federation. The extensive correspondence of these two men during that time attests to their close relationship, which was rooted in a mutual experience of the black Catholic community of St. Mary's County, Maryland—Turner as a youth and LaFarge as a priest. Edward D. Reynolds referred to LaFarge in 1949 as "the leading Jesuit publicist for the Negro." See Reynolds, <u>Jesuits for the Negro</u> (New York: The America Press, 1949), pp. 195-201.

[9]David I. Walsh, "Extracts from an Address of Sen. David I. Walsh of Massachusetts, delivered at Convention of Federation of Colored Catholics, St. Augustine's Church, Washington, D.C., Dec. 5, 1926," Thomas W. Turner Papers, Moorland-Spingarn Research Center, Howard University, Washington, D.C. This collection will hereafter be referred to as the Turner Papers.

assured us that the Holy Father is quite conversant with these problems. He spoke not only in terms of deepest sympathy, but led us to feel that efforts are being made to get rid of the impediments and obstructions thrown in the way of the colored Catholic. The committee left him feeling that our case was in good hands. Our chairman placed in his hands a copy of the paper which had been sent to the Bishops of the United States, with a request that he present the same to the Pope.[10]

At the request of several members, the 1927 convention was moved up from December to September (4 and 5). It was also held in a different location, New York City, where the delegates who gathered found they had reason to celebrate several accomplishments during the previous year. Not only had there been a favorable article on the Federation in the December 30 issue of Osservatore Romano (official Vatican publication), but the Catholic Commission on International Peace, meeting at the Catholic University in April 1927, had invited the Federated Colored Catholics to send a representative. Finally, the Catholic Students' Mission Crusade had listed the Federation as its prayer intention for May of that year.[11]

Archbishop John T. McNicholas of Cincinnati invited the Federation to hold its fourth convention there on September 1, 2 and 3, 1928. The third day was added for an interracial conference

---

[10]From minutes of the committee, quoted in Turner, "The Federation of Colored Catholics," pt. 2, chap. 5, p. 13.

[11]Minutes of the Third Annual Convention, "Report of the Secretary," Turner Papers, p. 3. The Catholic Students' Mission Crusade (C.S.M.C.) is a national federation of mission societies to acquaint students with Catholic missionary endeavors at home and abroad. Founded in 1918, the C.S.M.C. chose each month a deserving work for special remembrance in the prayers of its members. Recognizing the Federation in this way meant widespread publicity and approval for the group among American white Catholics.

arranged through the cooperative efforts of Fr. R. A. McGowan of the National Catholic Welfare Conference and a committee of the Federation, emphasizing the role of blacks in industry. This interracial discussion became a regular feature of each succeeding convention.[12]

At this point the Federation was publicizing its activities as best it could in Catholic and black journals, as well as a small house organ called "The Council Review."[13] At the fifth annual convention in Baltimore on August 31, September 1 and 2, 1929, this problem was solved. A young Jesuit priest from St. Louis, Missouri, Fr. William Markoe, the pastor of St. Elizabeth (black) parish, offered his parish newsletter,

---

[12]Dr. Turner had suggested the creation of such a committee in his address to the convention the preceding year, as quoted in Turner, "The Federation of Colored Catholics," pt. 2, chap. 5, p. 14. The Federation adopted the idea in its resolutions of 1927. See "Resolutions Adopted by the Federated Colored Catholics in the Third Annual Convention Assembled in the City of New York, Sept. 4 & 5, 1927," Turner Papers, p. 11.--The National Catholic Welfare Conference was an outgrowth of the National Catholic War Council, founded during World War I to coordinate the activities of Catholic societies in the war effort. The N.C.W.C. (originally National Catholic Welfare Council, after the war) was established in 1919 at the Third Plenary Council of American bishops in Baltimore. It is an executive agency of the American bishops, which meets annually in Washington, D.C. in November and maintains an Administrative Board with offices in Washington for the coordination of a wide variety of Catholic activities. In 1966 the N.C.W.C. offices were named the United States Catholic Conference, and the body of bishops themselves, the National Conference of Catholic Bishops. For a history of the organization see New Catholic Encyclopedia (1967), s.v. "National Catholic Welfare Conference," by F. T. Hurley.

[13]Smith to Turner, 17 September 1928, Turner Papers. Although no year appears on the letter itself, other correspondence verifies the date as 1928. Smith as Secretary reported that the executive committee had engaged the services of Mr. Dorsey to print the "official organ of the Federation." This letter and other advertisements in the Turner papers indicate that C. Marcellus Dorsey & Sons of Baltimore was the printing firm hired. On the hiring of Dorsey, see also "Official Record of the Proceedings of the Fourth National Convention of the Federated Colored Catholics of the United States," September 1928, Turner Papers, p. 10.

the "St. Elizabeth's Chronicle," to the Federation as its official journal. His proposal included some irresistable features: unlimited space for Federation matters, freedom of expression, and a low subscription rate, all at no additional cost to the organization itself.[14] The offer was gratefully accepted, and the Chronicle adopted as the new official organ, with Father Markoe as editor.

This same convention was considered important for other reasons: representatives from twenty states were present—107 delegates in all-- as guests in part of the Josephite Fathers and the Father Dorsey Chapter of Baltimore, with Fr. Louis Pastorelli, Superior General of the Josephites, celebrating the opening Mass. Since the Josephites were the only order of priests in the United States totally dedicated to the conversion of blacks, their support of the Federation was earnestly sought and welcomed.[15]

Despite the interracial emphasis introduced into the conventions of 1929 and 1930, some critics levelled a charge of black exclusivism at the organization about this time. The matter was brought before the executive committee, a group composed of the national officers of the Federation, along with several other appointed persons. It met

---

[14]Smith, "An Outline History," p. 5. Dr. Turner was to regret later that this agreement with Markoe was never notarized. See Turner, "The Federation of Colored Catholics," pt. 2, chap. 5, p. 15.

[15]The relationship between the Federation and the Josephites was never one of real cooperation. Even the attempt made here became the subject of controversy. See Turner to Louis B. Pastorelli, Superior General of the Josephites, 8 September 1931, Turner Papers, in which Turner denies rumors circulated that the Federation had chosen Baltimore for their convention site in order to embarrass the Josephites. Also see Pastorelli to Turner, 11 September 1931, Turner Papers, which does not deny the existence of such rumors, but minimizes their importance.

twice each year, in January and June, to conduct the administrative business of the Federation. Its primary role was to plan the annual convention and oversee the work of whatever committees has been appointed by the previous convention.[16] At the executive committee meeting in June 1929, Dr. Turner reported that there had been some criticism of the Federation as a "Jim Crow organization," since it was composed largely of black members devoted to a black cause. The result, said the critics, was that blacks themselves had created consciously the same racial isolation they were attempting to abolish. Markoe later wrote an article for the July 1930 issue of the Chronicle entitled "Our Jim Crow Federation," in which he raised the question of whether the name "Federated Colored Catholics" was responsible for the objection.[17] Although he affirmed that the name was a dignified one and need not be changed, Markoe had introduced an issue which was to appear in full force two years later.

By the time the sixth annual convention was convened in Detroit on August 31, 1930, the Federation's leaders were concentrating on two other important issues: the efficacy of working through existing Catholic organizations, and the necessity of maintaining ecclesiastical

---

[16]The executive committee included the national officers and such other members as the president should select. They were to "direct the general activities of the Federation." See Constitution of the Federated Colored Catholics, art. x, as published in the Official Record of the Fourth Annual Convention, September 1928, Turner Papers, p. 26.

[17]William M. Markoe, "Our Jim Crow Federation," Chronicle, July 1930, pp. 149-50.

approval.[18] This led the convention to adopt several new regulations, which emphasized that individual chapters of the organization were to be composed of persons who had gathered for some Catholic purpose other than membership in the Federation, and that all were to obtain proper ecclesiastical approval before joining the Federation. This meant, of course, that the Federated Colored Catholics were promoting both the entrance of established Catholic organizations into the Federation, and the organizing of individual black Catholics along existing Catholic lines (Holy Name Society, Sodality) as a first step toward Federation membership. This approach necessitated and enhanced the second objective, the gaining of greater ecclesiastical approval.

Since the convention took place in Detroit, another important topic of discussion was the black working man. Particularly noteworthy were addresses by Donald Marshall, head of black personnel at the Ford plants, who pointed out that his company was among the few to employ blacks in Detroit; Dr. Karl Phillips, United States Commissioner of Conciliation in Washington, D.C.; and John C. Dancy, Jr. of the Detroit Urban League.[19] All three men were prominent blacks in the industrial field.

During the next year two local incidents occurred which required the application of the Detroit rules. In Chicago a Federation organizer named C. J. Foster involved his chapters in several local controversies,

---

[18]Turner, "Our Detroit Regulations," Chronicle, June 1932, pp. 110-11. See also "The Federation--How It Works," Chronicle, September 1931, p. 542.

[19]John LaFarge, "What Do Colored Catholics Want?" America, September 20, 1930, p. 565.

at the displeasure of Fr. Joseph J. Eckert, pastor of St. Elizabeth's (black) parish. Dr. Turner's response, indicating the new policy of maintaining ecclesiastical approval, assured both Father Eckert and Mr. Foster that the Federation did not "go into local issues."[20] Writing to Foster, President Turner said that despite the merits of the case, ". . . we have reached a critical point in the organization, a point where we cannot grow larger or in deeper confidence, but through the existing organization, and with the approval of the ecclesiastical authorities."[21] Foster acquiesced, at least for the time,[22] while Father Eckert appeared somewhat appeased.[23] The second such local crisis arose in Philadelphia, where efforts to organize a strong branch of the Federation under Fr. Vincent Dever met opposition from a small committee of black Catholics, who claimed that they were already members of the organization. Father LaFarge, who had come down from New York to assist Father Dever, insisted that the small group in question had not received proper ecclesiastical approval, had no specific purpose as a Catholic Action organization (except to sell subscriptions to the Chronicle) and was therefore not a bona fide chapter. The case was appealed by both Father LaFarge and William B. Bruce, chairman of the committee in question, to Dr. Turner,[24] who ruled in favor of Fathers

---

[20]Turner to Rev. Joseph J. Eckert, 10 July 1931, Turner Papers.

[21]Turner to C. J. Foster, 25 July 1931, Turner Papers.

[22]Foster to Turner, 20 July 1931, Turner Papers.

[23]Mrs. Maude B. Johnston, local field agent in Chicago, to Turner, 24 July 1931, Turner Papers.

[24]LaFarge to Turner, 13 July 1931, Turner Papers. Also William B. Bruce to Turner, 13 July 1931, Turner Papers.

LaFarge and Dever. Again, Turner applied the principles of the Detroit convention: "Our plan . . . entails tactful cooperation with the clergy on the part of officers and field agents,"[25] he said in a letter to Bruce; and he remarked to LaFarge, ". . . the further growth of the work must depend upon the existing Church organizations rather than upon independent aggregations."[26]

At the same time that he used these new principles, however, Dr. Turner emphasized to Foster in Chicago that no clergyman could destroy the Federation if its members were patient and steadfast.[27] He wrote to Mrs. Maude Johnston, the deputy organizer in Chicago, that the new regulations did not imply submission to any local pastor in matters of organizational policy.[28] Finally, Turner informed the membership at large that the new regulations in no way meant a change in the basic lay control of the organization,[29] and that he as president was fully aware of the difficulties involved in promoting lay-clerical harmony in the local situations.[30] The coexistence of these two strains, cooperation with the established Church and the maintenance of independent policy, remained an important issue as the Federation developed in the early thirties.

---

[25]Turner to Bruce, 16 July 1931, Turner Papers.

[26]Turner to LaFarge, 25 July 1931, Turner Papers.

[27]Turner to Foster, 25 July 1931, Turner Papers.

[28]Turner to Johnston, 4 August 1931, Turner Papers.

[29]Turner, "Our Detroit Regulations," p. 110.

[30]Turner to Chapters, Organizers and Federation members, 28 July 1931, Turner Papers.

Largely because of its location and the growing influence of Father Markoe as editor of the *Chronicle*, St. Louis was selected as the site of the seventh annual convention. Invitations were sent to every black parish in the country in the hope of making this the largest and most successful convention yet held.[31] Markoe placed emphasis during prior publicity on an *interracial* program, with a special invitation to white friends of black Catholics, and a promise of discussion on the role of the clergy in work among blacks.[32]

Fr. Stephen Theobald, a popular young black priest from Minnesota, celebrated the opening Mass.[33] Reports from the secretary and the field agent showed that the organization had grown from a committee of five in Washington, D.C. to seventy-two separate chapters

---

[31]Markoe, "The Annual Convention," *Chronicle*, June 1931, pp. 457-58.

[32]Markoe, "Plans for the National Convention," *Chronicle*, July 1931, p. 488.

[33]Ibid. Stephen L. Theobald (1874-1932) was the protege of Archbishop John Ireland of St. Paul, Minnesota, who had declared earlier that any man qualified for the priesthood would be welcome in his seminary, regardless of color. Ordained in 1910, Theobald served on the Cathedral staff as an expert in canon law. Soon he was appointed pastor of a mixed congregation at the Church of St. Peter Claver in St. Paul, where he remained until his death. Theobald met Dr. Turner in 1914 in Baltimore, where he first learned of Turner's interest in organizing black Catholics. Theobald remained a strong supporter of Federation activities as they emerged. Father Markoe brought Theobald to St. Louis as guest speaker for a parish banquet in 1927. It was this talk which convinced Markoe to feature Theobald at the St. Louis convention in 1931. On this second occasion the black priest spoke from a podium at St. Louis University, and boldly took the opportunity to denounce the discriminatory entrance policies of the Jesuit institution! See Albert S. Foley, *God's Men of Color* (New York: Farrar, Straus, 1955), pp. 95-103. See also *Markoe to Turner*, 30 July 1931, Turner Papers. Finally, Markoe, "An Interracial Role," (memoirs, Milwaukee, 1968), pp. 100-101.

and forty-four individually enrolled members, representing areas as far removed as California and Washington state, Texas, Boston, and a number of locations in between.[34] The Chronicle was given much credit for publicizing the organization and its activities, although Father Markoe had to plead during the same convention for greater financial support to continue his work.[35]

Many pressures affected the Federation in 1931 and 1932: cooperation with the clergy, the relationship of the Federated Colored Catholics to the Church at large, white membership and influence in the organization, the differences in local situations, North and South, faced by each chapter, and finally, the economic depression which affected the entire nation. Although the St. Louis convention had produced two relatively substantial contributions,[36] the money was

---

[34]Smith, "Report of the Secretary," Chronicle, November 1931, p. 660. William M. Prater, "Report of the Field Agent," Chronicle, November 1931, pp. 665-66. Exact numbers of the Federation were always hard to determine, because individuals could be counted several times if they belonged to more than one organization (parish, Sodality, Holy Name Society) that was a Federation chapter. Smith estimated in August of 1932 that the Federation had 75,000 members. Smith to Turner, 20 August 1932, Turner Papers. The estimates in issues of the Chronicle immediately preceding the split went as high as 100,000. This is in a black Catholic population of approximately 250,000. Overestimating membership figures was an objection to the Federation raised by Rev. John T. Gillard, historian and author on black Catholicism, in a letter to Bishop Emmet M. Walsh on April 5, 1932, Gillard Papers, Josephite Fathers Archives, Baltimore, Maryland. This collection will hereafter be referred to as the Gillard Papers.

[35]Markoe, "Report on the Chronicle," Chronicle, November 1931, p. 664.

[36]Rev. Edward C. Kramer of the Catholic Board for Mission Work among the Colored People to LaFarge, 14 September 1931, Turner Papers, with a check for $500.00 enclosed. Smith to Turner, 15 September 1931, Turner Papers, indicating the receipt of a check from Bishop Hugh Charles Boyle of Pittsburgh.

insufficient to prevent the Federation and Chronicle from suffering the same hardships as most voluntary organizations and journals of the time. However, the Federation proceeded with its resolution to send a letter to each member of the hierarchy in October 1931, once again pleading for the right to practice the faith in churches and schools on an equal basis with every other member of the Church.[37] The letters were followed by a visit to the campus of the Catholic University in Washington, D.C. during the bishops' annual conference in November. Here a small committee of black Catholics spoke to any bishop who would listen, reiterating the message of their earlier letter, and emphasizing particularly the color bar at the Catholic University itself. Cardinal O'Connell of Boston, as chairman of the University's Board of Trustees, was especially sympathetic to this latter complaint and promised to act upon it.[38] Subsequent meetings with the university rector and of the trustees among themselves resulted, however, in a confirmation of the existing policy. "The time is not ripe," wrote the rector on behalf of the trustees in May of 1932.[39]

---

[37]Turner as President of the Federated Colored Catholics to the Catholic hierarchy of the United States, 10 October 1931, Turner Papers.

[38]Turner to Fr. Vincent Dever, 16 November 1931, Turner Papers, in which the former describes the visit to Catholic University and the talk with Cardinal O'Connell.

[39]The text of the letter from Rector James H. Ryan of the Catholic University to Dr. Eugene A. Clarke, President of Miner Teachers College, 27 May 1932, Turner Papers, was brief, and is printed in full here: "At the recent meeting of the Executive Committee of the Board of Trustees of the Catholic University of America, the question of admitting colored students to the University was placed before the members. Likewise, I presented the arguments of Dr. Turner and yourself favorable to this matter.--The judgment of the Executive Committee

Much of the executive committee meeting in January 1932 was devoted to planning the next convention, with New York chosen as the site.[40] The June meeting discussed the annual convention in greater detail, along with several other topics. One item not on the agenda proved most important. The *Chronicle* of July 1932 records:

> Communications were read by the Secretary . . . from several groups from Chicago, asking that the name of the Federation be changed to the Inter-racial Federated Catholics.[41]

In the same issue Father LaFarge wrote in his column "Doing the Truth" about this request made at the executive meeting, concluding that while a change in name was not necessary (since Dr. Turner had already satisfactorily refuted all complaints about "Jim Crow"), "National Catholic Inter-racial Federation" did indeed "express what has developed to be the primary purpose of the organization," the promoting "of relations between the races based on Christian principles."[42] An editorial appeared in the September 1932 issue of the *Chronicle*, immediately preceding the New York convention, entitled "A National Catholic Inter-Racial Organization." Although it did not address the

---

was that, without prejudice to the case, the time is not ripe to admit colored students to this University." The irony of the letter was twofold: that it was sent to a man who was himself the president of a teachers' college in the same city, and that it mentioned the name of a man, Dr. Turner, who had been a black student at the university for a brief time, under an earlier, more lenient policy.

[40]"Executive Committee of the Federated Colored Catholics," *Chronicle*, February 1932, pp. 37-38.

[41]"Executive Committee Meets to Plan Convention," *Chronicle*, July 1932, p. 140.

[42]LaFarge, "Doing the Truth," *Chronicle*, July 1932, p. 130.

subject of name at all, the use of the same phrase is too obvious to overlook.[43] In any event, it is significant that the issue of a change in name was raised at the executive committee meeting preparatory to the New York convention, for it was during that convention that the change occurred.

The eighth annual convention opened on September 3, 1932 with a Mass at St. Patrick's Cathedral, 4,000 black Catholics in attendance, and Bishop John J. Dunn, auxiliary of New York, as the celebrant.[44] During an executive committee session, a proposal was introduced to include the word "interracial" in the name of the organization. After much disagreement about the removal of the word "colored" from the title, Dr. Turner and the delegates from Washington, D.C. reluctantly acquiesced in a compromise. Neither word was used. The title chosen was the "National Catholic Federation for the Promotion of Better Race Relations."[45] Yet events to follow confirmed that more than a name was involved in the convention debate. When Father Markoe wrote to Dr. Turner two weeks later informing him that the magazine issue announcing the recent organizational name change would itself bear a new title, "Interracial Review," he initiated a controversy which was

---

[43]"A National Catholic Inter-Racial Organization," Chronicle, September 1932, p. 177. The article was probably written by Markoe, as editor.

[44]Hazel McDaniel Teabeau, "Federated Colored Catholics Make History in New York City Convention," Interracial Review, October 1932, p. 195.

[45]Turner to Clarke, 18 September 1932, Turner Papers, in which Turner laments Clarke's absence from the convention, convinced that together they would have been strong enough to resist the name change entirely.

to split the Federation permanently.[46] The old Federated Colored Catholics of the East and the new National Catholic Interracial Federation of the Midwest both lost momentum and eventually disappeared. Only the future Catholic Interracial Council of New York, under the leadership of Father LaFarge and composed of several members of the older Federation, was to survive into the present, publicized in the pages of the new Interracial Review. The controversy which brought about this split is my subject.

Frequent references are made in this paper to the relationship of the Josephite Fathers to the Federation. The nature of the disagreement between these two parties, as well as the larger question of the Josephites' influence on black Catholic history, deserve further investigation. It was not possible to explore either topic adequately here.

---

[46] Markoe to Turner, 23 September 1932, Turner Papers.

CHAPTER II

THOMAS WYATT TURNER

Thomas Wyatt Turner was born on March 16, 1877 in Hughesville, Charles County, Maryland. The son of Eli and Linnie (Gross) Turner, descendants of black Catholic slaves of Southern Maryland, Thomas was baptized as an infant at St. Mary's Church, Bryantown. He attended the county black schools for eight years, working in his spare time like other children of sharecroppers in the corn and tobacco fields of the region. Since Catholic secondary education for black children in Southern Maryland was limited to a three-month trade school,[1] young Turner enrolled in an Episcopalian black school at Charlotte Hall in St. Mary's County in 1892.[2] Its missionary-principal, the Rev. Joseph Y. Bryant, taught the young boy Latin, and thus a greater appreciation of his own Catholic faith. The school's other teacher was a female graduate of the New York Normal School (now Hunter College). She spoke to Thomas in French phrases and convinced him through her example that teaching was a noble profession.

At his graduation from Charlotte Hall in 1894, Turner was offered the opportunity of a scholarship to Bryant's alma mater,

---

[1] Interview with Thomas W. Turner, Washington, D.C., April 1974.

[2] Certificate of graduation from St. Mary's Parochial and Industrial School, 5 June 1894, Turner Papers.

Lincoln University. There was one condition, however; the scholarship recipient had to be an Episcopalian. The young black Catholic considered the alternatives, consulted a wise Quaker friend of the family, and decided to hold fast to his faith and make it on his own.[3] He set out for Howard University in Washington, D.C., determined to become as fine a teacher as his mentors had been. To overcome the weaknesses of a rural education he took remedial courses at Howard University Preparatory School from 1895 to 1897, working at odd jobs to support himself while studying. From 1897 to 1901 he attended Howard University, from which he received his A.B. degree in 1901.

Around 1900, Turner made a decision which seems profoundly important in retrospect. Nearing graduation from Howard University, he went to see General John Eaton, Inspector of schools in Puerto Rico. Eaton assured Turner of a teaching position in Puerto Rico, and also gave him some advice. The white man has kept the Jim Crow cars off the streets of Washington, the aging general said. But he is getting tired. Now the black man must take over. Turner left that interview with a new dedication to the cause of civil rights. Needless to say, he did not go to Puerto Rico.[4]

---

[3]Interview with Turner, Hampton, Virginia, 24 March 1973. Turner maintained all his life a particular love for the Quakers, and a long friendship with this family. "They were a part of my spiritual life, even spiritual . . . you see, my parents were the first generation out of slavery and they didn't know much about these things of all kinds . . . so I would go when it came to scholastic things, to this Quaker lady . . . which I did, asking her whether I should take this scholarship or not. Whether I should give up things I had now. I'd ask her any question, just as I would my own parents. 'Well,' she said, ". . . if you love God and love your church, stay it, and you can work and get by.' . . . I thought it was a very delightful answer to give."

[4]NPR, "Options," April 1974.

Convinced that he still had not learned nearly enough to teach school, Turner enrolled at the Catholic University of America for further study. His meager funds were spent so quickly for equipment and books, however, that he eagerly accepted a teaching offer arriving about this time from Booker T. Washington at Tuskegee Institute. The one-year teaching opportunity at Tuskegee enabled Turner to gain professional experience, and there he developed a life-long admiration for Washington and his work.[5]

In 1902 Turner returned to Maryland to be among the first group of black teachers hired at the Baltimore High and Training School for black students. He remained in this teaching position for ten years, except for one year (1910-11) at St. Louis High School in St. Louis, Missouri. During the same period the young teacher was also a student, in the summer of 1903 at the University of Rochester, then at the Cold Springs Biological Laboratory in 1904, at Howard University, where he received an M.A. in biology in 1905, and at Johns Hopkins for Saturday and evening classes in 1905 and 1906.

Turner's great love during these years was biology, particularly botany, an interest he had developed from his early years on a farm in Southern Maryland. His desire was to teach rural children the secrets

---

[5]Booker T. Washington had founded Tuskegee as an agricultural and trade school in 1881. Since Turner was from the country, and the South, he saw worth in Washington's efforts. Years later Turner still insisted that he never saw "any sense" in the controversy which arose between Washington and W. E. B. DuBois, Washington's most famous critic of the period. Primarily, Turner admired DuBois, but thought him mistaken in believing that Washington did not favor higher education for the black man. See NPR, "Options," radio interview with Turner, April 1974.

of the natural surroundings they would know all their lives. In 1913 he was offered a position as professor of the teaching of biology at his alma mater, Howard University. He often pointed out later that he and Woodrow Wilson came to Washington in the same year. In September of 1913, in fact, the new professor wrote to James Cardinal Gibbons, Archbishop of Baltimore, which See included the city of Washington, D.C., requesting that the prelate send a letter to President Wilson on racial discrimination. Gibbons politely replied that he "was not sufficiently acquainted with the President" to do so, but would certainly not hesitate to express himself should the occasion arise.[6] Turner's request was in keeping with his more active involvement in racial affairs. He had helped to establish the first chapter of the N.A.A.C.P. in Baltimore; upon arrival in Washington, he used that experience to recruit members for the newly formed, influential chapter in the District of Columbia.[7]

The next nine and one-half years at Howard were busy ones for Turner. From 1914 to 1920 he not only taught biology but served as Acting Dean of the School of Education. He attended Columbia University in the summer of 1913, taught at Hampton Institute the following summer, and in the summers of 1915 through 1917 attended graduate school at Cornell, where he received his Ph.D. degree in Biological Science after a sabbatical year during 1920 and 1921. During one of those summers at Cornell, Turner had the opportunity to travel to the South, lecturing

---

[6] James Cardinal Gibbons to Turner, 17 September 1913, Turner Papers.

[7] Interview with Turner, Washington, D.C., 24 December 1974.

for the National Security League of New York to black summer schools. He chose purposely the states of the deepest South, because he wished to experience the "nasty" discrimination which he believed had never truly touched him in Southern Maryland. In 1918 the U. S. Department of Agriculture sought an expert on white potatoes to conduct experiments at the Presque Isle Laboratory in Maine. Cornell University replied that they knew only one man who could do the work--a black scientist at Howard University. Professor Turner promptly landed the job.

Turner's published articles in biology at this period included several on the teaching of biology in rural schools. He wanted the farm youngster to have the opportunity to lay a solid scientific foundation for the work with nature which would be his life. City children were taught gardening far more often, he reflected, than rural students who were in greater need of methodology. Not only could they gain practical skills, he noted, but "the genuine respect for life in one form generally begets respect for it in other forms."[8] Speaking of the teacher's role, he said:

> I consider the one unpardonable sin of the teacher to be his inability to grasp the problem which embodies the needs of his community and his consequent failure to take proper means and methods to relieve them. Whether these needs be along economic, intellectual, or moral lines, the standard of the community should be raised because it has invested in a teacher.[9]

---

[8]Turner, "Nature Study in the Public Schools," Southern Workman 42 (September 1913): 503.

[9]Ibid., p. 800. Also Turner, "Rating Methods in Colored Schools,"Howard University Record 17 (January 1923): 189-94; Turner, "Biology Teaching and the Rural School," Southern Workman 55 (August 1926): 349-52; Turner, "Biological Laboratory and Human Welfare," Howard University Record 18 (January 1924): 180-87.

Turner was interested in the sociological and even ethical implications of his scientific study and teaching.

> We are beginning to see that an individual's reactions in regard to his neighbors are simply expressions of himself. We have about learned that the self, the personality, is a product. The biological laboratory with its data on the origin and development of personality offers a splendid opportunity to impart ethical values in their social relations and thus to contribute to building of better individuals and better communities.[10]

Turner could see the value further in laying a scientific basis for proper race relations.

> Another way in which the biological laboratory makes for ethical culture is the part which it has played and is playing, in trying to establish the true relationship of races and nations to each other. We know how persistently certain scientists only a few decades ago classified races as superior and inferior. We marvel at the sense of security they took in the absolute certainty of their conclusions after having applied their mathematical and chemical tests! This belief, of course, carried with it two types of conduct, one toward the superior and one toward the inferior. But the microscopists and naturalists working along other lines are fairly united at present that these terms have no meaning as applied to races and nations, and the additional fact that some of the so-called inferior peoples have forged ahead to the front ranks of civilized nations, while some so-called superior ones have become apparently decadent, has completely upset these older calculations.
> A universal ethical conduct which must be the same to all men will surely follow as the ignorance and superstition of former days shall be supplanted by the truths of the laboratory. We are nearer the goal of universal brotherhood, I feel, today than we were a century ago, largely, because the pursuit of science has developed a larger sympathy among men, by teaching them that they are truly of one flesh, with a common parentage.[11]

As Turner specialized in botany his professional work was further removed from these specifically human studies. He retained an interest

---

[10]Turner, "Biological Laboratory," p. 185.

[11]Ibid., p. 186.

in it, however, as will be seen later, particularly in his review of Fr. Gillard's book on black Catholics. He summarized his professional ideal thus:

> The teacher of biology then ought to be a person of high moral and religious ideals, large sympathies and breadth of character, working ever to develop right conduct, right attitude, and to prepare the young to render active service to the living. . . .[12]

Early Religious Concerns

While writing of improvements in public institutions Turner was also aware of religious educational needs. In correspondence with Fr. Walter Elliott, editor of the *Missionary*, Turner spoke of the needs of black Catholic children for education, particularly higher education, within their own church structure. Elliott sympathized with the genuine concern which Turner displayed, but claimed that racial mingling of students was improbable, for the argument would always be raised that such a move would only drain institutions of their white pupils and force eventual closings. Ultimately, the priest admitted, "I take refuge (let me confess it) in my prayers."[13] Elliott listened enough, however, to believe Turner's voice should be given some expression, and

---

[12] Ibid., p. 187.

[13] Walter Elliott to Turner, 8 September 1914, Turner Papers. The Society of Missionary Priests of St. Paul the Apostle to which Elliott belonged was founded in 1858 by the Rev. Isaac Hecker, for the conversion of non-Catholic Americans to Catholicism. It was the first religious community to open a house on the campus of the Catholic University of America in 1889. The *Missionary* was a community organ, conducive to the publication of articles about the largely non-Catholic black population. On the Paulist Fathers, see *New Catholic Enycyclopedia*, s.v. "Paulists," by V. F. Holden.

invited the latter to submit his ideas for publication in the Missionary.

In the first of two articles, entitled "After the Parish School, What?--For the Catholic Colored Child?" Turner (who himself was married but had no children) pointed out that black Catholic parents faced a crucial decision when their children first started to school. They were exhorted to give their children a Catholic education, which was sometimes available on the elementary level. But these same black parents were aware that when their children reached junior high or high school age, a Catholic education was denied those who sought it at the local Catholic high school. What damage, then, would be done to a child by the discontinuity in his education, and perhaps also by the awareness of Church discrimination against him in the field of education? Turner, the teacher, noted that he saw black Catholic youngsters in the local public high school (Baltimore High and Training School) who suffered disastrous results of discontinuity and discrimination. Some lost their Catholic faith; others left school. Still others lost their general focus in such a way as to make further education far less productive than it might have been. Catholic educators more than anyone else, Turner agreed, realized that the opportunity to reach the heights would be all that could motivate men to become leaders, and especially, to pursue the highest forms of religious calling in the Church.

> . . . I feel that this prejudice, which prevents Catholic colored youth from gaining an education within the folds of the Church, is too flagrant and positive a wrong to be tolerated for a moment by the Church after its attention has been sufficiently called to it.[14]

---

[14]Turner, "After the Parish School, What?--For the Catholic Colored Child," Missionary, November 1915, p. 653.

Turner mentioned that a priest with whom he had recently corresponded (he meant Elliott) was rather gloomy about possible solutions to the whole problem. He himself found no need for gloom, he said, but perhaps only an awareness of past guilt in the Church. The solution, after all, was very simple.

> Race prejudice stands in the way [of education], which is the child of ignorance and of racial conceit; if our priests and other authorities would ignore it and deal with it as they do other violations of the ten commandments, for this is certainly such, the monstrous falsehood would soon die like other slanders and calumnies. . . .[15]

The second article, "More Work and Less Talk," was a rebuttal to an earlier magazine article by a priest on missionary work among blacks. The author of the original article had tried to explain why black Catholics display so much apathy toward their religion. Turner found the priest's answers "zealous" but "mistaken." When the priest advanced the idea that black Catholics could be doing much on their own initiative to create lay organizations, Turner replied that most lay organizations, including the Knights of Columbus, had resulted from clerical initiative. Then he went on to state an opinion rather interesting in the light of his later work in the Church:

> Personally . . . I do not feel that a peculiarly colored organization within the Church is consonant with the teachings and ideals of Our Lord, its founder.[16]

His approach, he said, was to advise black Catholics to follow the laws and ideals of the Church herself. He insisted that black Catholics needed access to general organizations of their Church.

---

[15]Ibid.

[16]Turner, "More Work and Less Talk," *Missionary*, February 1916, p. 65.

Denied entrance into groups like the Knights of Columbus, and forbidden by the Church from joining such associations as the Masons, they were bereft of any supportive fraternal organizations.

Prior to the appearance of this article in the Missionary, Turner had requested of Rev. J. J. O'Connor, pastor of St. Augustine's, the mother church of black Catholics in Washington, D.C., the establishment of a Knights of Columbus unit for the men of his own parish. Having studied their foundation, he said, he knew that the organization could serve as an adequate alternative to other fraternal societies such as the Freemasons, which the hierarchy forbade Catholic laymen to join. The appeal was directed to a priest, Turner said, "because most of the orders have been established by priests and, of course, we look to priests to lead us into the larger field of temporal and spiritual graces."[17]

One Catholic organization which had been open to black men was the Holy Name Society.[18] Its activities formed the basis for one of Turner's first acts of protest within the Church. In February 1916, he wrote to Rt. Rev. O. B. Corrigan, the spiritual director of the Holy

---

[17]Turner to J. J. O'Connor, 8 January 1916, Turner Papers.

[18]A confraternity whose history dates back to the Middle Ages, the Holy Name Society was founded to promote reverence for the name of Christ. Promoted by the Dominican Order, usually in parish units, its members often hold processions in honor of the Holy Name. The Knights of Columbus as a fraternal organization sponsoring social activities was more likely to raise color barriers than a group such as the Holy Name Society. One argument given Turner for excluding blacks from the Knights of Columbus was that the group's insurance premiums would be increased if it included black members. See interview with Turner, March 1973.

Name Union of his area, to complain about newspaper accounts of the local Holy Name parade of October 15, 1915, which referred to black boys as "picanninies." Although he had introduced resolutions in his own Society meeting to send letters to the paper, he was told that the Washington reports he read were merely copies of accounts in the Baltimore <u>Catholic Review</u> and the Holy Name Journal. In any event, Turner explained to Bishop Corrigan, all accounts should be regretted by any true Catholic, and he sincerely hoped Corrigan would handle the matter.[19]

This was not the only time Bishop Corrigan was to hear from Turner, for later that same year Turner complained that his Holy Name group itself had been "Jim Crowed" into a special place at Corpus Christi Church in Baltimore during a Holy Name Mass.[20] To this letter the bishop replied, in a message to Father Griffith of St. Gregory's Church in Baltimore, that his only purpose on the day in question was to reserve good seats for the black men, who would be arriving from out of town. The point was to avoid the very trouble now being raised. The bishop added: "I am surprised that a man of Mr. Turner's education and standing should lend himself to such an unwarranted complaint."[21]

Not all Turner's dealings with priests during this period were unpleasant ones. He wrote to Fr. Ignatius Smith of the Catholic University, for example, congratulating him for a talk delivered to the

---

[19]Turner to Rt. Rev. O. B. Corrigan, 4 February 1916, Turner Papers.

[20]Turner to Corrigan, 2 May 1916, Turner Papers.

[21]Corrigan to Father Griffith, May [1916], Turner Papers.

Holy Name men. He asked the priest to speak out against race prejudice:

> Race prejudice is the greatest sin in the world to-day. The prejudice within the Church by white men against their fellow Catholic colored co-workers is probably the greatest menace which aims at her perpetuity. She cannot withstand the hypocrisy of men who claim they are following Our Lord when they are not. It seems to me to be the duty of all of us who claim to be true Catholics to guard our Holy Mother Church against this evil.[22]

The letter did contain one critical note on the clergy. Prejudice, he said, "is growing worse just in proportion to the silent treatment given it by our spiritual Fathers."[23] A positive outgrowth of the *Missionary* articles was a letter from Fr. P. J. Wendel in Mississippi, who introduced himself as the pastor of a black school and parish who had authored a pamphlet entitled "Our Negro Missions." Having read the article, "After the Parish School, What?", Wendel said he was convinced of his agreement with Turner on most issues. The priest himself had tried to get a Catholic college started that would prepare blacks for the priesthood, but had failed. Had Turner any advice to offer on other laymen, black or white, who would support such an endeavor? In a subsequent letter, the priest explained: "We fellows here in the South are looking to you in the East for help in our efforts for the Catholisation of the Negro in the South."[24]

---

[22]Turner to Rev. Ignatius Smith, 8 February [1916], Turner Papers.

[23]Ibid.

[24]Rev. P. J. Wendel to Turner, 22 November 1916, Turner Papers. See also Wendel to Turner, 16 November 1915, Turner Papers.

Committee Beginnings

At the outbreak of World War I Turner's position at Howard University involved him directly in a problem unique for black Catholics. United States troops were racially segregated. Welfare services were provided in segregated cantonments for the non-Catholic soldiers, black and white, by the Y.M.C.A. and Y.W.C.A. The Catholic Church coordinated its services, as was mentioned in chapter one, through an agency entitled the National Catholic War Council. No facilities were provided, however, for black Catholics, or for their employment in serving the troops.[25]

Turner became aware of this problem when a trustee of Howard University who was also a Y.M.C.A. officer began sending him applications for cantonment positions from black Catholic laymen, largely teachers. Turner arranged for a small committee of black Catholics to meet first with the pastor of St. Augustine's Church, where it was decided that the group should visit Cardinal Gibbons in Baltimore. After a sympathetic session with the committee, the cardinal referred its members to the National Catholic War Council. Here they met with Col. P. H. Callahan, director of welfare services provided for the Council by the Knights of Columbus. Callahan saw the need for some immediate solution and placed qualified black Catholic workers in cantonments at several camps, where they served until the end of the war.

---

[25]The information for most of this section on black Catholics and the National Catholic War Council was taken from Turner, "The Federation of Colored Catholics," pt. 2, chap. 2, pp. 3-4.

Not all problems of discrimination, of course, required the immediate attention of the cardinal himself. Turner and his black Catholic friends in Washington felt the irritation of local conditions. They experienced discrimination in Catholic education and at church services in certain parishes. Black priests were a rarity.[26] As his consciousness of these issues grew more acute, Turner began to discuss them in informal meetings in his own home. The original group of five men grew eventually into the "Committee of Fifteen." An early letter from the group to the Most Rev. Edward F. Prendergast, Archbishop of Philadelphia, contained its own self-description:

> We, the Committee of Fifteen, a body of practical Catholic men and women, organized (1) to bring about a better feeling and closer union among all Catholics, (2) to eradicate any and every obstacle which tends to prevent colored men and women from enjoying the full temporal graces of the Church, (3) to raise the status of the Colored Catholic and (4) to cooperate with orders, Priests Societies and any other efforts within the Church to promote the spiritual and temporal welfare of all Catholics, respectfully solicit your good will and influence to secure for the Colored Catholic full opportunity for educational, economic and spiritual uplift.[27]

This particular letter, interestingly, was a petition for the Archbishop's aid in securing admission of black Catholics to the "two most powerful organizations within the Church, the Knights of Columbus and the National Catholic War Council."[28]

---

[26]Ibid., p. 5. There were five black priests in the United States in 1925. See John T. Gillard, The Catholic Church and the American Negro (Baltimore: St. Joseph's Society Press, 1929), pp. 85-86.

[27]Turner to the Most Rev. Edward F. Prendergast, December 1918, Turner Papers.

[28]Ibid.

Turner always maintained later that the organization was never meant to be a permanent one, but was merely an "ad hoc" committee, meeting for as long as there were problems to be solved. And the problems were tenacious.[29]

Another letter in 1919, this time apparently a standard form mailed to a number of bishops, called for an increase in black priests and indicted the Josephite Society for failing to admit black candidates at St. Joseph Seminary in Baltimore, Maryland (a charge always vehemently denied by the Josephites). The committee protested the new policy of refusing black students at the Catholic University of America, and the general lack of educational facilities for black Catholics. The group observed that other churches, such as the Methodist and the Presbyterian, spent much larger sums of money on black education. Finally, it requested representation on all Church boards affecting the welfare of blacks: "We do not feel that adequate opinion of the needs and necessities of the Negro can be received from any one except the Negro himself."[30]

While black Catholics themselves were meeting in Washington, another group interested in their welfare gathered in Richmond. In November of 1918 several priests and teachers involved in black Catholic work met in Richmond to form the National Catholic Association for the Advancement of Colored People. Their purpose was to "labor for the

---

[29]Interview with Turner, March 1973.

[30]Committee of Fifteen to the hierarchy, 1919, Turner Papers. See also Turner, "The Federation of Colored Catholics," pt. 2, chap. 2, pp. 6-7.

conversion of the Negro population of the United States, to advance their moral and social well-being, and to promote their Christian education."[31] Bishop D. J. O'Connell of Richmond welcomed the group to his diocese and attended all its sessions over a four-day period. He noted that what the work among black Catholics needed most desperately was coordination, among the various societies engaged in ministry and education, and the various parishes scattered across the country. Perhaps this new organization could help to accomplish that, he said. Among the officers, all white, elected at this first session were Bishop O'Connell as Honorary President; Rev. L. B. Pastorelli, Superior of the Josephites, as President; Rev. Thomas Wrenn of Philadelphia as Vice-President; Rev. Charles Hannigan as Secretary; and the Rev. T. B. Maroney, rector of St. Joseph Seminary, Baltimore, as Treasurer.

On the last day of the conference Rev. Dr. Howard, Secretary General of the Catholic Educational Association, attended the sessions. He indicated that he would not be opposed to an affiliation of the educational branch of the new organization with the C.E.A.; in fact, he had tried ten years before, he said, to start a section on black Catholic education within the C.E.A. Arrangements were made by Father Hannigan as Secretary with the Parish School Department of the C.E.A. for papers to be delivered on black Catholic education at the next annual meeting in St. Louis in June 1919.

---

[31]A brief history of this organization was presented by its secretary, Rev. Charles Hannigan, at the Catholic Educational Association convention in June 1919. See Hannigan, "Report of the Formation of the National Catholic Association for the Advancement of the Colored People," Proceedings, Catholic Educational Association Bulletin 16 (November 1919): 418-22.

Bishop O'Connell contacted Dr. Turner at Howard and Dr. W. P. Dickerson, a black Catholic of Newport News, Virginia, to ask if they would deliver papers. Both men agreed. Dickerson addressed the conference with "A Plea for Social Justice," and Turner spoke on "Actual Conditions of Catholic Education Among the Colored Laymen."

To demonstrate that the work ahead in the field of black Catholic education was enormous, Turner used U. S. Census Bureau statistics--an illiteracy rate of 30.4 percent or higher among blacks in 1918, and possibly as many as five million blacks not affiliated with any religion out of a population of ten to twelve million. Much of his remaining address was similar to the earlier Missionary article on the black Catholic child. Educational facilities were utterly vital to real growth, and almost non-existent on higher levels for black Catholics.

As for present facilities, there were a few industrial and vocational schools, and two high schools, one with a complete course leading to college entrance.[32] In contrast, the Baptists had twenty-two schools in Louisiana, sixteen in Mississippi, and forty-three in Georgia, many on the secondary level. Over 1100 Catholic white high schools existed and more than 100 white colleges, with ten universities, Dr. Turner remarked, so that it was not hard to understand why the

---

[32]Xavier University in New Orleans, presently a coeducational institution directed by the Blessed Sacrament Sisters for the higher education of black students, was founded by Mother M. Katherine Drexel as a high school in 1915, and had a normal department added in 1917. The teachers' college and liberal arts and science programs were not in existence until 1925. See New Catholic Encyclopedia, s.v. "Xavier University of Louisiana," by M. N. Conroy.

Catholic white population outstripped the black one. "No one kind of training is sufficient for any class of people," he went on. While vocational education may be valuable, black students must be given the opportunity for more. The Church has capitalized on the Catholic leaders emerging out of the recent War; she should educate blacks and capitalize on her best products to convince "hard-headed" Catholic businessmen that black Catholic education is a good investment. The need for a native clergy and religious vocations presented all the more reason for beginning now.

Turner concluded with a declaration. Any sin against democracy, whether Bolshevism, autocracy or racial antipathy, was a sin not only against the country but against the Church as well. Catholic schools could prevent these evils because they could inculcate democracy.[33]

The Committee of Fifteen was convinced above all that the answer to converting black people and maintaining them in the Church was a native clergy. It was the primary reason for their emphasis on Catholic education, in which vocations to the ministry could be inspired and fostered. Entrance into the seminary itself was a further problem. With this in mind Turner wrote in 1919 to Rev. E. R. Dyer of St. Mary's

---

[33]Turner, "Actual Conditions of Catholic Education Among the Colored Laymen," Catholic Educational Association Bulletin 16 (November 1919): 431-40. See also Turner, "The Federation of Colored Catholics," pt. 2, chap. 3, pp. 6-7. The Catholic Educational Association was founded in 1904, through the union of three existing groups: the Educational Conference of Seminary Faculties, the Association of Catholic Colleges, and the Parish School Conference. In 1927 its name was changed to the National Catholic Educational Association. It has at present more than 14,000 member institutions and educators. See New Catholic Encyclopedia, s.v. "National Catholic Educational Association," by M. Irwin.

Seminary in Baltimore. Was it true, he asked, that the seminary would not accept any candidate "if he were dark enough to be identified with the Negro race?"[34] Dyer replied that such was not the case. St. Mary's had gladly accepted black students from St. Joseph's Seminary (Josephites) in some of its courses. As for allowing black students to board at St. Mary's itself, however, the seminary had to consider "conditions not at all of our making or of our choice." He elaborated:

> We could not admit colored students as members of our Seminary Community because this would make it impossible for us to serve a great many Bishops and dioceses who now depend upon us for the education of their clergy, and who would be unwilling to commit their subjects to us if we received colored students. To quote the words of Mr. Cleveland, which have since become a proverb: "It is a condition and not a theory which confronts us."[35]

Dyer advocated instead segregated seminaries.

> It seems to me that the principle governing the relations of the two races in present conditions should be <u>distinction without and sense of inferiority on either side</u>.[36]

Turner's reply expressed no surprise that bishops shared responsibility for present conditions. But how could the hierarchy be respected, he asked, if it showed such discrimination? For his own part and that of the committee, there was an alternative:

> The Catholic colored people have tied themselves, in the Church, up to the Banner of the Lord Jesus Christ, which we think we recognize quite clearly; but when a white majority in the Church shall for social purposes abandon this Banner we shall certainly not be mislead. If all the white priests

---

[34] Turner to Rev. E. R. Dyer, 11 October 1919, Turner Papers.

[35] Dyer to Turner, 14 October 1919, Turner Papers.

[36] Ibid.

> and laymen decide that segregating and discriminating Catholics are reasonable in the Catholic Church we shall still cling to the undefiled Banner of the Lord even though we may have to tread the "wine press alone."[37]

Turner's response to Dyer's suggestion of segregated seminaries was sharp: the same reasoning had been used in the South for generations. It was based on a conviction of black inferiority.

> We can see no reason for color segregation either in Church or elsewhere except that some class is always seeking an opportunity to exploit a weaker class and by keeping them distinct they can be rounded up more easily.[38]

Civil and religious segregation in a democracy was un-American and unCatholic, declared Turner, and its ultimate logic would be that the black Catholic have separate priests and bishops and even his own pope.

> No, Father, the sense of self-respect of the colored man is to be appealed to in exactly the same way as that of the white man by urging him to move forward, to become allied to and to take possession of every civil and religious privilege along with other men, and to seek to blot out every distinction that would necessitate an adjective before his Catholicism or his Americanism.[39]

The black layman felt, he said, as though he were the prophet of old, saying, "Jerusalem, Jerusalem, convertere ad Dominum Deum tuum."[40]

Father Dyer responded to this letter. He advocated a two-fold approach: to acknowledge conditions, and to study ways to meet them effectively. The condition of prejudice, he said, was not merely a Southern attitude. It existed against national groups, such as the

---

[37] Turner to Dyer, 18 October 1919, Turner Papers.

[38] Ibid.

[39] Ibid.

[40] Ibid.

Italian and Irish--wherever there were people with varied ideas, education and tastes. The problem in the seminary was one not so much of the classroom as of the common life of the students.

> It is in no way necessary for the full religious, civil and social development of a people or race that they mix and comingle [sic] indiscriminately with a distinct people or race. Each one has within itself all that is required for its own full and complete development.[41]

The Church had always preferred to face conditions as they were and act slowly, when as in the case here a matter of faith and morals was not involved, Dyer reflected. He did not think that he was prejudiced, since he knew many educated and refined blacks. Indeed, prejudice seemed to be lessening generally, although it would never fully disappear. Ultimately the Church had the only answer to the problem: an uplift of blacks that would diminish prejudice.[42]

Turner did not remain silent, but chose to respond to this letter by telephone rather than by the written word.[43]

Meanwhile the Committee for the Advancement of Colored Catholics, as it was now calling itself, also expressed itself on the issue of seminary discrimination. Its letter to Cardinal Gibbons shortly before his death, complaining that black students were not being admitted at the Josephite seminary in Baltimore, drew a strong denial. Gibbons replied that the Josephites were willing to accept all qualified candidates; the records showed that many who had applied were over age

---

[41] Dyer to Turner, 23 October 1919, Turner Papers.

[42] Ibid.

[43] There is a note to this effect in Dyer's letter above.

or unfit for college work. He advised Turner to "use your influence with your people and cause them to see what we are doing with such a limited means of men and money."[44]

Gibbons himself had donated money before the war for the establishment of a black Catholic school in Southern Maryland. The task had been turned over to the Jesuits, but the war interrupted their efforts. After Gibbons' death in 1921, plans to construct an institute were resumed.[45] Dr. Turner and several other black Catholics were invited to join the Board of Trustees of what became the Cardinal Gibbons Institute. Originally the Jesuits had decided that the greatest need in Southern Maryland was for a reform school. After the black Catholics on the board pointed out that Protestant churches were building black secondary schools and even colleges in the South, the rest of the board relented. It was decided to establish a national black secondary school offering academic and industrial training for boys and girls. Since the school was to be located in rural Southern Maryland, attention would also be centered on agricultural courses. Dr. Turner was offered the opportunity to become the principal when the school was completed.

---

[44] Gibbons to Turner, 15 March 1920, Turner Papers.

[45] Most of this section on the Cardinal Gibbons Institute was taken from Turner, "The Federation of Colored Catholics," pt. 2, chap. 3, pp. 7-9. The Jesuits in Southern Maryland had the original idea for this school, which was to be called St. Peter Claver Institute, and be the counterpart to St. Mary's Industrial School for white boys in Baltimore. The latter was administered by the Xaverian order, who were to take charge of the new school as well. Cardinal Gibbons became interested and donated money to purchase acreage. When the Xaverians were unable to take part in the project, the Jesuits took full responsibility. John LaFarge was involved in the plans from the very beginning, and more will be said later in his connection about the Institute. See Reynolds, Jesuits, pp. 78-82.

Although he declined, Turner did remain a member of the board for a number of years, working with Father LaFarge, who was deeply interested in the project.

When after World War I the National Catholic War Council was made a permanent administrative body, the National Catholic Welfare Council, the American bishops began a practice of meeting annually in November at the Catholic University of America. The Committee for the Advancement of Colored Catholics used this occasion each year to address a letter to the hierarchy, and also to meet with as many bishops personally as it could. In 1919 its message contained a reference to the Josephites and discriminatory admission policies at their seminary, the charge answered by Gibbons in 1920.[46] Two years later the committee wrote Gibbons' successor, Archbishop Michael Curley, recalling the earlier charges, and adding a specific complaint against the actions of a Josephite priest during a meeting on the Cardinal Gibbons Institute. The committee requested the removal of the priest in question from his parish and of the Josephites from that parish generally, and from consideration for the pastorate of a proposed new black parish in Washington.[47] Such strong language indicates the resentment which had begun to build toward the Society of St. Joseph, and was to continue (despite the committee's protests of "no axes to grind" and some personal friendships between members and Josephite priests) in one form or another throughout the Federation's history.

---

[46]Committee of Fifteen to the hierarchy, 1919, Turner Papers.

[47]Committee for the Advancement of Colored Catholics to Bishop Michael Curley, 30 December 1922, Turner Papers.

In 1923 and 1924 Turner served as a judge in a Catholic Historical Society essay contest on black Catholic missionary activity, an event which helped renew a valuable acquaintance with Fr. Stephen Theobald, second place winner in the contest. In a frank letter to Turner, Theobald remarked that he as a black priest was probably just as effective living in the West and encouraging an active lay black movement in the East, for if he were in the East his activities would undoubtedly be limited.[48]

Federated Colored Catholics

In 1924 Dr. Turner, having received his Ph.D. in 1921, became head of the department of biological sciences at Hampton Institute in Virginia.[49] On December 29 of the same year a group of black Catholic laymen, consisting of members of the original committee and representatives from the Knights of America and the Knights of St. John, met at the N.C.W.C. headquarters in Washington to establish the Federated Colored Catholics of the United States. The N.C.W.C. news release stated as the purpose of the new organization:

---

[48]Theobald to Turner, 23 May 1924, Turner Papers. Theobald had greater ministerial opportunities as the protege of Bishop John Ireland of Minneapolis-St. Paul. Interestingly, the same letter contained a reference to Theobald's encounter with a "Claver Club" in the Midwest. "It is an attempt," he said, "to realize the theory enunciated by Markoe, S.J. in one of his articles in America."

[49]Turner was asked to come to Hampton at the time it was developing a four-year collegiate program. Although he was responsible specifically for biological sciences, his broader aim was to develop a research attitude in the student body generally. The school was one of several black agricultural and technical institutions established after the Civil War, this one by the American Missionary Association. Turner was the only black faculty member with his education at the time. Interview with Turner, March 1973. Also NPR, "Options," April 1974.

. . . to bring about a closer relation and a better feeling among all Catholic negroes, to advance the cause of Catholic education throughout the negro population, to seek to raise the general Church status of the negro and to stimulate colored Catholics to a larger participation in racial and civic affairs.[50]

One year later Turner sent out invitations for the first annual convention of the Federation at the N.C.W.C. headquarters in Washington in December 1925. From the beginning the purpose was to get every black Catholic organization and parish to join, the invitations noting that "this organization is established to supply a need which colored Catholics have long felt."[51] In his first convention address President Turner pursued this theme. Sporadic efforts in the past to unite black Catholics had failed, he said, but the hope of the Federation, which arose "almost spontaneously," is to serve as "a voice of the Catholic Negro in America."[52] Turner listed Catholic education as a primary goal.

As for clerical participation at this early stage, Archbishop Curley addressed the convention and listened patiently to its members; Father Alonzo Olds of St. Augustine's Church served as a host; and Father Theobald sent a paper, which arrived too late for reading but was printed with the proceedings in the new Council Review.[53]

---

[50]News clipping, 29 December 1924, Turner Papers.

[51]Form letter, Turner to "Friend," 1925, Turner Papers.

[52]Turner, "The Federated Colored Catholics of the United States," address at the first annual convention of the F.C.C., December 1925, Turner Papers.

[53]Turner to Curley, 9 December 1925, Turner Papers. Turner to Olds, 9 December 1925, Turner Papers. Turner to Theobald, 9 December 1925, Turner Papers.

In December Turner traveled to Kansas City, Missouri, to deliver a paper at the annual convention of the American Association for the Advancement of Science. He attended these conventions as often as he could and used the opportunities not only to improve professionally, but also to speak to black Catholics locally on the newly formed Federation. Turner described an experience en route to Kansas City. Stopping over in St. Louis on Sunday, December 27, he had sought out a Catholic Church for Mass. When he sat down in a pew in the middle aisle, being careful to note that it was not someone else's, an usher approached to direct him to the back of the church, the "place" for black people.[54] When Turner refused to move, the usher insisted that these were "the pastor's orders." Turner replied that he took his orders from Jesus Christ in the Church, not mere man. The usher did not pursue the matter, but Turner remarked that the man later received Holy Communion piously.

Turner mentioned discrimination he had learned of in Kansas and Missouri, as well as recent reports of discrimination in Philadelphia and New York. Why do black Catholics remain in the Church, he asked rhetorically.

> . . . the black man's connection with the Church of Jesus Christ far antedates most of those who would have him leave it; thus it would be quite painful for him to leave.[55]

Charging that in many cases parish priests of black people were "marking time," Turner wondered why they had not yet learned the lesson Protestant churches had: ". . . real, permanent progress,

---

[54]Turner, "Experiences of a Colored Catholic," Fortnightly Review, 1 April 1926, pp. 143-45.

[55]Ibid., p. 145.

spiritual or temporal, is assured only when a racial group is helped to fall in line behind its own leaders."[56] Priests made the mistake of presuming that they were sufficient in themselves to speak for black people and that "colored leaders are superfluous and troublesome."[57] The Church had learned better in every other mission area of the world. Why not, Turner asked, among blacks in America? "It would be interesting to know who is responsible for this, and how the situation may be improved."[58]

Meanwhile the Federation was already experiencing reactions to its existence. Eugene J. Marshall, a Chicago attorney, repeated his address at the first Federation convention to an audience at St. Elizabeth (black) Church in Chicago. In a later letter to an F.C.C. member in Washington, Marshall complained that his speech had incurred the displeasure of St. Elizabeth's pastor, Father Eckert. Further, Eckert was discouraging participation of his parishioners in the Federation because it was a "segregated affair." That charge, and Father Eckert's attitude generally, reappeared to plague Turner in the next few years.[59]

The November 1926 message to the hierarchy—the first that the F.C.C. sent as an official organization—recalled the original letter of 1919 and concluded,

---

[56] Ibid.

[57] Ibid.

[58] Ibid.

[59] Eugene J. Marshall to Prater, 25 January 1926, Turner Papers. At the same time, Eckert himself must have attended the first convention of the Federation and later wrote Turner asking if the latter would deliver a paper at the Eucharistic Congress in Chicago in June of 1926. See Eckert to Turner, 30 April 1926, Turner Papers.

> Since presenting the first paper to you, our further investigations of the status of the Catholic colored people do not indicate that there has been any particular consideration given to the welfare of our people in the Church by the authorities in this country. In fact, there is the clearest indication everywhere that the extensive provision made for Catholic education and Catholic progress (as shown by the annual proceedings of the Catholic Educational Association) are not meant to include the Catholic Negro at all.[60]

The letter went on to quote from an article which appeared in a 1926 issue of <u>Crisis</u> on the Catholic Negro:

> And the reason for this [discrimination] is clear: the Irish hierarchy which dominates the Catholic Church in America is defying the whole Catholic world in its attitude toward black folk.[61]

The tone of the letter was not entirely negative. Several positive developments were mentioned. The first of these was the papal encyclical of March 5, which urged the establishment of native clergies. A major reason for the difference between results in Africa and those in America—here the Federation was quoting from Our Negro Missions—was that Africa had forty-two native priests and America five. The members of the Federation were also grateful for the establishment of the Cardinal Gibbons Institute, the founding of St. Augustine's Mission House for the education of black seminarians by the Society of the Divine Word at Bay St. Louis, Mississippi,[62] and finally, of course,

---

[60] Federated Colored Catholics to the American bishops, November 1926, Turner Papers.

[61] Ibid.

[62] Ibid. St. Augustine's Mission House in Bay St. Louis, Mississippi was established by the Society of the Divine Word in 1920 to educate black candidates for their own community. It was the only black Catholic seminary per se in the country. See <u>New Catholic</u> <u>Encyclopedia</u>, s.v."Negroes in the United States, IV (Apostolate to)," by P. E. Hogan and J. B. Tennelly.

for the organization of the Federated Colored Catholics. Speaking of the latter, the members explained to the bishops:

> Our effort is to have every Catholic Negro organization in the country affiliated with the central body which will act as a clearing house for Negro Catholic opinion and will serve as a medium for making presentations to the American Hierarchy and to the Holy Father.[63]

The remainder of the letter was devoted to the results of a collection of black Catholic opinion already taken in various parts of the country. The survey revealed that the attitude within the Church toward the black Catholic was a very uncatholic one. Indeed, the Church lagged far behind secular thought on blacks. Many discriminatory practices had never been revised, such as those found in Southern Maryland. The Federation offered to provide additional data on the subject, and referred the hierarchy also to Turner's article of that year in the *Fortnightly Review.*

Although an elementary education was the Church's spiritual foothold, the Federation's study showed that it did not exist in many areas for black Catholics, or did so in an unacceptable manner. The black Catholic did not mean to be a lawbreaker in the South, where separate schools were required (though he did not understand the need for them), but in the North the Church had no excuse for maintaining separate schools. What better place to teach tolerance, asked the Federated Colored Catholics, than in the Catholic school?

The same study addressed the question of black parishes. The results indicated that few priests and bishops seemed to understand

---

[63] Ibid.

that blacks, especially in the North, objected strongly to the establishment of black parishes within white ones. Even when this was done in good faith, the black Catholic was suspicious, and not intimidated by accusations that he sought "social equality." Although members of the Federation were not certain whether canon law allowed the erection of parishes within parishes, coercion was hardly the answer in any event, they claimed, especially where segregation was not otherwise common. Their findings seemed to pinpoint Philadelphia as one city which suffered particularly from its parish arrangement for blacks.

Finally, the survey considered the current state of a native clergy. Since the Federation's first letter to the hierarchy in 1919, two black men had been ordained. The F.C.C. still sought to know the true policy of the Josephites, and expressed hope that two Jamaican students studying as Jesuit seminarians might produce a new trend in that order. Thanks was given to the Society of the Divine Word, the Lyons African Mission Fathers, and the seminaries of St. Paul and Detroit for admitting black seminarians. This was the greatest act of sincerity bishops and priests could perform for the black Catholic, concluded the Federation report: to prepare black Catholic children for ordination and religious life.

The entire letter ended on an ironic note. If the Catholic Church placed color above catholicity, declared the F.C.C., then she had assumed that viewpoint on race which they considered characteristic of protestantism. The black Catholic would be pushed toward a position of racial separatism and forced to conclude that:

... if color of his skin outweighs every other consideration in the white Catholic mind, then the more completely the spiritual and material accumulations of the race are fused on that basis, the greater will be his protection and his progress. And, thus, in the United States, we have the sad spectacle of colored people being driven in conversion to protestantism through the interactions of the Church authorities.[64]

The reason this message to the hierarchy has been outlined at such great length here is that many future letters were based on it. The words were largely Turner's, as so many of the specific references make clear, although Father LaFarge had commented on particular passages, especially the one on canon law for parish boundaries.[65]

The Federation met for its second annual convention in 1926. Turner stressed in his opening remarks that the organization was not a grievance group, even if it was meant to support black Catholics in their problems. He reiterated the main purposes of education and a black clergy.[66] There is some indication that LaFarge also spoke at this meeting on the use of the press. The resolutions of the gathering (prepared largely under LaFarge's direction) included many expressions of gratitude: to the Pope for his recent encyclical on native clergy; to the editors of America and Our Colored Missions for articles on blacks; for the growing trend toward a native clergy; for contributions of friends to the Cardinal Gibbons Institute; to Archbishop Curley as Spiritual Director. Father Olds arranged a successful meeting of a

---

[64]Ibid.

[65]LaFarge to Turner, 3 October 1926, Turner Papers.

[66]Minutes of the second annual convention of the Federated Colored Catholics, 5 December 1926, Turner Papers, p. 1.

committee of the Federation with the Papal Delegate during this convention.[67]

One interesting address of the annual meeting was the sermon of Fr. Norman Duckette, a black priest from Michigan, and a former parishioner at St. Augustine's. He stressed black pride. Why should not a black Catholic become a bishop, he asked. If no one here wanted to be one, we could bring a black man from Africa, where the Church was blossoming.

> I feel honored to know that my parents were slaves. It is nothing to be ashamed of. It is an honor to know that even though a few years ago your parents were slaves, your race is not a slave race today. So you cannot make a fixed law and the minute you say "There will be no more prejudice from now on," there will be no more prejudice. Work gradually. Do not try to get everything overnight. Persevere. Do not give up too early.
> . . . I trust that you will always remember that we are all Negroes, whether we admit it or not; we are all black people fighting for the same thing, and going to the same heaven. . . .[68]

The convention decided to meet next year in New York City and adjourned. In a letter of April 1927, Turner thanked Fr. P. Matthews Christman, at Bay St. Louis, Mississippi, for his favorable coverage of

---

[67] Ibid., pp. 6-9.

[68] Ibid., pp. 10-11. The Baltimore Afro-American in December 1926, listed these statistics as having been reported at the second annual convention: 250,000-300,000 black Catholics in the U. S.; 87 churches with resident pastors and schools; 132 churches; 22,000 black children in parochial schools; 134 black Catholic schools, five academies; 3 Catholic industrial schools; 11 Catholic orphan asylums;, 7 parochial high schools; 2 colleges preparatory to priesthood; 175 priests in work among blacks; 50 priests in work parttime; 20 sisterhoods representative in work, 700 sisters fulltime; 66 schools aided by the Catholic Board of Missions to the Colored People; 160 black sisters of the Oblates of Saint Francis; 151 black sisters of the Holy Family order; 12 black sisters of the Handmaids of the Most Pure Heart of Mary; 5 black Catholic college graduates [of Catholic colleges].

the last convention in the March issue of that black seminary's newsletter, the St. Augustine's Messenger. Impressed also with a recent article on the Federation in Osservatore Romano, the president told the priest:

> We need your advice and shall welcome it at all times. We may not always be doing things that are entirely agreeable to all, and it is unfortunate that we do have to say occasionally things that are not, but we hope as time goes on our aims and our methods can be so unified that every organization working for the elevation of the Negro can put forth a solid, united front. That is the hope underlying whatever efforts we are putting forth.[69]

Father LaFarge wrote to Turner in July that he wished to discuss the future of the Federation before the next convention. A recent study of Catholic organizations had convinced him, he said, that the Federation could not succeed unless certain changes were made soon. While not wanting to create alarm, LaFarge was sure that the New York convention might well be a turning point for the group. He had several suggestions to offer. Actually, his more detailed organizational plans followed several years later.[70]

Meanwhile, invitations had been sent to prominent political figures, such as Governor Al Smith of New York. Important New York Catholics, many of them friends of LaFarge, and clergy involved in work among blacks also received special attention.[71] In his remarks to the

---

[69]Turner to Rev. P. Mathews Christman, 2 April 1927, Turner Papers.

[70]LaFarge to Turner, 27 July 1927, Turner Papers.

[71]Smith to Turner, 20 June 1927, Turner Papers. See also Rev. Harry A. Quinn to Turner, 18 July 1927; Turner to Eckert, 22 August 1927; LaFarge to Turner, 23 August 1927, all in Turner Papers.

third convention, Turner described the unique set of pressures endured by any black Catholic group attempting to organize itself. First, there was the task of uniting on a racial basis. Scattered in parishes across the country, Catholics had been particularly slow to do this, although they possessed a heritage of black saints and popes to inspire them. One difficulty had been the lack of black clerical leaders, resulting in a peculiar dependence on the sympathetic aid of white priests in organizing. Once on its feet, however, the group could make a unique contribution to efforts for racial improvement in the country, Turner believed. It must also look to its religious responsibility:

> It is confronted at one and the same time with the problem of conserving the specific interests of the group within the Church, of conserving the interests of the Church as a whole and of conserving the general interests of the race in cooperation with other organizations having similar aims.[72]

A Mr. C. F. Clarke of Philadelphia gave an address, "The Value of a Native Clergy." Fr. Edward Kramer, director of the Bureau of Colored Missions, referred to Clarke's speech and suggested that the Federation would do better by assuming a different attitude on such matters. He was interrupted by Dr. Eugene Clarke of Washington, D.C. who said that if the clergy would act differently, there would be no cause for complaint. The minutes then recorded:

> At the conclusion of Dr. Kramer's remarks the President [Turner] further explained the position of the colored man, that it is impossible for others to know the feelings of

---

[72]Turner, "The Federation of Workers among Catholic Negroes," announcement of third annual meeting of the F.C.C., September 1927, Turner Papers.

colored men in matters of discrimination, that only those who suffer a particular thing know what that suffering is, and therefore much of the advice given misses its mark, because it does not involve knowledge of the colored man's point of view.[73]

The incident, indicative of the general tension created by the situation of black Catholic laymen in a Church of white clergy, was pursued by another white priest, Fr. Mark Moeslein, in a letter to Turner. Moeslein considered Clarke's interruptions rude, and his further objections to the words "black" and "white," puzzling. The priest confessed that he found it difficult to discover any word which was truly acceptable to black people as a reference to themselves.[74]

Moeslein had described the recent Federation convention in the Sign magazine, in an article entitled "Colored Catholicism."[75] His remarks were generally favorable, although he regretted the almost total absence of white Catholic laity and the black Catholics of local Harlem. Quoting Pope Pius XI on native clergy, he remarked that the

---

[73]Minutes of the third annual convention of the Federated Colored Catholics, 4, 5 September 1927, Turner Papers, p. 5. At least one local newspaper considered the question of native clergy, and this exchange particularly, as central to the convention. See the New Jersey Monitor, 17 September 1927.

[74]Rev. Mark Moeslein to Turner, 20 October 1927, Turner Papers. Moeslein himself was an interesting individual. After building a successful black parish in Corpus Christi, Texas, he turned the church over to a black priest, the Rev. Joseph A. John. Ironically, Father John was later transferred from his parish, possibly because white sisters who came to teach there could not have a black pastor. Moeslein was in his seventy—fourth year when he wrote Turner, but indicated that he had just agreed to take a small black parish in North Carolina. See the editor's note to Moeslein's article, "Colored Catholicism," Sign, October 1927, p. 135. Also see Smith to Turner, 29 September 1928, Turner Papers, on Father John's departure from Texas.

[75]Moeslein, "Colored Catholicism," pp. 135-38.

Pope would probably abolish the color line for America if it were not that the result would only be empty churches and resentment on the part of white Catholics. No, the Church preferred "mental reconstruction," Moeslein said. Moeslein missed any reference at the convention to spiritual improvement of the individual and the family. Black Catholics could do without the Federation, but the Federation could not survive without spiritual improvement.[76]

In a letter to Turner, Moeslein elaborated on the point about individual improvement among blacks. Moeslein said that all complaints about blacks were of individual and family faults, yet when blacks talked about improvements, they seemed only to see the need for a better education.

Although Moeslein had publicly endorsed the Council Review, he did warn Turner in this same private letter to refrain from criticizing white priests, as a recent issue had done. "Priests of the white race laboring among your people have enough to put up with, without the added annoyance of slurs from colored persons writing for the Review," he said.

Several other letters between Moeslein and Turner in the latter's collection indicate the priest's sincere desire to engage in interracial dialogue, learning all he could from the race he continued to serve.[77]

---

[76]Ibid.

[77]Moeslein to Turner, 20 October 1927, Turner Papers.

The 1928 Federation convention was held in Cincinnati, Ohio, at the invitation of Archbishop John T. McNicholas. A third day added to the schedule accommodated a new joint program sponsored by the N.C.W.C. office of Social Action and an interracial relations committee of the Federation. The topic was blacks in industry. This was the first real discussion between blacks and whites introduced into the convention and easily became a part of every succeeding convention. It was opened to the public and often included prominent non-Catholic speakers. The announcement of the Cincinnati meeting made note of the innovation:

> Emphasis will be placed, as in former conferences, upon efforts to further education and a Race clergy. Greater emphasis than formerly will be given to health, social conditions, and interracial relations.[78]

The first industrial relations program included speakers from both races on topics such as unemployment, blacks in business, and in unions. One of the most widely discussed papers was by M. P. Webster, Division Organizer of the Brotherhood of Sleeping Car Porters of Chicago, which was then engaged in struggles with the Pullman Company. Other broad economic and social issues such as housing and health also received attention.[79]

The subsequent resolutions of the meeting reflected these broader interests; for example, support for industrial and vocational training (although not to the detriment of students capable of advanced

---

[78]Announcement of the fourth annual F.C.C. convention, September 1928, Turner Papers.

[79]Minutes of the fourth annual convention of the F.C.C., September 1928, Turner Papers, pp. 3-5.

work in Catholic institutions of higher learning); encouragement of business activities among blacks, especially in commerce; affirmation of the dignity of all labor; development of an appreciation of public health programs. Here a committee was appointed to investigate the particular problem of tuberculosis, especially among black children.

> We recognize the fact that to be good, useful, practical Christians, the soul must live in a morally clean and healthy body. We know that bad sanitation, crowded living conditions, lack of personal cleanliness encourage and promote immoral living and is a big factor in increasing social diseases. We urgently appeal to the Church and all religious organizations to unite with us in our endeavor to remedy these evils.[80]

In this same vein the Federation declared that Catholic hospitals which discriminated against black physicians were injuring the public health.[81]

The annual report of the Field Agent-Organizer, William Prater, contained some strong language on conditions as he found them in traveling for the Federation, and receiving reports from others.

> In traveling about in the interest of the work, I have found some unfortunate conditions. In some places I found a separate door for the Colored people to enter Church and a stall like arrangement for them to sit and try to worship their God. A good Sister is on hand as guardian to see that little Colored boys and girls wait until all the other boys and girls have reverenced the communion alter [sic] before they are allowed to go. This condition is found in Maryland, the very cradle of the Catholic Faith in America. There is in a town in Pennsylvania, a Colored Chapel, the good Father insists on separation by segregation, not only in the Church but also during the entertainments in the basement. The good Father, in person, seeing that these arrangements are carried out. I have found that where

---

[80] Ibid., p. 6.

[81] Ibid., p. 17.

the Church practices this vicious form of race prejudice, not
only is its gain in new members very small, but [it] is losing
many of its active members who are a credit to the Faith.[82]

Prater noted also discrimination in schooling, particularly at the Catholic University, and a tendency toward exclusively black parishes. His own recommendations were simple.

> The Federated Colored Catholics of the United States is unalterably opposed to segregation in all forms, because it is sinful and certainly not Catholic. It is openly charged in some quarters that the Catholic Church does not want the colored people. These rumors are a great hindrance to my work. It should be proved or denied. I urge the discontinuance of segregation in Church and School. I do hereby urge the committee on resolutions to take the matter up at once and prayerfully beg the Church Officials to heed our appeal because they are sewing [sic] the seeds of discontent in every section of the land.
> . . . We are not asking for any special treatment, all we want is to be treated like the other members of the Church, and we mean to keep up the fight until we get that treatment and the same opportunities.[83]

Prater suggested sending Turner to Rome as the Federation's representative to the Holy Father.

Apparently the existing method of publishing the convention proceedings and other publications of the Federation, through the <u>Council Review</u>, had proved unsatisfactory. Consequently, the organization accepted the offer of C. Marcellus Dorsey of Baltimore to take over the work. He began publication with the proceedings of the Cincinnati convention.[84]

---

[82]Ibid., p. 20.

[83]Ibid., p. 19.

[84]In that same issue the official constitution of the Federation was also printed. Its prologue contained a succinct summary of the organization at that period: "This organization known as the Federated Colored Catholics of the United States, was undertaken in response to the earnest and pressing demand coming from all parts of the country,

One final result of the Cincinnati meeting was that George W. Conrad of Cincinnati was elected first vice-president. Conrad would later serve charges of misconduct upon Turner, and replace him as president.

Prater's proposal during the convention to send Turner to Rome as the representative of black Catholics to the Pope was not as farfetched as it may have sounded. The president actually did receive a leave of absence from Hampton for the academic year 1929-30, to study microbiology at Louvain. Father LaFarge wrote many letters of introduction to his Jesuit friends from student days. He also helped raise additional funds for the trip. A letter of introduction to the Pope was arranged through the Papal Delegate and Monsignor Eugene Burke of the North American College in Rome. All these efforts were in vain, for Turner became ill shortly after arriving abroad, and had to return home before accomplishing any work.[85]

---

for closer union of all Colored Catholics, in order to gain through conference and discussion, a clearer understanding of their common problems and to work out the most effective solution.--It aims to federate all Catholic organizations and individuals of the race into one comprehensive organization, and to focus their attention upon the single purpose of improving the conditions of the Catholic Negro temporally and spiritually. While local conditions will not be overlooked, this organization is especially concerned with setting forth the true plight and the urgent needs of the Catholic Negro throughout the country, in order that each community may have an intelligent ideal towards which to work." (Ibid., p. 25.) On the hiring of Dorsey, see also Smith to Turner, 17 September 1928, Turner Papers.

[85]Interview with Turner, March 1973. For letters of introduction, see LaFarge to Turner, 16 August 1929; Rev. Paul Marella to Turner, 21 August 1929; Rev. P. Fumasoni-Biondi to Rev. Eugene Burke, 21 August 1929; LaFarge to Turner, 22 August 1929, all in Turner Papers.

Turner (far left), on route to Europe, intending to see the Pope, 1929

The 1929 convention was held in Baltimore, hosted by the local chapter whose name was that of a black Josephite priest, Fr. John Dorsey. The same format of three days was followed with Fr. R. A. McGowan of the N.C.W.C. handling the first day's sessions on blacks in industry. Advance notices had emphasized that all sessions would be open, and that pastors, especially of black parishes, were most welcome.[86] Two incidents involving the Josephite Fathers, whose headquarters were located in Baltimore, are noteworthy. The first was the opening Mass, which was celebrated by the Superior General of the Josephites, Fr. Louis B. Pastorelli. He preached before 107 delegates, representing twenty states.[87] The second event was a major address delivered to the convention by Fr. Thomas J. Duffy, who discussed with frankness a ten-year-old issue with the Federation, the question of whether the Josephites were systematically excluding black candidates.

Duffy asked that whatever was said be recorded accurately, since he meant to present the "official position" of the Josephite order, and did not wish to be misquoted. "St. Joseph Society," he began, "believes absolutely and unqualifiedly in colored priests."[88] Indeed, it had been in the forefront of that movement. Naming several black priests,

---

[86]Prater, "F.C.C. to Convene in Baltimore," St. Elizabeth's Chronicle, September 1929, p. 13. Oddly enough, this article on the Federation appeared in Markoe's publication before it became the F.C.C. organ, possibly because Markoe was seeking news items from other localities.

[87]"The Convention," Chronicle, October 1929, p. 14.

[88]Thomas J. Duffy, address at the fifth annual convention of the F.C.C., 1 September 1929, Gillard Papers.

Duffy remarked that these were the candidates who made it and he could supply the names of others who did not, usually leaving on their own accord. What must be kept in mind, he urged, was that the Josephites just like any other order would take only qualified candidates. The society was not a dumping ground for other orders, nor would it treat seriously the applications of those who came merely to test the Josephites' willingness to accept black men. Many who had the ability lost interest at sixteen or seventeen. The society had tried to build schools to prepare boys. It was easy for "armchair" missionaries to criticize, who did not know the conditions in the South (where most Josephite missions were located) and the inability of black people to support the work among them. Future plans were being laid, but these were for the society to know until it decided to disclose them.

From here on the address took a strange turn. Duffy recalled his initial request that his words be precisely understood. Then, protesting his honesty, he told of hearing from some of the convention's officials that Father Pastorelli, the Josephite superior, had been invited to the meeting for the purpose, quoting his unnamed source, of "forcing his hand and that of the Josephites on the question of colored priests."[89] While accepting the challenge himself, Duffy said, the Federation must realize that its own frankness and freedom from pettiness were the means to true success. Then it would have God's approval, and human approval would become irrelevant.

---

[89] Ibid.

The address did not mend the breach between the Federation and the Josephites. Indeed, the rumor Duffy mentioned near the end was still a subject of discussion nearly two years later.[90]

Markoe and the Chronicle

Another priest had come to this convention whose future role in Federation activities was to have much greater significance. After listening to the proceedings, Fr. William Markoe, offered his own parish newsletter, the St. Elizabeth's Chronicle, to the organization as its official organ. Renamed the Chronicle, the periodical began appearing monthly, with Markoe as official editor in St. Louis, Missouri. The conditions were simple: unlimited space for Federation matters, freedom of expression and a low subscription rate, with no added financial obligations on the group.[91] This last attraction was somewhat modified later, when chapters were asked to contribute specified amounts toward a directory in the magazine. The obligations did remain minimal, however, and no official contract was ever drawn between Markoe and the Federation. The October issue of the Chronicle contained a brief statement of its purpose:

> . . . the Federated Colored Catholics of the United States must have a medium of expression, a journal or publication. The Chronicle, official organ of the Federation, will fill this role. The Chronicle will assist in bringing the more or less loosely organized units of the Federation closely together so as to form an enduring, closely knit body of sterling Catholic men and

---

[90]Turner mentioned the rumor in his invitation to Pastorelli for the seventh annual F.C.C. convention in St. Louis. See Turner to Pastorelli, 8 July 1931, Turner Papers.

[91]Smith, "An Outline History," Chronicle, December 1929, p. 4.

women. It will express to the world the thoughts, feelings, and aspirations of the colored Catholics of the United States.[92]

Soon after the Baltimore convention, Father LaFarge made some suggestions in writing to Turner, who himself proposed some revisions in the constitution.[93] In June 1930, the accusation of "Jim Crow" was raised against the organization in its executive committee meeting. No one answered that objection at the time, but Markoe did write an article in July asking whether the organization's name might be at fault.[94]

Other factors were at work at the approach of the 1930 convention, scheduled for Detroit. Turner was still recuperating from the illness which had cut short his European trip, and was uncertain of his own attendance at the convention. George Conrad, newly elected first vice-president, was not sure that he could be there. Dr. Eugene Clarke, Turner's mainstay for many years in Federation affairs, was about to be appointed President of Miner Teachers College in Washington. Finally, there was some agitation for a permanent headquarters, with the suggestion from H. M. Smith that the Holy Name Guild hall in Washington could serve that purpose.[95]

Meanwhile, Markoe had been busily gaining subscriptions for the Chronicle, promoting the Federation in its pages, and in general, helping to plan a successful Detroit convention. Indeed, Markoe was

---

[92]"Why the Chronicle?", Chronicle, October 1929, p. 15.

[93]LaFarge to Turner, 11 February 1930; Smith to Turner, 5 July 1930, both in Turner Papers.

[94]Markoe, "Jim Crow," pp. 149-50.

[95]Smith to Turner, 5 August 1930, Turner Papers.

working so hard that he had already arranged with Cardinal Glennon of St. Louis to hold the next convention (1931) in that city. During this period members of the Federation expressed very high regard for both LaFarge and Markoe.[96]

Since the 1930 convention was held in an industrial city, Detroit, its program on blacks in industry was an obvious focal point. The addresses by Donald Marshall, black representative for the Ford plant, John C. Dancy, Jr., Industrial Secretary for the Detroit Urban League, Dr. Karl F. Phillips, U. S. Commissioner of Conciliation in Washington, and Dr. James E. Hagerty, Director of the School of Social Administration at Ohio State University, provided much material for discussion. Priests also made their contribution: Monsignor Edwin V. O'Hara of the Rural Life Bureau of the N.C.W.C. and Fr. William A. Bolger, of St. Thomas College, St. Paul, Minnesota.[97]

Turner, despite his illness did attend the convention, and struck some new themes in his address. After reviewing the past work of the Federation, including its thrust toward obtaining adequate facts on racial discrimination, he turned in a new direction. This year's topic, he recalled, was Catholic Action.

---

[96]On Markoe's acquisition of an invitation for the F.C.C. to hold the 1931 convention in St. Louis, see Markoe to Smith, 20 August 1930, Turner Papers. For expressions of appreciation for the work of LaFarge and Markoe, see Smith to Turner, 12 July 1930; Constance E. H. Daniel to Turner, 7 August 1930, both in Turner Papers.

[97]Official program of the sixth annual convention of the F.C.C., September 1930, LaFarge Papers, Woodstock College Library, New York, New York. This collection will hereafter be referred to as the LaFarge Papers.

> . . . it behooves us to be concerned less and less with the differences that may be found among us and to place more and more emphasis upon the things which we all have in common as Catholics.[98]

Whether Federation members were concerned with the rural life, the liturgical or the retreat movement, they should relate their actions as laymen to the Church. As for the need of one more organization, Turner replied that the question could only be asked in a society suspect of black activity--new organizations were born in the Church every day. Those who would remove themselves from this one as limited or segregated in character were merely seeking an excuse to remain on the sidelines of a vital struggle. For those who expected accomplishments from an organization so young, at least the Federation could point to a new absence of parish "clannishness" among its members.[99]

The most important work of the Detroit meeting was *internal*, inasmuch as the Federation attempted to incorporate the thrust emphasized in Turner's speech. The organization effected new regulations which required that new chapters to the Federation have as their end some form of Catholic Action beyond mere membership in the Federation, and that they have hierarchical approbation. A motion to limit voting delegates at the convention to individuals representing at least twenty-five members (again, stressing a Federation of *organizations*) was tabled after much discussion.[100]

---

[98]Turner, "Address Made at the Detroit Convention," *Chronicle*, December 1930, p. 289.

[99]Ibid.

[100]Russell J. Cowans, "Turner Re-elected to Lead Catholics," *Chicago Defender*, 6 September 1930.

Although there was some repetition of the tension between white clergy and black laity which had emerged at other conventions (for example, Father LaFarge rising to the defense of the black Catholic in the face of a fellow white clergyman), the ultimate thrust of the convention, at least in Turner's subsequent actions, was toward greater Catholicity. In a letter to a white Catholic layman from the Midwest in late 1930, Turner reflected:

> We have been striving for some time to interest white Catholics in an inter-racial movement which would insure justice in spiritual and temporal practices throughout the country. It is well known that Catholic institutions have been as intolerant racially as any other, and this matter can be corrected only by cooperative action of both races.[101]

A book appeared in 1930, however, which strained the new efforts at interracial cooperation. It brought with it the specter of the always difficult relationship between the Josephites and the Federation (particularly, perhaps, with Dr. Turner). The book was The Catholic Church and the American Negro by John T. Gillard, S.S.J., subtitled:

> An investigation of the Past and Present Activities of the Catholic Church in Behalf of the 12,000,000 Negroes in the United States, with an Examination of the Difficulties which Affect the Work of the Colored Missions.[102]

The first five sections of the book, devoted to a scientific survey of the state of Catholic work among blacks in America, received generally favorable reviews in every quarter. It was the last sections, in which Gillard ventured his own analysis of problems and

---

[101]Turner to J. J. Heithaus, 1 November 1930, Turner Papers.

[102]Gillard, The Catholic Church, title page.

suggestions for improvements, that evoked negative responses.[103] Turner's review in the September issue of the Chronicle was no exception. He began by objecting to the "decidedly non-Negro point of view" in the book and the author's use of several offensive terms to refer to the race: "primitive," "fledgling," and "uncultured."[104] Indeed, Turner remarked, he could not believe that Gillard would actually repeat fallacies about blacks which had been dead theories for twenty-five years. Gillard's hesitations about a black clergy discarded the Church's wise experience in reaching varied peoples, and could only be attributed to an "Americanization" of the Josephite attitude, which had been more receptive at an earlier period.[105] Basically, Turner went on,

---

[103]LaFarge, "Fr. Gillard's Study of the Catholic Negro," review of The Catholic Church, by Gillard, in Chronicle, July 1930, pp. 151-52. Carter G. Woodson, review of The Catholic Church, by Gillard, in Journal of Negro History 15 (July 1930): 373-76. Woodson's closing comments are particularly interesting: ". . . the author seems to deliver a veiled attack on the liberal attitude of the Rev. John LaFarge and the Rev. Wm. M. Markoe, who denounce those of their Catholic brethren who have permitted race hate and caste prejudice to reduce their religion to a mockery. It is interesting to note, too, that with a saner approach to the Negro and his problems these two clergymen have won a place in the hearts of the Negroes whom they have served while the Josephite Fathers with a different policy are all but hated by the very Negroes among whom they have toiled for generations." (376) Constance E. H. Daniel, review of The Catholic Church, by Gillard, in Opportunity, August 1930, pp. 247-48.

[104]Turner, "Fr. Gillard's Book," review of The Catholic Church, by Gillard, in Chronicle, September 1930, pp. 205-206.

[105]The "earlier period' Turner spoke of had to be prior to 1919, when the Federation first started publicly criticizing the Josephites. The actual separation of the Josephites from their parent body, the Mill Hill Fathers of England, occurred in 1893. Turner implies that the earlier Josephites, recently arrived from England, had not imbibed the negative racial attitudes of white Americans. An account of that early history is given in Richard H. Steins, "The Mission of the Josephites to the Negro in America" (master's thesis, Columbia University, 1966). Gillard sketched

Gillard must be criticized for his lack of awareness of progressive forces at work in the black community, his disregard for the value of black leadership, his unscientific assumptions about the inherent biological makeup of the black race, and his rationalization of "separatist" practices in the Church. It should be remembered here that Turner as a biologist was peculiarly sensitive to discussions of racial heredity, a subject he dealt with professionally, at least on occasion.[106]

This rather harsh review was the perfect motive for the Josephites to renew their hostility toward Turner. The latter acted to prevent that by sending a letter to the editor of the Chronicle in November 1930, criticizing another black (Carter G. Woodson) for a statement in his review of Gillard's book that blacks hated the Josephites.

> It is true that certain practices of the Order have been subjects of criticism by thinking colored men and women from time to time, but there is no basis for the assertion that these criticisms have come from a spirit of hatred. The Federated Colored Catholics have had the friendship and encouragement of the Superior of the Josephites, the Very Rev. L. B. Pastorelli, and many of the priests of the Order from its beginning. . . . My impression is that a fuller understanding is maturing between the Josephites and the thoughtful of the group. As the fathers of this Society come to see more fully the Negro at his best, I predict a much more productive cooperation than we have had in the past.[107]

---

the later history up to his own time in the book under discussion, and later in Colored Catholics in the United States (Baltimore: St. Joseph's Society Press, 1941).

[106] Mention has already been made of Turner's interest in genetic theories on race. He published a book review involving this subject just one month after his review of Gillard's work. See Turner, review of The Biological Basis of Human Nature, by H. S. Jennings, in Southern Workman 59 October 1930): 430-31. He applauded the book for dealing with the interrelations of races as impartially as with those of the salamander and fruit fly! (p. 321.)

[107] Turner to the editor of the Chronicle, 6 November 1930, Turner Papers.

In another letter to a white student friend at Catholic University Turner went on to say that if he was at times harsh, it was not with a feeling of personal animosity, but rather out of a sense of Christian duty. This was for him true Catholic Action.

> We must all stand for loyalty and humility as far as faith and dogma are concerned, but we must be conversant with the canon law in the Church and for the enlightened practice for which He stands and then carry on eternal and aggressive warfare upon all of those temporal segregations and Jim-Crowism which are outcomes of attitudes of mind that regard accident of color as making one less entitled to the graces of God. You use the term docility. This word has a respectable origin, but its present use makes it not a term to be applied to intelligent Catholic people.[108]

Referring once again to the Josephites, Turner remarked:

> . . . I think . . . that the Josephite Order is beginning more and more to return to its original moorings and to develop a policy which will meet the approval of intelligent Catholic colored people. Certainly a policy that does not cannot be expected ultimately to succeed. I am not speaking words simply of my own, but I am speaking through innumerable laymen and clergy.[109]

On another occasion the student who was the recipient of this letter provided an insight into Turner's thought. Writing about an awkward interracial social situation in which he found himself, the white student remarked that Turner had always recommended the works of Dr. Gilligan on the subject. The reference was to Dr. (Fr.) Francis Gilligan, whose doctoral dissertation at the Catholic University was entitled "The Morality of the Color Line." In it Gilligan had recommended "social separation"; for example, separation of the races "in those

---

[108]Turner to Alan C. J. M. Bates, 18 November 1930, Turner Papers.

[109]Ibid.

circumstances and activities in which friendships conducive to marriage might naturally be formed."[110] Turner seemed by this time to have abandoned that position, however, for he wrote back:

> The trumping up of the old statements about social equality and the like has no place whatever in the Church's activities. The term social equality, as used by the whites, is very obnoxious to Negroes, but it must be understood that any self respecting person, whether he be white or black, expects to have the same privileges and preferences as any other. This means that he expects the highest and best that his station affords anywhere; he expects to eat when he is hungry and sleep when he is tired at any place where his money will pay. Nor does he expect to be turned away because he is black. It is a part of the duty of the Church to see that this type of justice is meted out to all Christians alike.
> I think if Christ came on earth He would drive many out of the Catholic University. He would expel many of the pastors of the Catholic churches, and many of the Catholic laymen, he would excommunicate. The idea of separating your religion from your politics is the basis of the discriminatory practices carried on today, and I think if you will examine your attitude pretty carefully, you will agree with me that you are placing the Church in a very untenable position when you seek to approve many injustices because there is no explicit statement to the contrary. I do not hesitate to say that I think that Christ expects men and women to resent with fervor the un-Christlike things that are done; that he expects us to follow scrupulously in His path.[111]

When the student, who was from Missouri, expressed a need for some kind of bridge between himself and the black race, Turner replied that he already had the perfect bridge, Jesus Christ. It was not possible, he continued, for any Christian to remain in the middle. Either he was the good Samaritan or one of those who walked by the man

---

[110]Francis J. Gilligan, "The Morality of the Color Line," (Ph.D. dissertation, The Catholic University of America, 1928), p. 97. Gilligan was a frequent contributor to the Chronicle. There are some indications that he wished later to revise the above work. See Victor H. Daniel to Turner, 1 July 1931, Turner Papers.

[111]Turner to Bates, 12 January 1931, Turner Papers.

on the road, because he was not of their own. It was a matter not of choosing one race over the other, Turner said, but of treating all equally.[112]

During this period Markoe had been traveling when time would permit to promote the Chronicle and the Federation. He went to Philadelphia in the spring of 1930, where he formed a committee which later claimed to be the first authentic Federation chapter in that city (see Chapter I). At the end of the year he went to the South for the same purpose.[113] LaFarge had written a favorable report of the Detroit convention in America and had drawn up and publicized its resolutions wherever possible, including an article in Osservatore Romano.[114] All these efforts prompted Turner to write Gustave Aldrich, a Federation member in Tacoma, Washington, praising both priests for their work. Thanking Aldrich for his own work in the Washington state area, Turner observed:

> I know further that both white and colored have accused us of setting up a jim-crow organization. But I believe that we have succeeded in convincing the colored Catholics, east, that it is the only organization in the Church which will ultimately succeed in breaking down jim-crowism, and certainly it is the only vehicle through which Negro Catholics have had a chance for free expression on questions of policy in the Church.[115]

---

[112]Turner to Bates, 7 February 1931, Turner Papers.

[113]Markoe, "An Interracial Role," pp. 144-48, 164-67.

[114]LaFarge, "What Do Colored Catholics Want?", pp. 565-67. LaFarge to Turner, 28 November 1930, Turner Papers, in which he enclosed a copy of the translation of the convention resolutions which appeared in the Osservatore Romano.

[115]Turner to Gustave Aldrich, 18 March 1931, Turner Papers. News reports of that period also indicated that Federation members

It is noteworthy that as early as 1931 Turner was distinguishing East from West in Federation membership. Local views were to play a great part in the controversy less than two years later.

Turner also urged Aldrich to read Fr. Gillard's book and then work in every way he could to set priests straight who worked among black Catholics but did not properly represent them.[116]

Turner took his own advice by writing to *Commonweal* magazine in April 1931 in response to an editorial which expressed the thought of Fr. Augustine Walsh, newly appointed white chaplain of the Howard University Newman Club. Turner agreed with Walsh's contention that people should not speak about a black "problem," but objected that the rest of the essay treated the black man in just that way. In explaining possible approaches to black Catholic in secular institutions, Walsh missed the whole point that the problem would not exist if blacks were just admitted to Catholic institutions of higher learning. The priest was wrong to assume, Turner said, that blacks can find peculiar advantages in a secular institution, such as association with educated non-Catholic blacks. The truth was that blacks did not practice religious discrimination among themselves to the degree that white men did. In short, education at a Catholic institution of higher learning would not create obstacles to later professional relationships with non-Catholic blacks. Indeed, black men of various faiths defended one another whenever white men discriminated against any one black religious group.

---

generally approved the work of these two priests. See *New York Amsterdam News*, 29 July 1931, p. 14. Also the *New York Age*, 1 August 1931, p. 5.

[116]Turner to Aldrich, 18 March 1931, Turner Papers.

Secondly, while Walsh was correct that a "back-to-the-farm" movement was not the best approach for the Church to assume generally with blacks, efforts such as the Cardinal Gibbons Institute should be applauded as the sole attempt being made to meet the needs of rural blacks. Turner observed rather pointedly that in the end what any clear presentation of the "correct point of view" on the black man required was an intimate knowledge of his life.[117]

As the time approached for the 1931 convention in St. Louis, correspondence quickened between Turner and Hazel McDaniel Teabeau, editorial assistant for Markoe, and between LaFarge and both parties. Obviously every effort was being made to see that this year's meeting was the most successful to date. LaFarge was once again urging Turner to reorganize the Federation along lines similar to those of other strong Catholic organizations.[118]

---

[117]Turner, letter to the editor, Commonweal, 29 July 1931, pp. 325-26. LaFarge had urged Turner to write Commonweal, because the editorial criticized back-to-the-farm movements in the Church for black Catholics. The Jesuit thought that was an obvious reference to Cardinal Gibbons Institute (apparently learning later it was not), but hesitated to write himself, for reasons not completely clear. See LaFarge to Turner, 7 April 1931, Turner Papers. The first Newman Club was founded by Timothy L. Harrington, a medical student at the University of Pennsylvania, in 1893. Other such clubs arose elsewhere as organizations of Catholic students on secular campuses. How much of an educational role the Newman Clubs should play was, incidentally, a subject of controversy in Catholic circles at this time. See New Catholic Encyclopedia, s.v. "Newman Apostolate," by C. Albright.

[118]What he proposed was that the presidency become a nominal position, with the individual serving one year, and to be re-elected only once (Turner had been re-elected every year). The office should be filled by men from various sections of the country, who would travel about promoting the Federation. The real administrative work would be delegated to a permanent secretary, with or without a staff or board of trustees, who would maintain contact with the Social Action Department of the N.C.W.C. (now sponsoring the interracial day of the conventions). LaFarge suggested that Turner and Smith (secretary) could form such a

In the midst of these preparations, however, two incidents occurred which threatened the relationship between the Federation and the clergy. The first was in Philadelphia, where LaFarge had gone to aid Fr. Vincent Dever, who had recently been placed in charge of the work among blacks by Cardinal Dougherty of that city. When the two priests set out to organize the Federation there, they met opposition from the small committee Markoe had established earlier to promote the Chronicle. This group claimed it was already a bona fide chapter of the F.C.C., and that its chairman, William B. Bruce, was an official deputy field organizer for Philadelphia. The second controversy involved Father Eckert of St. Elizabeth's (black) Church in Chicago, who objected to the race-related activities of the local chapter headed by C. J. Foster. As mentioned in the last chapter, Turner ultimately ruled in favor of the priests in both instances, citing the thrust of the new Detroit regulations as his rationale. In some respects, however, it was these very regulations which made the conflicts possible. For the new rules in promoting efficiency called for local chapters to form organizations in each section or city, thus creating a situation in which the clergy, sometimes even the bishops, were confronted with the activities not merely of one chapter, but of local black Catholics from various parishes or units. In Philadelphia the difficulties arose as the city began organizing on that scale; in Chicago, after the local organization began acting as a unit.[119]

---

secretariat, perhaps with a rotating board and power to outvote the president. See LaFarge to Turner, 19 June 1931, Turner Papers.

[119]Markoe, "The Annual Convention," pp. 457-58. Here Markoe repeated the regulations of the 1930 convention. Numbers seven and eight read: "7. In each city the recognized chapters shall each appoint

A second factor in the conflicts may have been the field organizer himself, William Prater. The strong language his annual reports contained about discrimination in the Church indicated his forthright approach. There was some dissatisfaction expressed about his handling of the Philadelphia situation, where he had apparently appointed William Bruce a deputy field agent, thus giving Bruce reason to believe he had some authority over Federation affairs in that city.[120] Some complaints came to Turner about Prater's lack of judgment, with requests that the field agent be "kept off the road."[121] Turner's response in these cases was interesting. Apparently recognizing the potential harm in alienating the clergy (LaFarge himself had threatened to quit the Federation if Bruce rather than Father Dever were placed in charge of the Philadelphia Federation), the president wrote both to Bruce and to C. J. Foster that the organization was at a critical stage, in which it was imperative to seek the closest possible cooperation with the local clergy. He also emphasized that when the field agent did not promote that cooperation, it was the duty of the president and executive committee to intervene.[122]

---

a representative, which representatives shall meet together once a month, constituting a board to be known as the Federated Colored Catholics of the city in question; for example, the Federated Colored Catholics of Chicago. 8. On occasion the whole federated group of any city can hold general meetings as deemed expedient."

[120]Turner to Bruce, 29 July 1931, Turner Papers.

[121]Victor Daniel to Turner, 1 July 1931, Turner Papers. LaFarge to Turner, 13 July 1931, Turner Papers. LaFarge felt Prater was "imprudent," and Bruce, personally "unworthy," for his rudeness to Father Dever.

[122]Turner to Bruce, 16 July 1931; Turner to Foster, 25 July 1931; Turner to Bruce, 29 July 1931, all in Turner Papers.

On the other hand, when Turner traveled to Philadelphia to settle the issue personally, he wrote first to Bruce asking the layman to meet him at the train. This gesture let Bruce know that meetings with Father Dever would take place after Bruce had had his say. The president added that he might bring along Field Agent Prater. With regard to the curtailment of Prater's activities, Turner merely admonished him to select deputy agents in the future who would cooperate with the clergy.[123]

The same pattern appeared in Chicago: while upholding Father Eckert's objection to Federation involvement in local racial issues, Turner wrote to C. J. Foster and Mrs. Maude Johnston, a deputy field agent, that cooperation with the clergy could never mean domination by them. Turner was particularly strong in his approval of Foster's dedication and "deep racial consciousness."[124] The letter sent to all chapters, organizers and members on the subject stressed the need for ecclesiastical approval and urged the development of harmony between the Federation and the clergy, but admitted that local situations often made the task difficult.[125]

---

[123] Turner to Bruce, 16 July 1931, Turner Papers. Turner to Prater, 25 August 1931, Turner Papers. Turner wrote the field agent, "It is not against a man personally that he does not get along with the spiritual authorities but the progress then made must be found in those who pull together." Prater's response was a degree of puzzlement, asking whether he should have gone to Dever for the name of a field agent, but trusting in the wise guidance he felt Turner always gave. See Prater to Turner, 29 August 1931, Turner Papers.

[124] Turner to Foster, 25 July 1931; Turner to Johnston, 4 August 1931, both in Turner Papers.

[125] Turner to F.C.C. Chapters, Organizers and Members, 28 July 1931, Turner Papers.

Perhaps as a contribution toward this effort, the invitation to the 1931 convention sent to Father Pastorelli of the Josephites contained a note from Turner about past difficulties. Turner said he was concerned about rumors only recently brought to his attention that the real motive behind the Baltimore convention of 1929 had been to face the Josephites on the question of a race clergy. (Apparently Turner had been unaware of the remarks in Father Duffy's speech of that year.) The Federation president wished to know the source of the rumors, since "my insistent aim was to bring about better feeling between the clergy and the lay people in that city. . . ."[126] Pastorelli's only reply was that the matter if true at all had long since been forgotten. He would not attend the convention, but Father Gillard would represent him.[127] Gillard delivered the sermon at the opening Mass and an historical address during the sessions. (Despite the Federation's outspoken criticism of his book, Gillard had finally consented to come upon the insistence of John LaFarge)[128]

The plans for the 1931 convention emphasized the broadest possible cooperation of clergy and laity, black and white Catholics. Programs were planned to include these various concerns. The Detroit rules on convention representation were publicized in the Chronicle, which urged Federation chapters to form local organizations quickly in every city, along with their "white friends," in time to send delegates

---

[126]Turner to Pastorelli, 8 July 1931, Turner Papers.

[127]Pastorelli to Turner, 11 July 1931, Turner Papers.

[128]Gillard to L. J. Welbers, 5 May 1932, Turner Papers.

to St. Louis.[129] The program would feature the "thought of inter-racial philosophy and the status of the Negro in the Catholic Church."[130] Specific emphasis would be placed on the role of the clergy, and those priests who could attend were offered hospitality at St. Louis University. The desire for white participation was evident: "white people have much to learn about the Negro Catholic as a preliminary step to the Negro's salvation," Markoe wrote.[131] He had already organized in his own parish the "White Friends of Colored Catholics."[132]

Miss Linna E. Bresette, field secretary of the Social Action Department of the N.C.W.C. arrived in St. Louis one week before the convention in order to settle last minute arrangements and stimulate as large an attendance as possible, particularly at the opening day's conference on blacks in industry.[133] These first sessions were held on Saturday, September 5 at the People's Building, which Markoe described as "St. Louis' finest all-colored office building."[134] The speakers included Fr. Francis J. Gilligan; John T. Clark, secretary of the St. Louis Urban League; James A. Jackson of the Marketing Service Division, Department of Commerce; and W. F. Rohman, treasurer of a

---

[129]Markoe, "The Annual Convention," pp. 457-58.

[130]Markoe, "Plans for the National Convention," Chronicle, July 1931, p. 488.

[131]Ibid.

[132]Teabeau, "Sept. 5, 6, 7—The Seventh Annual Convention, St. Louis, Missouri," Chronicle, August 1931, pp. 522-23.

[133]"Annual Convention of Colored Catholics Opens this Saturday," St. Louis Argus, September 1931, p. 1.

[134]Markoe, "Plans," p. 488.

credit union in a St. Louis parish. Dr. Thomas E. Purcell of Kansas City and Father McGowan of the N.C.W.C. spoke at the evening session.[135] The day's acttivties also featured an interracial luncheon and a round-table discussion at which black laborers and white union men talked together about attitudes black and white workers held toward each other.[136]

Sunday's schedule began with a procession of over 500 clergy and laity from St. Elizabeth's (black) Church to the college church, St. Francis Xavier, at St. Louis University. Here a solemn high Mass was celebrated by Fr. Stephen Theobald, with the sermon preached by Father Gillard. He read from Ps. 26: "The Lord is my light and my salvation; whom should I fear?" Blacks faced two preeminent dangers, he warned. The first was the conclusion that God either must not exist or did not care about the black man his suffering. Here the black man must recall his forefathers who, in greater need, remained conscious of the God who saved Israel. The second temptation was to see the end of Christianity as mere social progress, and to blame that religion when problems still remained. But Christianity meant more than that; it was established to bring the Kingdom of God, not man. The forms of Christianity which blacks had known thus far, however, had been inadequate.

There were only two choices left for blacks, Gillard claimed: Catholicism or socialism. If the latter was to be judged by the events

---

[135]N.C.W.C. news release, 8 September 1931, Turner Papers.

[136]Newspaper account, 30 September 1931, LaFarge Papers.

in Russia, the poor would not gain much more from socialism than from the old order. Quoting three atheists who viewed Catholicism as the best choice for blacks, Gillard proclaimed that the primary end of the Church was to save souls, and secondarily, to improve the social order. Although some Catholics were truly un-Catholic in their attitudes (one reason for the existence of the Federation) all those present should unite to rid the land of "un-American, un-Christian, unCatholic discrimination in the things of God and man."[137] Might it not in fact be the role of blacks to lead others to Calvary, teaching them brotherhood? "Members of the Federated Colored Catholics, yours is a privilege of speaking in the name of thousands of your fellowmen. Catholic Action is your slogan," Gillard concluded.[138]

On Sunday evening at an open meeting at St. Louis University, Father Theobald spoke on "Our Hopes and Aspirations." He was introduced by Fr. R. S. Johnston, president of the university. With his host sitting on the same platform from which the black priest spoke, Father Theobald addressed the issue of closed doors at Catholic universities, specifically at St. Louis University. Although no one present voiced objections to Theobald's bold words, one newspaper later described the moment as "tensely dramatic."[139] The speech was followed

---

[137]Gillard, "The Catholic Church and the Negro," sermon delivered to the F.C.C. assembled at their seventh annual convention, St. Louis, 6 September 1931, Gillard Papers.

[138]Ibid. One of Gillard's objections later was that this sermon and the historical address he gave the following day were the only speeches not printed by the Federation.

[139]Newspaper account, 30 September 1931, LaFarge Papers.

by closing remarks from Fr. Vincent Dever of Philadelphia. He mentioned the growing realization among white priests of the black man's need to be better understood, for better opportunities, and his own priests. Only one thing the priests did not understand: "We do not know how to get these things as quickly as we would like," Dever said.[140] At first he had thought to write books on the subject, but he soon discovered the black man was already saying it all himself. Presentation of the facts was important, but then they must be studied and acted upon. Dever pleaded for blacks to tell white friends how to help. He went on to cite an official booklet printed by the Archbishop of Philadelphia commanding an end to the color line in Catholic schools. The bishop had not only published the command, but enforced it. When white objections were raised, Dever as the bishop's representative had defended the new policy. The priest closed with a reference to a sermon he had given at the funeral of a black priest, in which he noted that the only goal of white priests ministering to blacks was to be replaced by black clergy.[141]

The Monday meeting was devoted to Federation affairs. The nominating committee presented its list of officers, most of them already serving, which the convention accepted. Dr. Turner was reelected president. It should be pointed out that the method of election was largely a committee function. The nominating committee would merely

---

[140] Vincent Dever, "Closing Remarks," corrected text, by the author, September 1931, LaFarge Papers.

[141] Ibid.

present a slate of proposed officers, which was then accepted by the convention, often unanimously. LaFarge's suggestion to Turner that two names be submitted and voted on was not adopted.[142]

Father Markoe reported on the poor financial condition of the Chronicle. He proposed a solution already endorsed by the executive committee: each chapter would purchase a two dollar advertisement each month in the magazine. After some debate, the motion was adopted.[143]

Victor Daniel, the principal of Cardinal Gibbons Institute, reviewed briefly the history and statistics relating to the school. He announced the donation of property by J. Goddard Mattingly, who had read of the Institute in the Chronicle. The acreage would be divided into small farms which would be sold to graduates of Cardinal Gibbons as they worked the land and acquired it gradually. We advocate, Daniel declared, not a "back-to-the-farm movement," but a policy of "stay-on-the-farm."[144]

---

[142]LaFarge to Turner, 19 June 1931, Turner Papers. There are some indications in the correspondence of Father Gillard that attempts had been made both at Detroit and in St. Louis to have Turner replaced. Apparently, LaFarge backed down in St. Louis, after some backstage maneuvering, declaring that Turner was the only logical candidate. This especially irked Gillard, because he had gone to the convention on the promise of LaFarge to do something about Turner. See Gillard to Welbers, 5 May 1932; Gillard to Curley, 10 October 1932, both in Gillard Papers. G. A. Henderson of Pittsburgh indicated in later correspondence that he had maintained control of the nominating committee, and had even failed to read a letter of resignation from Turner to the committee at Detroit, in order to insure the latter's re-election. See Henderson to Smith, 18 November 1932, Turner Papers.

[143]Markoe, "Report," p. 664. See also Smith to Turner, 15 September 1931, Turner Papers.

[144]Victor Daniel, "Seven Years of Cardinal Gibbons Institute," Chronicle, November 1931, pp. 664-65.

In what may have been a defense of his past handling of the office, William Prater in his report recalled the early history of the Federation, and declared that his object had always been to instill in each new chapter an understanding of "the true spirit which caused the Federated Colored Catholics to have its birth."[145] Noting the roles of clergy and laity in the Federation, he warned:

> We cannot reach the goal by depending on a few good priests to lead the fight. It is our job and we must take the initiative to accomplish the best results.[146]

The young were leaving the Church; they were limited in education and refused entrance even at the Catholic University. The conditions called for immediate action under black leadership.

> . . . I trust that there will be no misconception placed on my object in recommending that we maintain the initiative and keep the body strictly officered by race men and women. It is well known that every good man of the opposite race that takes an active leadership for the cause of the Negro suffers in the end.[147]

As for those in the Church who would limit the Federation's activities, Prater was emphatic:

> The Federation is not enslaved; Catholic men and women in the United States can come together for any good purpose without the sanction of any church head. If this is not true, we are not free. I urge the Federation on. Don't stop this side of Rome. The truth is known only by us—the victims. You are fighting for what God has intended for you. For your children's sake, demand your place in the Catholic world.[148]

---

[145]Prater, "Report," p. 666.

[146]Ibid.

[147]Ibid.

[148]Ibid.

He believed "so firmly in a Racial consciousness," the field agent declared, that he could not carry out his office in any other way.

The secretary's report by H. M. Smith listed seventy-two groups affiliated with the Federation and forty-four individual members. (The convention to which he spoke had representatives from twenty-six states and the District of Columbia.) For most of the new membership Smith gave credit to publicity on the organization in the Chronicle, and he urged support of it. He also advocated that local chapters organize into larger bodies as recommended by the Detroit regulations.[149]

The resolutions from the convention, drawn up once again by LaFarge, reflected the Federation's concerns in 1931. After the usual expressions of gratitude to the hosts of the convention, and of loyalty to the Pope and the bishops, the delegates reaffirmed the thrust of the Detroit convention. They spoke, too, of the present depression, brought on by the greed of a few, and affecting most deeply black Americans. They denounced the current trend toward birth control as contrary to the law of God and "an insidious attempt to weaken and ultimately to destroy the very physical existence of the race, while placing it at the mercy of unscrupulous experimenters with human rights."[150] Equally dangerous, the resolutions went on, was the outrageous existence of lynching and judicial murder.

The group praised the broadening of admission policy at several Catholic colleges, and urged that a committee visit the assembled

---

[149]Smith, "Report," p. 666. For figures on the convention attendance, see "The Convention," p. 632.

[150]Resolution of seventh annual convention of the F.C.C., September 1931, LaFarge Papers.

hierarchy at its November meeting to present a full picture on black Catholic education. The convention was also grateful for the consecration of a black bishop in Africa and for the new feasts of St. Peter Claver and the Blessed martyrs of Uganda.[151] Finally, the Federation sent greetings to Dr. James Hardy Dillard, recently retired from the administration of the Jeanes Fund on behalf of blacks. H. M. Smith, secretary of the Federation, later wrote to Father LaFarge, expressing the hope that these resolutions would "be the means of drawing many more good white friends in our ranks," and thanking the priest on behalf of the Washington members for his good work on behalf of "the entire Negro Race."[152]

Apparently LaFarge himself was caught up in other results of the convention. He rejoiced that a list of proposed amendments to the Detroit regulations which had been sent by the disgruntled Chronicle committee of Philadelphia never reached the convention floor. He was also enthusiastic about the election of Elmo Anderson of New York to the position of "national organizer." LaFarge suggested that Anderson use his office at the headquarters of Father Kramer's Mission Board

---

[151] The blessed martyrs of Uganda were twenty-two young men who were put to death by the ruler of Bugunda between 1885 and 1887. Most were Christian pages who refused the ruler's homosexual demands. They had been raised to the status of blessed (last step before canonization) by Pope Benedict XV in 1920, and were finally canonized by Pope Paul VI in 1964. See New Catholic Encyclopedia, s.v. "Uganda, Martyrs of," by J. F. Faupel. St. Peter Claver was a Jesuit missionary, called Saint of the Slaves, who ministered to African slaves arriving in Cartagena in the early seventeenth century. He was canonized by Pope Leo XIII in 1888. See New Catholic Encyclopedia, s.v. "St. Peter Claver," by H. Vivas Solas. Also A. Valtierra, Peter Claver: Saint of the Slaves (Westminster, Maryland, 1960).

[152] Smith to LaFarge, 20 September 1931, Turner Papers.

staff in New York to appoint deputies and perhaps even lay a foundation for a regional vice-presidential system LaFarge had been advocating.[153]

One concrete result of the convention was financial; substantial contributions were received from Fr. Edward Kramer of the Catholic Board for Mission Work among the Colored People and from Bishop Hugh Boyle of Pittsburgh.[154] Apparently a second result was extended publicity, for even W. E. B. DuBois of *Crisis* requested material on the Federation.[155]

The first business flowing from the convention was the annual letter and visit to the hierarchy. Father Dever gladly accepted the task of drafting the letter. The small committee appointed to visit the hierarchy at its annual meeting was composed of Turner, Eugene Clarke, and H. M. Smith. Father Theobald had been asked to join the group, and apparently was willing but unable to make the trip. Father Kramer came down from New York for the meetings and was available to the small group for consultation.[156]

The Federation's general letter to each member of the hierarchy was mailed in October. Its emphasis was on education, as the previous convention had recommended. The members urged the bishops as spiritual shepherds to bring into the fold the sheep missing through discrimination

---

[153]LaFarge to Turner, 12 September 1931, Turner Papers.

[154]Kramer to LaFarge, 14 September 1931, Turner Papers. Smith to Turner, 15 September 1931, Turner Papers.

[155]On DuBois' request for information see Turner to DuBois, 16 September 1931; also Turner to DuBois, 17 September 1931, both in Turner Papers.

[156]Turner to LaFarge, 31 October 1931, Turner Papers. Clarke to Turner, 31 October 1931, Turner Papers. Kramer to Turner, 7 November 1931, Turner Papers. Turner to Theobald, 8 October 1931, Turner Papers.

by Catholic institutions. Open Catholic schools on all levels, that black Catholics might fulfill the obligation preached to all the laity: to educate their children in a religious atmosphere. Such a grave obligation must mean a "potent right to the means necessary."[157] Several acknowledgments of sincere concern reached the Federation in response to this letter, and served as some encouragement when the committee set out to meet with the bishops during their November meeting.[158]

These individual conferences at Catholic University resulted in an effort to open that institution itself. The attempt in that year failed. When the color bar was lifted several years later, however, Federation members took some credit for their initiatives in 1931.[159]

Turner requested the right to address all the bishops in assembly. He was informed by Bishop Emmet Walsh, secretary of the N.C.W.C., that the Federation should submit a letter embodying its concerns to a sympathetic bishop who would be willing to present it, with his endorsement, at the next Administrative Committee meeting. This suggestion was taken up at the Federation's executive committee meeting in January, and a letter subsequently prepared.[160]

---

[157]Turner as President of F.C.C. to the hierarchy, 20 October 1931, Turner Papers.

[158]W. J. Giroux, Chancellor, to Turner, 21 October 1931, Turner Papers. Bishop Joseph Schrembs to Turner, 21 October 1931, Turner Papers. Bishop Frank J. Beckman to Turner, 2 November 1931, Turner Papers.

[159]Turner to George Conrad, 17 December 1938, Turner Papers.

[160]Bishop Emmet M. Walsh to Turner, 13 November 1931, Turner Papers.

During the same month the two cities which had been of such concern to Turner that year--Chicago and Philadelphia--were once again on his mind. The newly formed organization in Philadelphia under Father Dever invited Turner to speak there. He returned from the city enthusiastic about the work being accomplished there.[161] Chicago--or rather, Father Eckert--remained a source of problems. Turner had heard rumors that the priest was displeased with the president's address at the St. Louis convention because it contained no reference to the work of the Society of the Divine Word, of which Eckert was a member. Turner wrote to Eckert explaining that the speech referred to no religious group by name, and that in fact the Federation and its president had always maintained a close relationship with the society. The priest's criticism, he added, would be harmful to future cooperation between the Federation and the clergy. A copy of this letter, with a word of explanation, was sent to the Divine Word superior.[162] Such controversies seem petty now, but so few persons from either race were involved in the Federation that each such breach posed a major threat to the organization's future.

A third city became the center of Turner the biologist's attention as the end of the year approached. The annual meeting of the American Association for the Advancement of Science was held in New Orleans, the home of a large number of black Catholics. Seeing the opportunity for organizing the Federation in the deep South, Turner

---

[161]Turner to LaFarge, 31 October 1931, Turner Papers.

[162]Turner to Superior, S.V.D., 18 November 1931, Turner Papers.

wrote to Louis Israel, Supreme Commander of the Knights of Peter Claver.[163] He inquired about the possibility of his meeting with a group of black Catholics and explaining the aims of the Federation. Israel referred Turner to A. W. Arnaud, with whom arrangements were made. Turner's comments later in the <u>Chronicle</u> indicate that he was pleased with the vitality of black Catholic life in New Orleans and with the opportunity to spread the work of the Federation.[164] Another source indicates, however, that the trip was a cause of bad feeling, particularly among the Josephites. Correspondence between Father Gillard and priests of his order complained that Turner, who purported in his article to know conditions in the city, had not visited a single Josephite pastor or the Holy Family Sisters while there.[165] Fr. L. J. Welbers wrote to Markoe that Turner did not seem acquainted with the Josephite's missions. Markoe sent the letter on to Turner, who responded to Welbers: "First, I want to assure you that I am no armchair novice at the work undertaken. I have been living in it all my life."[166] He proceeded then to speak plainly on discrimination in the Church.

---

[163] The Knights of Peter Claver were founded in 1909 by four Josephite priests and three black Catholic laymen in Mobile, Alabama. Its purpose was to provide "Catholic fraternalism, Christian charity, and insurance protection for Negro Catholics." See <u>New Catholic Encyclopedia</u>, s.v. "Negroes," by Hogan and Tennelly.

[164] Turner, "A Visit to Catholic New Orleans," <u>Chronicle</u>, February 1932, pp. 52-53.

[165] Welbers to Gillard, 30 April 1932, Gillard Papers. Actually, Turner mentioned in his article that he had met Father Cassilly, president of Xavier College and pastor of the church there. He added that the Blessed Sacrament Sisters at Xavier were on retreat at the time.

[166] Turner to Welbers, 15 February 1932, Turner Papers.

> The remedy for the situation has hardly been sensed remedially yet. The Negro will remain, in saecula saeculorum, as you describe him until our clerical leadership help him through the same incentives and through the same channels as are offered other groups in the Church. There are no Race leaders among Catholic Negroes. Up to the present time the way has been closed whereby they may come into positions of leadership. . . . It is impossible to stifle the aspirations of those qualified for Holy Orders and for advance ment without at the same time degrading the group.[167]

Turner was not optimistic for the future; the only hope lay in immediate changes. This was the rationale for visits to the hierarchy. Apologizing for his frankness, the layman closed with the comment that he knew several non-Catholic efforts which had resulted in a significant advancement for blacks in a much shorter time than Welbers proposed for his own San Antonio. The letter did not satisfy the priest, and the Josephites in general continued to be dissatisfied with Turner.[168]

The January executive committee meeting was devoted to arrangements for the next annual convention. New York City was selected as the site, and some discussion held on the program. Dr. Turner reported on the visits to Catholic University in November, and Father LaFarge, observing that the president could not reach all parts of the country, argued for elected regional vice-presidents who could hold general meetings in their areas and visit individual chapters. The idea was favorably received and turned over to Father Dever, who chaired a committee on the revision of the constitution.[169]

In the spring Miss Anita Williams, a black Catholic social worker of Baltimore, tried to reorganize the almost defunct Federation

---

[167] Ibid.

[168] Welbers to Gillard, 30 April 1932, Gillard Papers.

[169] "Executive Committee of F.C.C.," pp. 37-38.

there. Father Gillard refused to assist her, writing to Archbishop Curley why he could not support the organization. (Earlier Gillard had written in the same vein to Bishop Emmet Walsh, when Walsh proposed using the Federation as a vehicle for a sub-department of black Catholic societies in the N.C.W.C.)[170] Dr. Turner traveled to Baltimore to speak, but warned Miss Williams to seek members who had no "axes to grind."[171]

Contacts with various clergymen, such as Father Welbers, convinced Turner that the greatest misunderstanding about the Federation was that its primary end was to fight discrimination. The major goal, he declared in a May article in the Chronicle on the "Spirit of the Federated Colored Catholics," was Catholic Action. Other organizations, such as the N.A.A.C.P., had been founded to fight discrimination, he had written to Welbers. The Federated Colored Catholics largely created an atmosphere and inspiration in which groups could work for the specific ends of Catholic Action that concerned them.

> Of course, we shall seek to eradicate anything that stands in the way of our Catholic Action Program. If such happens to be discrimination, certainly our logical leaders would not be expected to ban our efforts as being "radical" or to withdraw their flocks from the opportunity of helping to solve this problem.[172]

When the executive committee met at the home of Elmo Anderson in June, plans for the convention were perhaps uppermost in everyone's

---

[170]Gillard to Curley, 13 April 1932, Gillard Papers. Gillard to Bishop Walsh, 5 April 1932, Gillard Papers.

[171]Turner to Anita R. Williams, 4 April 1932, Turner Papers.

[172]Turner, "The Spirit of the Federated Colored Catholics," Chronicle, May 1932, p. 92.

mind. Two other items already in process received some attention: the revision of the constitution, for which Dever had by then made some definite proposals, and the annual letter to the bishops, which was presented to the meeting. Another matter not on the agenda proved ultimately of greatest importance. Several members from Chicago had written to the national secretary requesting that the Federation emphasize interracial activities, externally and internally, and toward that end, change its name to the "National Catholic Inter-Racial Federation."[173] Fathers LaFarge and Markoe treated this event in later articles in the Chronicle. While neither priest directly advocated a change in name, they did support the emphasis on interracialism which it signified.[174]

Several letters exchanged in the months between June and September indicate that there was some concern about the proposed revision of the constitution. Father LaFarge rejected Dever's changes as too complicated and superfluous, and had several reforms of his own to offer. Some of these he outlined in a letter to Turner. What the Federation needed was a program of action. Otherwise it would appear too aloof from the problem.

> Our primary task as I see it, abstracting from what we can tell non-Catholics, is to <u>educate the general Catholic public</u> and that on three main lines:
> 1. The sense of social responsibility as a general principle.
> 2. Specific facts as to what the Negro experiences, what he needs in trying to fulfill his obligations as a Catholic and as a citizen; these specific facts to be obtained through the expression of authentic Negro thought.

---

[173]"Executive Committee Meets," p. 140.

[174]LaFarge, "Doing the Truth," Chronicle, July 1932, pp. 130-31. "A National Catholic Inter-Racial Organization," p. 177.

3. The APPLICATION of social responsibility to remedying the situation revealed by these facts.[175]

LaFarge explained that white Catholics could be educated about race relations only if they saw the proper correlation between the instances of discrimination and the body of Catholic doctrine that applied. The correlation was what must be made apparent, for otherwise it was all too easy for individuals to agree to a principle, lament the instance, and do nothing. The Federated Colored Catholics as a body would have to agree to a systematic procedure for accomplishing this correlation. Even though they were laymen, Federation members could act effectively. They must not wait for a native clergy. That would flow from their forceful activity.

Toward this end LaFarge had three suggestions: the program should have the widest possible appeal; financial support would come if the program were effective; and if the Federation did not act quickly it might defeat its own purpose by causing another organization to be imposed in its place. LaFarge concluded by reminding Turner that the latter had put his "life's blood" into the work, which should not be in vain.[176]

Turner's reply was in general agreement, only adding that the past practice of allowing individual memberships (discouraged in Detroit) should be reintroduced. At least that would prevent the possibility that large segments of the membership would be withdrawn by the mere "fiat" of a pastor.[177]

---

[175]LaFarge to Turner, 8 August 1932, Turner Papers.

[176]Ibid.

[177]Turner to LaFarge, 17 August 1932, Turner Papers.

Eugene Clarke also expressed strong criticisms of Dever's proposed constitutional revision. He feared that it placed the Federation under even greater hierarchical control. While Clarke agreed that the organization should be approved by the Church, he saw the new changes as removing all initiative from the members. After a few other technical criticisms, he concluded with the hope that the original aim of the Federation would remain in sight: "to eliminate any and all barriers within the Church organization which limit the opportunities of the Negro Catholic in his enjoyment of all his religious rights and privileges."[178]

LaFarge saw this letter and was prompted to send Turner his reaction. The priest agreed with Clarke that no further word was needed on obtaining ecclesiastical authorization of individual chapters. He went on to point out, however, that all Catholic organizations engaged in public activity must be subject to hierarchical control, which could advise, but also "prescribe the norms according to which it shall be conducted in specific instances."[179] Regarding the object of the Federation, LaFarge argued that Clarke was being too narrow in referring only to religious rights. The Federation should seek "the establishment (in general) of race relationships based upon Christian principles"--whether they be civic, social, or religious. Christianity, in fact, is necessary for secular justice: "without the invocation of the general principles of justice and charity drawn from the Faith,

---

[178]Clarke to Turner, 18 August 1932, Turner Papers.

[179]LaFarge to Turner, 20 August 1932, Turner Papers.

there can be no effective means of attaining the righting of particular wrongs,"[180] and justice, "though theoretically self-sufficing, is actually not capable of being actuated save through supernatural love."[181]

Another original member of the Federation, H. M. Smith, wrote in somewhat the same vein as Clarke. He hoped the new constitution would emphasize the original purpose of the Federation--the discrimination black Catholics experienced--and that the convention would seek remedies [182]

Shortly before the convention, on July 5, 1932, the Federation lost one of its most beloved members, Fr. Stephen Theobald. His death left two black priests in the United States.[183] Father Markoe preached the funeral sermon, and the Chronicle printed an editorial eulogy that included the words of a former mayor of St. Paul, Minnesota: "This plain, quiet man had lived in order to make humble folk happier and better. . . . So he is remembered by many whose hearts learned a new song through him, whose souls leaped to new spiritual vision under his unfailing tutorship."[184]

In the week preceding the convention a letter was composed from the Federation to Pope Pius XI pleading for an end to discriminatory

[180] Ibid.

[181] Ibid.

[182] Smith to Turner, 20 August 1932, Turner Papers.

[183] Antoinette Banks, "Fr. Stephen L. Theobald," Chronicle, August 1932, p. 160.

[184] "Fr. Theobald," Chronicle, August 1932, pp. 157-58.

practices in the Church, particularly the refusal to admit black students to the Catholic University. Pointing out that the black Catholics supported the university (through annual collections), the letter observed that the school refused even black Sisters at the same time that it accepted non-Catholic white students, while many prominent non-Catholic institutions admitted blacks. The group said it did not wish to embarrass the board of trustees, for the Federation was certain that a small number of Southern faculty members were responsible for the present policy. Indeed, the institution had a number of black graduates from an earlier, more lenient period.[185]

In the flurry of preparations preceding the convention, LaFarge sent Turner a number of thoughts on the Federation. He mentioned in passing that he was not recommending a change in the name, but did think it should be given serious consideration. Then he explained his own understanding of the F.C.C. With regard to principles of organization, LaFarge emphasized that as a *Federation*, the group should not consider individual memberships. It should be organized like any Catholic lay group under the approval and direction of the bishops.[186]

At the last minute two people declined to attend the convention. One was Constance Daniel, assistant principal of Cardinal Gibbons Institute, who had earlier refused a speaking role at the meetings.

---

[185]Federated Colored Catholics to Pope Pius XI, 24 August 1932, Turner Papers. It is not evident whether this letter was actually sent. The copy available to me was itself incomplete.

[186]LaFarge to Turner, 25 August 1932, Turner Papers. Enclosure, LaFarge, "Principles Underlying the Federated Coloured Catholics: as seen by Fr. LaFarge," LaFarge Papers.

She indicated to Turner that all was not well at the Institute, she was dissatisfied with LaFarge, and she feared becoming a "stick of dynamite" on the platform.[187] The other expression of regret came from Father Dever of Philadelphia. He wrote that another member of the committee could read his report on constitutional revisions. As for his position on the executive committee, he asked to be withdrawn for reasons apparently given at its last meeting.

> As I said in June, I do not think it wise to let the impression grow that a few of us white members of the Federationa are running it, and I think we could do as much good, if not more, in an advisory capacity.[188]

The Controversy

Published accounts of the convention in New York painted a sparse portrait of all that occurred there. Little of the discussion on the name change, so vital to the future history of the Federation, could appear in the reports since it took place in the closed door sessions of the executive committee. The *Interracial Review*—the new name for the Chronicle beginning with the first issue after the convention—related only a successful, progressive change for the Federation. The procession of black Catholics preceding the Sunday Mass celebrated by Cardinal Hayes in St. Patrick's Cathedral was described in full. Included also were the sessions on Saturday about

---

[187] Constance Daniel to Turner, 27 August 1932, Turner Papers.

[188] Dever to Turner, 1 September 1932, Turner Papers. Dever's place as chairman of the constitutional revision committee was taken by Markoe. See Markoe, "An Interracial Role," p. 241. For LaFarge's authorship of the new constitution, see Clarke to the executive committee, 29 November 1932, Turner Papers, in which he mentioned this fact.

blacks in industry, and on Monday, the addresses outlining black history. As for the internal affairs of the Federation, the magazine printed the new constitution (which had deleted all uses of the word "colored" wherever possible) and a small description of the name change.

> The new name is intended to symbolize a widening of interests in the organization, which now becomes identified with the whole Catholic body and is no longer exclusively a Negro group.[189]

And in a later reference to the clergy:

> The change in the name of the Federated Colored Catholics was made in recognition of the important part played by white clergy in the group's activities which hitherto have been of an unofficial nature.[190]

Father LaFarge was also quoted: "An organization designed to promote better racial relations should itself be interracial in character."[191]

A later editorial in the *Interracial Review* explained the issues in the name change debate more fully:

> In debating the merits of the old name as compared to suggested new titles, the arguments always centered around a fundamental point of difference. The old name contained the word "colored," the exclusion being symbolic of the interracial idea which was suggested as definitely expressive of the true nature of the organization. So the debate was racial versus interracial. Lines were clearly drawn and it was made plain that if the old name were retained, it would mean that the body had definitely put itself on record as a racial group, whereas the adoption of a new name excluding the word "colored" would put the organization's final seal of approval upon itself as an interracial body.[192]

---

[189] Teabeau, "Federated Colored Catholics," p. 195.

[190] Ibid., p. 199.

[191] Ibid., pp. 199-200.

[192] "Federation's New Name Spells Progress," *Interracial Review*, December 1932, p. 245.

As for Dr. Turner's reaction, he wrote plainly to Eugene Clarke that the change had occurred because a large number at the convention were from above the Mason-Dixon line, and had a "phobia" about the word "Negro." They had the support of Fathers LaFarge and Markoe, who threatened to resign if changes were not effected. Turner revealed that in acquiescing, he had not really changed his own mind.

> It was not that I considered the name entirely satisfactory, but the motive for changing was based upon queer reasoning supported by the two clergy that it was better to put effort primarily on interracial activity than upon increasing racial solidarity and racial improvement.[193]

Although Turner expressed fear that he had fallen out with the clergy by implying they were not indispensable, he seemed more concerned about future control of the organization. "We shall need very strong hands," he told Clarke, "to keep it as an instrument of the Negro layman."[194]

In a letter to Elmo Anderson, Turner stressed this same set of priorities about black control.

> It is essential in my judgment to line up the Negroes throughout the country as solidly as possible around the ends and aims of the organization. And following that of course to bring the white friends, as many as possible, into an inter-racial committee to aid.[195]

Turner noted that Father Markoe had offered to become a deputy organizer for the Federation. Turner thought the priest had enough work as the head of publicity, although he left the final decision to

---

[193]Turner to Clarke, 18 September 1932, Turner Papers.

[194]Ibid.

[195]Turner to Elmo Anderson, 16 September 1932, Turner Papers. Anderson apparently later revealed the contents of this letter to Markoe and the Midwestern group, because it formed the basis of one of the later charges against Turner.

Anderson (the national organizer). In any event, the Federation must "avoid the condition that we had with the officers and constitution saying one thing and the editor of the journal presenting another" (apparently a reference to material on the interracial aims of the organization which Markoe had printed with the program for the New York convention. Turner had objected to it strongly).[196]

The climax, however, came in a letter from Markoe to Turner on September 23, 1932, in which the editor announced a change in the name of the Chronicle. Originally the name had been the St. Elizabeth's Chronicle to signify a parish newsletter, and then the "St. Elizabeth's" was dropped when the magazine became the Federation organ. Several people in the past, LaFarge for example, had complained that the journal's name hindered its promotion; and it did not indicate what the magazine contained. Therefore, Markoe announced, the October issue would bear a new title: Interracial Review. Not only would the name be more significant, but it would aid library listings and appearances in the Catholic Periodical Index. Markoe enclosed sample copies of the cover in his letter.[197]

Turner's reaction was to compose two letters, one to the executive committee and one to Archbishop Curley, the spiritual director of the Federation. The letter to the committee he sent to H. M. Smith for his perusal, and the latter he mailed to the Archbishop in Baltimore.

---

[196]Markoe, "An Interracial Role," p. 229.

[197]Markoe to Turner, 23 September 1932, Turner Papers. Markoe wrote in his memoirs that LaFarge had suggested the new name for the magazine as Markoe was leaving the convention to return to St. Louis. p. 244.)

In that letter he related the compromise that had occurred, reluctantly, at the New York convention. It might not be enough, however, because Markoe had recently without approval changed the name of the journal. While the Federation was grateful for clerical assistance, Turner wondered whether it had been at the price of orderly procedure. He explained that his purpose was not to seek action from Curley, but only to inform. Enclosing a copy of the new magazine, Turner declared he would tell Markoe it was no longer an official organ. The priest had admirable zeal, he admitted, but his methods were not helpful.[198]

Curley's response was twofold: he sent the letter on to Gillard for his information, and then wrote a brief reply to Turner himself. In it he expressed surprise at the news, about which he was sure he could do little since the delegates at their convention had acted officially. As for Markoe, he knew nothing of him, but had spoken to Father LaFarge occasionally about the Federation. From these conversations he was convinced of LaFarge's sincerity. The letter ended on that note.[199]

Apparently Turner also wrote Markoe of his disapproval. The priest answered immediately, expressing his regret that the matter could not be handled in "a good heart to heart talk." He had no personal animosity for Turner, he explained, and had in the past often defended the layman from others' criticism. Concerning the present issue,

---

[198] Turner to Curley, 6 October 1932, Gillard Papers.

[199] Curley to Turner, 8 October 1932, Turner Papers. Evidence that Curley had sent Turner's letter of October 6 to Gillard was found in a letter from Curley to Gillard, 8 October 1932, Gillard Papers, and in the presence of the letter among Gillard's collected papers.

> I write only that the truth may appear and that we may have a
> clearly mutual understanding pertaining to fundamentals for the
> sake of harmony in our actions so necessary as we agreed in our
> last convention in New York.[200]

Denying any desire for power, and requesting the opportunity merely to serve, Markoe pointed out that he had been elected to the position of editor by the officers, and was responsible to that entire body for his actions. He could not be removed from office except by a two-thirds vote of the executive committee.[201] The magazine, he reminded Turner, had been adopted by the convention assembled in Baltimore, a move that had been reaffirmed every year thereafter. Markoe carefully distinguished between ownership and use.

> In New York, before the full National Executive Committee, I
> carefully explained that the magazine which I have been editing
> for nearly five years is owned and edited by me in the name of the
> Society of Jesus to which religious Order I belong. More than three
> years ago in Baltimore, purely to help the Federation, I graciously
> informed the Convention in full session that I would gladly allow
> them to use *my* magazine as their official organ in which event it
> would become *our* magazine merely by virtue of my new official
> relationship to the Federation.[202]

As Jesuit owner, Markoe declared that he had the perfect right to name the magazine what he would. Good editorial policy dictated that the title be changed to suit the new thrust of the Federation taken at the last convention. Regarding that decision,

> You may be sure, Doctor, that if you had not consented to
> a change of name for the Federation, it would have been changed

---

[200] Markoe to Turner, 10 October 1932, Turner Papers.

[201] The new constitution included this provision, which was later used as the mechanism for removing Turner. Whether there was actually a two-thirds vote in that instance was always a matter of dispute.

[202] Markoe to Turner, 10 October 1932.

> over your protest and you could not have been re-elected
> President. You may not believe me when I tell you this, but
> I know that you were beaten by two to one, and I would not
> have organized one vote against you. Others were vitally
> interested.[203]

If the Federation wished to run its own magazine, Markoe went on, it could do so. To own this one, thousands of dollars of deficit would have to be paid. If he was to continue bearing the financial burden, at least he should be able to call the magazine what he chose. Urging a compromise for the sake of unity, Markoe proposed that the name remain "Interracial Review" for the time, for practical considerations, and that a poll be taken of the Federation members. It would stimulate interest, and promote democratic rather than one-man rule.

Then Markoe turned to a second issue, his appointment to the role of deputy organizer. Markoe reviewed a set of facts about the last executive committee meeting and convention in New York which he thought supported his case.

> Moreover, just as I informed the full Executive Committee
> that I intended to change the name of the magazine and after my
> explanation no further objection was raised, so I informed them
> that I intend to ask Mr. Anderson to appoint me a Deputy
> Organizer, but did not wish to do so if there was any objection.
> There was no objection! . . . So I really already have the
> Executive Committee's endorsement, or at least non-objection, to
> my appointment as a Deputy Organizer and also for the change of
> name of the magazine. This will appear in the minutes if they
> are properly written. It was a long assumption on your part
> when you intimated that in organizing new Chapters I would sow
> propaganda against the idea of colored groups organizing along
> racial lines. I only object to a Catholic organization being
> racial instead of Catholic, because it is a contradiction in
> terms and is logically a surrender of all we are advocating which
> point was thoroughly debated and settled at the last Convention.
> In coming to New York, moreover, I had no idea of changing the
> name of the magazine. It developed as a logical after-result

---

[203]Ibid.

> of the change of name of the Organization. So your assumption
> about my having followed a completely prearranged, clever plan
> is all wrong.[204]

What makes this paragraph interesting is that Turner wrote alongside it, "not true, not true." The issues were puzzling, because Markoe always insisted that his actions had been taken gradually and with the express approval of the executive committee, whereas Turner always maintained that they had been sudden changes brought upon the Federation. It seems evident that while Turner had expected constitutional revisions for greater efficiency, the Markoe and LaFarge groups had taken the opportunity to create a new thrust in the organization.[205]

Meanwhile, Eugene Clarke was conducting his own poll in Washington. He wrote to Markoe shortly after hearing of the change in the magazine's title that there was a good deal of bitterness among those he interviewed.

> The fight which the clergy and certain northern Negroes who
> are comparatively new members of the Federation put up to
> change the Federation's name convinced our representative
> to the Convention that there was a conspiracy to modify the
> character of the organization so that it would be ineffectual
> in representing the true sentiment of the whole Negro group.[206]

Furthermore, local Federation members thought that Markoe was now misrepresenting the majority opinion expressed at the convention. In

---

[204] Ibid.

[205] What is also obvious is that agreement for the changes in name and constitution was pulled reluctantly from Turner in the executive session, because he had not been prepared for them and had not the votes to prevent their passage. The unanimous vote on the convention floor, made for the sake of harmony, did not reflect either Turner's or his group's views. The minutes for the executive session were not published in the Interracial Review, and no copy was found in the collections I examined. See also footnote 195.

[206] Clarke to Markoe, 7 October 1932, Turner Papers.

fact, they were concerned that LaFarge and Markoe were attempting to take over the Federation. Expressing personal regret at the evident discord, Clarke implored Markoe to settle his differences with Turner, whom he described as "a man of strong convictions and great determination."[207] Clarke's concluding remarks were a rebuke:

> It is my conviction that none of us, priest or layman, should attempt innovations in the Federation, however well intended, without getting the consent of the President and the Executive Committee.[208]

Despite the urgency of the situation, Turner put Markoe's long letter aside, writing to Clarke that he would answer it "in a few weeks," when he had more time. Meanwhile, Turner's words to Clarke indicated that he had already developed a strong suspicion of Markoe. He described the priest's work with Federation groups in New York, Chicago and St. Louis as "tricky political plays" and attempts, with LaFarge, to turn these cities against the Federation as a Jim Crow organization. They have had success, he said, only because the cities are such "out-ofthe-way places" for the Washington group to reach.[209]

In late October (after the first issue of the <u>Interracial Review</u> had appeared) Conrad wrote to Turner congratulating him for his broadmindedness at the convention. The Cincinnati man expressed loyalty to LaFarge and Markoe: "Let us renew our faith and trust in them until we have reason to believe otherwise."[210] The Federation would need such

---

[207] Ibid.

[208] Ibid.

[209] Turner to Clarke, 21 October 1932, Turner Papers.

[210] Conrad to Turner, 29 October 1932, Turner Papers.

priests if the black Catholic was to reach his true place in the Church. While he thought Markoe should have gotten permission from the executive committee to change the organ's name, Conrad was pleased with the result. In any event, "Peace and good-will should be our slogan, ever holding inviolate those lofty purposes for which the Federation was organized."[211]

Once the Interracial Review appeared, Turner no longer maintained public silence. Refusing to allow the magazine to represent the Federation, he sent a press release to Catholic and secular periodicals, particularly the black press. The statement denied that the new Interracial Review was the official organ of the Federation, as it stated. Rather, it was Father Markoe's property. Although the Federation had accepted the Chronicle "at Fr. Markoe's request" as its magazine four years ago, whether it would do the same now with this new one remained to be seen.[212] Turner added that his declaration was for the benefit of all those who had been asking by what authority the change was made. When the original release was handed to a Norfolk journalist for release to the black press, the newsman added a paragraph which was interpreted by some Catholics as anti-clerical in tone. Turner later had a sworn statement issued by the journalist to that effect, in an effort to counteract criticism of the release.[213]

---

[211]Ibid.

[212]Turner, "Letter to Catholic and Secular Press by the President," press release, October 1932, Turner Papers.

[213]Sworn statement, G. James Fleming to whom it may concern, 15 December 1932, Turner Papers.

Attempting to mediate the conflict, Clarke invited Turner and Markoe, along with several long-time members of the Washington Federation, Father Olds included, to meet at his home in early November. In a letter to Turner before the meeting, Clarke urged cooperation. Markoe had done much good work, he said, and a name meant little. Besides, many blacks were now supporting interracialism.[214]

Apparently the personal confrontation produced no positive results. Indeed, it only widened the split between the two men. Markoe described the incident later in his memoirs:

> When [I] entered the private home where the meeting was held, there assembled in the spacious, comfortable living room was the opposition with Dr. Turner at their head, like so many lions waiting to devour the defenseless lamb. [I] warmly greeted the group and began moving from one to the other, cordially shaking each one's hand, until [I] pulled up short in front of Dr. Turner. "Dr. Turner," I said, "I will gladly shake your hand and as of old be your loyal friend as soon as you apologize for your false charges published in the Afro-American." He refused to apologize. But [I] could see that my taking the initiative threw them all somewhat off balance. [I] told them I presumed there was no need for further discussion. Our host then helped by announcing that there were refreshments waiting in the dining room. I told them pleasantly that while I would not shake hands with Dr. Turner who had double crossed me, I would not object to taking a drink and a bite to eat because I was both thirsty and hungry. So we all had a pleasant, if somewhat restrained, visit. At its conclusion [I] bade them farewell and went on to report to Father LaFarge in New York.[215]

Meanwhile, Turner received a reaction from one black supporter of Markoe. R. Augustine Skinner, a Chicago attorney, reported to Turner on local interracial meetings he had arranged in accordance with the new constitution. He had invited Markoe to speak and was much pleased with

---

[214]Clarke to Turner, 6 November 1932, Turner Papers.

[215]Markoe, "An Interracial Role," p. 249. I have substituted "I" for "we" in the original manuscript. Markoe used the editorial "we" to refer to himself.

the results. Then he took up two issues which concerned him as a national officer: the change of the organ's name, and the question of Markoe in the role of national organizer. Skinner saw no reason why Markoe had not the right to do as he wished with his own magazine. The Federation should be grateful for Markoe as a deputy organizer (a post to which he was duly appointed) because he could travel at his own expense. The Chicago chapters favored both moves, and Skinner urged Turner to put his personal feelings aside. In a postscript Skinner expressed shock at an article in the St. Louis American, severing ties between the Federation and the Interracial Review. His objection was that Turner consulted no officers in making this announcement.

> I further am of the opinion that you have contravened the spirit and intent of the Constitution which gives you no right as our President to arrogate powers unto yourself without the sanction and approval of your Executive Committee where the Constitution does not specifically set out certain acts of an officer, then the conduct in common usage must prevail.[216]

The issue of proper authority, particularly black lay authority, was uppermost in Turner's mind during this period:

> Our aim is to keep the organization strictly in the hands of laymen. We must make it clear if the clergy come in it is coming into our set up to which they must conform. I thought Markoe and LaFarge understood this, but evidently they decided they could grab the land, put up their flag and claim the country for their own. This is what the white has done through the ages.[217]

Meanwhile, the business of the Federation continued. The annual statement to the hierarchy, approved at the convention, was sent to each

---

[216]R. Augustine Skinner to Turner, 10 November 1932, Turner Papers.

[217]Turner to Prater, November [1932], Turner Papers.

bishop, with the hope that it would be discussed at the next bishops' meeting. The requests made in 1932 were more forceful than ever.[218] Despite all the controversy at the time, Turner did appear before a committee of bishops of the N.C.W.C. to present a personal appeal.[219]

Announcements of an extraordinary executive committee meeting were sent out by George Conrad in his official position of first vice-president. The purpose of the meeting, scheduled for December 4 in Chicago, was to consider charges against Dr. Turner as president, under article III of the new by-laws.

---

[218](1) Every bishop should order an end to all discriminatory regulations in his diocese. (2) Where civil law imposed segregation, the bishops should work to repeal laws. (3) No Catholic institution--college, hospital, orphanage--should bar black Catholics. (4) A campaign of education should be conducted among white priests, Sisters, and laity on the true Catholic attitude on race. (5) Bishops should see to it that priests preach against race prejudice as a violation of the commandment to love thy neighbor. (6) They should also instruct confessors to urge penitents in correcting the grievous sin of race prejudice. (7) The above instructions should appear in diocesan periodicals or pamphlets. (8) Priests and Sisters should be urged to encourage religious vocations among black Catholic children as much as among white. (9) Bishops should handle sternly any public act of discrimination by Catholic institutions or individuals under his care. (10) No restrictions should exist at the Catholic University of America or in movements such as the N.C.W.C. (11) The interests of black Catholics should be included as an "integral part" of all Catholic Action efforts. (12) Bishops should speak out nationally through the N.C.W.C. press on such outrages as lynching. (13) Cases outlining abuses listed above could be supplied on demand. Turner as President of the F.C.C. to the hierarchy, 14 November 1932, Turner Papers.

[219]For Turner's appearance before the bishops, see Walsh to LaFarge, 21 December 1932, LaFarge Papers. Walsh was aware of the controversy when he wrote LaFarge, regretted it, and said he felt Turner's appearance before the bishops had done some good.

Article III—Suspensions
Section 1. In the case of misconduct or neglect of duty in office on the part of any National Officer, the Executive Committee, by the affirmative vote of at least two-thirds thereof, may declare his (or her) office vacant and may fill the same for the remainder of his (or her) term.[220]

The reaction of several Washington members was that the meeting was illegal, since only the president could call the executive committee into session. Smith sought legal advice, convinced also that the Federation, incorporated in Washington, must hold its board meetings there. He sent a note as national secretary to all executive committee members declaring that the December meeting was not authorized by the president, who would call a regular meeting in January.[221]

Markoe's response to these objections was that the relevant article would have no meaning if the officer being charged had to call the meeting. He could stall forever. Conrad as first vice-president was not only within his rights but obligated to arrange a meeting. Markoe concluded that two lawyers had informed him Conrad's action would be upheld in a court of law.[222]

Turner himself sent the letter to the executive committee which he had composed a month earlier. After reviewing the facts of the

---

[220]"Constitution of the National Catholic Federation for the Promotion of Better Race Relations," *Interracial Review*, October 1932, p. 207.

[221]Smith to Turner, 17 November 1932, Turner Papers. G. A. Henderson of Pittsburgh expressed horror at Conrad's announcement of a meeting, to consider charges against Turner. "I hereby protest against any actions that occur in or at any special meeting, not called by the president, in accordance with law on the matter." Henderson to Smith, 13 November 1932, Turner Papers.

[222]Markoe to Prater, 18 November 1932, Turner Papers.

controversy, he declared:

> The defiant publication of the untrue statement [that the Interracial Review is the official organ] had necessitated my setting forth the truth in the Catholic and the secular press. Though errors may creep in with these press communications such method may be called for until something better is worked.[223]

Turner insisted that the constitution gave him the power to act as he had, and that he would give a fuller explanation at the executive committee meeting in January. At that time the members would also receive a full report on his meeting with the bishops on November 14. Then Turner addressed the question of authority.

> Defiance of authority by a priest as well as a layman is a serious matter in the Church and must not be tolerated by anyone.
> . . . I wish to assure the members of the Committee that with the help of God and you this body shall not, so long as I am President be dominated by any extra-constitutional assumptions of authority which are now being attempted in case by the Editor of the Chronicle [224]

On November 25, 1932 Conrad sent Dr. Turner the formal charges against him. In the letter he demanded that Turner call a meeting for December 4, and he present himself, this despite the fact that all other committee members had already received notices to appear. The meeting was for the purpose of hearing charges brought by Father Markoe, and if Turner were not present, the committee would take whatever action "as it deems proper and fit."[225] The charges were "unwarranted

---

[223] Turner to members of the executive committee, 16 November 1932, Turner Papers.

[224] Ibid.

[225] Conrad to Turner, 25 November 1932, Turner Papers. For evidence that notices had already been sent out for the meeting Turner was supposed to call, see Smith to members of the executive committee invalidating said notices, 17 November 1932, Turner Papers.

assumption of authority" by Turner, when he repudiated the <u>Interracial Review</u>, "imprudence" shown in endangering the future of the Federation over the name of the magazine, and "false publicity" about clerical plots, evident in articles appearing in the <u>Afro-American</u>, the <u>Journal and Guide</u>, and material sent to the <u>St. Louis American</u> and the N.C.W.C. News Service. Turner was also accused of "scandal," because he had raised the anti-clerical issue in public, and "treason" for denying the interracial idea adopted by the New York convention.[226]

Turner decided not to respond to the charges in themselves, but he did take steps to see how the new group could be prevented from using the Federation name at its meeting or in its publicity. He also retained a copy of the formal letter from Conrad to the committee members, and asked Clarke to do so with whatever other correspondence might be sent to the executive committee. His plan was to write later on "the Federation and its struggle to continue under the control of Negro laymen."[227]

Among the older members of the Washington group, the question was whether to attend the "rump" session, as it was being called. Prater expressed a willingness to do so, but pleaded he had not the funds, and the Federation treasurer was a St. Louis man. He mentioned having written to C. J. Foster in Chicago, whom he felt would support Turner. Then he urged Dr. Turner to stand firm.

---

[226]Enclosure with Conrad to Turner, 25 November 1932, Turner Papers.

[227]Turner to Clarke, after 25 November 1932, Turner Papers.

> . . . this thing, as I wrote in my special is unchristian, unmanly, unethical and illegal so I hope and pray that if they are so degraded as to attempt to do as they say that you will go to the mat with them without fear of publicity.[228]

Clarke responded with an open letter to the executive committee in support of Turner. The form was that of a personal testimonial.

> I have known this gentleman for more than fifteen years. . . . He is not a politician. We don't want a politician to head Our Organization.[229]

Some accused him of being anti-clerical, Clarke went on. But just as many said he had been too generous with the clerical role. During his term of office, Archbishop Curley had been the spiritual director, LaFarge wrote the resolutions for the last convention, and Markoe directed the publication. LaFarge prepared the constitution accepted at the New York convention. Indeed, so strong was clerical participation, Clarke revealed, that immediately preceding the last convention, LaFarge wrote Turner an ultimatum. LaFarge, Markoe and Devers had agreed, said Clarke, that if the New York meeting were not handled differently from the others, there would be no more conventions.

> This assumption of dictatorship was more than even the liberal Dr. Turner could stand.
> Apparently, then, if Dr. Turner has erred it is because he has been too generous in accepting the services of the clergy. If our two good friends, Fathers Markoe and LaFarge have erred it is because they have thrown themselves too wholeheartedly into the affairs of the organization.[230]

All these men had value in the Federation, Clarke pleaded. The time to settle differences, then, was not at a meeting called by those

---

[228]Prater to Turner, 28 November 1932, Turner Papers.

[229]Clarke to the executive committee, 29 November 1932, Turner Papers.

[230]Ibid.

who had decided the case in advance. Turner's record deserved better than that.

>I, therefore, appeal to those who appreciate the splendid work which Dr. Turner has done to stay away from Mr. Conrad's meeting. The presumption of the Vice President in arrogating so much authority to himself is an insult to the intelligence of our Executive Committee.[231]

Turner responded to the announcement of the meeting, if not to the charges. Pleading a previous engagement, he wrote Conrad: "I assure you that nothing would give me greater pleasure than to be present and to clear up any matters which I may."[232] It must remain clear, he added, that the meeting nonetheless was not an Executive Committee one. Smith would send notices on that, to be held in Washington in January. Any charges could properly be settled there.

Next Turner wrote to Archbishop Curley, again merely as a matter of information. He expressed the view that Markoe had disrupted the organization, was calling an illegal meeting on December 4, and was generally bringing scandal to the Church. The president would not attend the meeting, Turner said, but would reply through the press later. Mentioning that Markoe never reported his financial transactions as other officers, and that all but the Northern groups supported the president, Turner asked whether Markoe could be relieved. Otherwise, the issue might have to go to the courts. Turner closed by referring the archbishop to Father Olds or Father McGowan for further details.[233]

---

[231]Ibid.

[232]Turner to Conrad, 30 November 1932, Turner Papers.

[233]Turner to Curley, 30 November, 1932, Turner Papers.

Curley did nothing about Markoe or the meeting, however, and on December 5, 1932, Conrad wrote Turner to inform him that he had been removed from office. Noting that the meeting had been the most representative ever held, with members present from all over the country, Conrad mentioned that the group had also decided the January meeting was unnecessary.[234]

Reaction in the press, especially the black press, was immediate and varied. The Pittsburgh Courier reported that Dr. Turner had been deposed for two reasons, false publicity and scandal.[235] The report traced the difficulty to a conflict between two schools of thought at the New York convention, one favoring a "purely colored" organization and one seeking an "interracial organization."[236] Turner was charged because he had accepted reelection knowing the interracial mind had triumphed, and then repudiated the idea in print. Listing the names of those present, the article quoted spokesmen as explaining the constitutional power by which the group had acted. It also mentioned puzzlement from Turner's friends about his attitude. A description of the new president, George Conrad, and an endorsement of Father Markoe's Interracial Review by the committee concluded the report.[237]

The Philadelphia Tribune gave first page coverage to the meeting, but concentrated on George Conrad rather than on Turner. Describing

---

[234]Conrad to Turner, 5 December 1932, Turner Papers.

[235]"False Publicity Charged to "Professor' by Federation," Pittsburgh Courier, 17 December 1932, p. 7.

[236]Ibid.

[237]Ibid.

Conrad's elevation to the presidency, the paper noted that Turner had been "unexpectedly relieved of his high position at the same meeting."[238] The rest of the article was devoted to a biographical sketch of Conrad, and quoted him in praise of the Church's work for blacks. His aim, Conrad declared, would be to "bring about a clearer union and better feeling among all Catholics."[239]

On the other hand, the Baltimore Afro-American came out in full support of Turner. Two articles appeared in the December 17 issue. The paper interpreted the ouster as an attempt by white priests to control a black organization. After a brief history of the Federation, the first article listed Turner's main concerns while he was president, a native clergy and the end to segregation in Catholic churches and schools. Relating part of Turner's address at the 1932 convention, which had outlined these abuses, the paper claimed that "Catholic leaders here" thought Turner too advanced for the Church, and that priests wished to "muzzle" him. The clergy urged him to drop racial solidarity and combat Communism instead. After reviewing the main events of the controversy, the Afro-American mentioned that Baltimore, Washington, and Philadelphia Catholics had earlier been approached but always refused to oust Turner. The article closed by quoting an executive committee member who said the issue was how the clergy would come into the Federation, as regular members on a level with laymen, or as exalted authorities dictating policy.[240]

---

[238]"Catholic Church Praised by Dr. Turner's Successor," Philadelphia Tribune, 22 December 1932, p. 1.

[239]Ibid.

[240]"Catholics Oust Dr. Turner," Baltimore Afro-American, 17 December 1932, p. 1.

A second article on the same page reported the Chicago meeting. It was, interestingly, the official Associated Negro Press release from Chicago, the same which had appeared in the Pittsburgh Courier.[241]

Apparently the group which met in Chicago decided to ask each national officer his intentions. A note was appended to Turner's official notice inquiring whether Smith wished to remain as secretary. The latter replied to Conrad that since the meeting had been illegal, the question was whether Conrad intended to retain his office! Smith explained what he meant by illegality.

> Article III, Sec. 1 upon which you based your action provides that at least two-thirds of the members of the Executive Committee must cast an assenting vote in order to declare an officer's position vacant. Since there were only eleven members present who were entitled to vote, the entire procedure was without effect. I hope that you will consider it agreeable to continue to hold your office of First Vice-President.[242]

In a subsequent note to Turner, Smith mentioned "putting off" the black press, telling it the president wished to consult the archbishop before releasing a story. Apparently Turner was being urged during this period by friends to see Curley. The president did wire the archbishop and later wrote requesting an appointment during the Christmas holidays, when Turner would be on his way to science meetings in Atlantic City. The stress was always on keeping the archbishop merely _informed_, however, not seeking his involvement.[243]

---

[241]"Catholic Body Ousts Turner, Elects Conrad," Baltimore Afro-American, 17 December 1932, p. 1.

[242]Smith to Conrad, 9 December 1932, Turner Papers. There were twenty-five members in all on the committee.

[243]Turner to Curley, 21 December 1932, Turner Papers. Smith's advice was in a letter to Turner, 13 December 1932, Turner Papers.

Meanwhile, Turner was busy soliciting the support of others. He wrote to Father McGowan asking whether the priest would handle the "false publicity" Conrad was sending the N.C.W.C. about the ouster. He also requested McGowan to write the truth to the archbishop.

> The trouble is that Fr. Markoe has come into the organization with a missionary attitude "to give his life," as he put it in New York, to the Federation. He doesn't understand that the Federation is not to be dealt with on such basis, so in his anger he thinks he can get a few people together, ignore the Constitution, and remove the President . . . and that in the face of the fact that we have an incorporated organization.[244]

Turner sent a message to a Chicago member, reminding her that another priest had opposed him in the past--the not-too-popular Father Eckert of that city. A contact in St. Louis also received a letter, requesting help in getting the truth to the black press there.[245] Father Olds and Father Kramer heard from Turner as well. Kramer replied that he had been away during recent weeks, but feared such a break. He had advised Turner earlier to make the group, begun in protest, a more constructive one; otherwise, such organizations "carry the germ of destruction within themselves."[246] Kramer also revealed that he had warned Markoe at the last convention that any name change should be hammered out on the convention floor. But instead it had been fought out in the executive committee session and then passed (with Dr. Turner presiding) unanimously. Noting an _Afro-American_ article claiming the issue was over black priests, Kramer asked, will

---

[244]Turner to Rev. R. A. McGowan, 15 December 1932, Turner Papers.

[245]Turner to Mrs. Margaret Cope, 15 December 1932, Turner Papers. Turner to Charles H. Anderson, 16 December 1932, Turner Papers.

[246]Kramer to Turner, 28 December 1932, Turner Papers.

you correct such false publicity? The same people will later turn on you, he warned.[247]

Father McGowan expressed regret about the split, in the light of the achievements cooperation had wrought and the success of the recent meeting with the bishops' committee. The N.C.W.C. press department was printing both sides. Although he did not feel a letter to the archbishop would help, McGowan promised to speak to him.

> You have done a splendid job. The charge that you are anticlerical is, of course, ridiculous, and I feel sure that your service to the Church and to your own people has just begun [248]

Since the two factions of the Federation had failed to come to terms, the obvious difficulty was which was the "true" Federation. Smith announced an executive committee meeting for January 8 in Washington. Meanwhile, the Conrad group had announced plans to hold the annual convention in Cleveland, and its next executive committee meeting in June. The *Interracial Review* was continuing to publish, of course, as the new official organ.

Turner wrote again to McGowan at the N.C.W.C., this time to request a meeting. One reason was to head off any plans for the N.C.W.C. to participate in the convention sessions of the new group.[249]

Both organizations attempted to reach the public through the press. When Turner traveled to Atlantic City in late December, he took the opportunity to visit Federation chapters in Washington, Philadelphia and Baltimore, and released the results to the press. Most of the

---

[247] Ibid.

[248] McGowan to Turner, 22 December 1932, Turner Papers.

[249] Turner to McGowan, 1 January 1933, Turner Papers.

executive committee was behind him, he declared, and opposed to the "self-appointed bossism of Fr. Markoe." Turner went on to describe the priest's actions as unsurprising.

> The Reverend is most regular historically in carrying out this attempt to force undoubted conviction that might makes right. It has ever been the way of unprincipled exploiters when they find their hidden motives thwarted to make such a coup as he has made in miniature in the Federation of Colored Catholics. His cry was "get the chief" and the rest will follow like lost sheep, and he can very easily place on the throne a puppet chief. . . . [250]

The result, however, was only fewer subscriptions for the Interracial Review, Turner insisted. It no longer represented the organization nor the effort to

> . . . build an organization having strong racial solidarity in some such way as is done for the Irish through the Ancient Order of Hibernians, for the Germans through their many Turnvereins and for the Poles, and other racial groups which need organization for their special protection and development.[251]

A December 24 edition of the Baltimore Afro-American carried an article announcing the January executive committee meeting, along with the full text of Turner's letter to the committee. In it the president spoke of the "insidious forces which are tending to destroy the morale of our organization."[252] Referring to the December 4 meeting in Chicago, Turner stated that only eleven persons besides Father Markoe were present from the executive committee. After Markoe had delivered a "violent invective," nine of the members, and the president, voted against Turner. One non-voting member there did cast a vote illegally.

---

[250] Baltimore Afro-American, 31 December 1932.

[251] Ibid.

[252] "Catholic Head to Disregard 'Rump' Ouster," Baltimore Afro-American, 24 December 1932, pp. 1-2.

Questioning Markoe's right any longer to be considered an officer, Turner concluded that at least an insufficient number of votes had been cast for an ouster. "The attack here is made not upon us," he proclaimed, "at least, I do not take it as such--but it is an attack upon Negro leadership, carried out with a lack of scruples and with most indecent propaganda."[253]

Markoe for his part granted an interview to the Associated Negro Press in St. Louis (published in the St. Louis Courier) when the announcement was made of a "regular" executive committee meeting in January. He declared that there would be no more meetings until June. As for the charge that he had attacked "Negro leadership," he replied,

> . . . I believe the intelligent Negro leaders of the organization are more than competent to handle any situation which might arise, for which belief there is already abundant evidence in their prompt removal of Dr. Thomas W. Turner as president, when the occasion demanded such action.[254]

Markoe denied as well that the issue was between clergy and laity.

> The recent developments, resulting in Dr. Turner's removal, have in no sense been a question of clergy versus laity. The issue was interracial versus racial, or progress versus reaction. It was the lay executive committee, and not the clergy, who removed Dr. Turner from office and elevated George W. B. Conrad to the presidency. Nor was the issue opposition to Negro leadership. The new president is as much of a Negro as his predecessor.[255]

Turner was quick to respond, of course, to the "erroneous interview by Rev. William M. Markoe."[256] The president's description

---

[253] Ibid.

[254] "Catholic Editor Talks," St. Louis Courier, 5 January 1933.

[255] Ibid.

[256] Turner, "Erroneous Interview given by Rev. W. M. Markoe to American Negro Press," press release, after 7 January 1933, Turner Papers.

of the meeting which ousted him read like a mystery story: Markoe was "secreted" in an adjoining room when the group met, and only appeared when it seemed the executive committee members would declare it an illegal meeting. He demanded and received their vote under threat that he would resign. Regarding the question of whether he had opposed the interracial idea, Turner declared that cooperation had existed with the N.C.W.C. for a long period, and that whatever interracial concept Markoe promoted was not that of the Federation membership.

The Midwestern group answered the charge of an illegal meeting through an attorney, R. A. Skinner, a second vice-president of the Federation. In an A.N.P. article which received widely scattered coverage, Skinner declared that the meeting in Chicago had been held in complete accordance with the constitution. Concerning the number of votes needed to depose the president, the group had interpreted the constitution to mean that two-thirds of those members "actually assembled" was needed for an ouster. Skinner went on to accuse Turner of a complete reversal in attitude in the past few months. After public praise for the Chronicle and his election on an interracial platform, the president had suddenly condemned these same aspects of the Federation.

There were the usual letters to the editor and expressions of support during the period. See, for example, letter to the editor, Baltimore Afro-American, 24 December 1932; "Conrad's Former Neighbor Will Support Dr. Turner," Afro-American, 7 January 1933; "Pa. Catholics Back Turner," Afro-American, 7 January 1933. When DuBois wrote for information on the controversy, Turner took that opportunity as well to state his position: "I organized the Federation about eight years ago to get at the discrimination and inequalities practiced. The white men who have [come] in have worked and cooperated admirably with us until we got [sic] of a young Jesuit Clergyman from the West who feels that everything is wrong which we have been doing and that the Lord has called him to change it. I am the chief obstacle in his way and thus his efforts to change me." Turner to DuBois, 6 January 1933, Turner Papers.

Dr. Turner is a Catholic gentleman and should be aware of the fact that any organization in the church having the imprimatur of the church must work in harmony with the clergy. Without the services of Father LaFarge and Father Markoe, men who have given their very all to the bringing about of a feeling of amicability among all Catholics in the church, the organization might have ceased to exist.[257]

Seventy-five persons gathered at the Holy Name Guild hall in Washington on January 8 for the "regular" executive committee meeting. All were from nearby states: Maryland, Virginia, Pennsylvania, and the District of Columbia. Twelve were members of the executive committee (one having also attended the meeting in Chicago, William Prater). Letters of support were read from three members unable to be present: Byron Peters of Pittsburgh, L. V. Abraham of Jacksonville, Florida and C. J. Foster of Chicago (who had attended the December meeting there. Prater and Foster had voted against ouster). The audience was boisterous in its response when Turner delivered his official address. Briefly adverting to the recent controversy, Turner reviewed the founding of the organization.

> It was conceived and organized by a group of Colored persons, after mature and prayerful consideration. Its efforts and activities have never been plaintive, but always truthful and constructive. Its aims have been clearcut, simple, and unequivocal. Equitable consideration of the Negro in the Church with reference to every sacred calling and every temporal opportunity is the basic stimulus that has brought us together from year to year to take counsel with each other and with our Spiritual Advisor as to the best method of improving the deplorable condition.[258]

---

[257]"Chicago Officer Sustains Action," <u>Californian</u>, 30 December 1932, p. 12. This article also appeared in the <u>Pittsburgh Courier</u>, 31 December 1932.

[258]Turner, address to members of the executive committee, 8 January 1933, Turner Papers. The meeting was reported in "Rump Catholics Are Denounced in Washington," <u>Baltimore Afro-American</u>, 14 January 1933, p. 1. One member only of the executive committee did not attend either meeting, in Chicago or Washington, Caroline Cook of

Then Turner noted the importance of the Detroit meeting. Quoting from his address on that occasion, Turner reiterated the value and necessity of a specific black Catholic organization, and the accomplishments of the Federation in recent years. The "remarkable unanimity" of the group, he went on, had been destroyed by two priests: Markoe and LaFarge. They began with "straddling" articles on the Federation as a Jim Crow organization, then went on to writings about an interracial purpose. None of these reflected the thinking of the ordinary member, Turner declared. The real difficulty grew during the summer, he explained, when LaFarge threatened to quit the organization if it did not change, and Markoe brought a group to the convention with that purpose in mind. "I realized that some sinister forces were at work," said Turner. Finally, Father Markoe announced at the convention that he was leaving parish work for full-time dedication to the Federation.

> We had not asked the Reverend Father to do this, nor had he consulted a single one of the presiding officers. The extirpation of the term, "Negro," from the constitution and the destruction of the Negro's aims seemed to be quite secondary to his inordinate ambition to have his own way and to impose his own questionable ideas upon the organization; in short, to become the self-imposed boss.[259]

As Turner continued his speech, the question of clerical involvement was obviously paramount.

> It might be said that we have never felt the need of advice from these Fathers as to our aims, though we have needed many other helps. The organization must not be considered a field for missionary activity. Cooperation in the same way as we find

---

Baltimore. She claimed when questioned that she wanted to remain "neutral." See <u>Baltimore Afro-American</u>, 21 January 1933.

[259]Turner, ibid.

laymen and clergy working together among the Knights of
Columbus or the various Catholic societies organized along
racial lines in different parts of the country and the world
is our plan.260

Then Turner reviewed events at the convention and immediately following, pointing out that he had rejected the term "Interracial Federation" as meaningless, and little approved of the change actually made. Describing press coverage as most generous in clarifying the major struggle, black leadership, as a "basic aim of the organization," Turner explained the changes made in his original press releases that had drawn charges of anti-clericalism. He also submitted supporting evidence. Ultimately, he told the committee, "I submit the matter to you for your judgment and action."261

The predictable response was overwhelming approval for the past president of the Federation. In a series of resolutions the committee members present endorsed Turner, condemned the "rump" session and its leaders, and repudiated the Interracial Review. In a specific but veiled reference to Markoe, they asserted that no members should hold more than one office (the editor was also a deputy organizer at that point) and that all deputy organizers should be approved by the president. The group warned that use of its name was an invasion of corporate rights, and expressed appreciation to the press for supporting its cause.

The eternal question is, "Are we capable of managing our
own affairs or are we to surrender all initiative to the
dominant group?" This organization believes in capable Negro

---

260 Ibid.

261 Ibid.

leadership. We don't want to wait for our so-called friends to "sell us." We want a fair chance to prove our own worth.262

The committee members appointed Mrs. Helen Pinckett, who had been in charge of publicity before the adoption of the Chronicle, to reassume that position. They announced the next committee meeting would be held on June 11, and the annual convention in September, in Washington, D.C. They expressed hope that the interracial industrial conference would remain a feature of the convention. Finally, the members voted to send copies of the January proceedings to all executive committee members, including Markoe.263

The January meeting received rather wide press coverage. When Markoe was asked to comment on the proceedings, he described them merely as a "consolation party," or "cry fest" given by Turner's followers to "soothe his wounded feelings."264 As the same article pointed out, however, the true test would come in September, when each group held "the" annual Federation convention.

Toward that end, Turner once again solicited the support of McGowan.265 Secondly, he secured the offices of a lawyer in the hope

---

262Resolutions of the executive committee, 8 January 1933. Reported in Baltimore Afro-American, 14 January 1933, pp. 1-2.

263Ibid.

264"Markoe Calls D.C. Catholic Meeting a "Cry Fest,' " Baltimore Afro-American, 21 January 1933. As for the coverage of the Washington meeting, see "President Is Vindicated by ational Executive Committee of Catholics," Washington Tribune, 13 January 1933; "Our Catholics Need Organization," Pittsburgh Courier, 21 January 1933. The Courier had heretofore printed articles favorable to the Midwestern group, but sided with Turner in this editorial.

265Turner to McGowan, 9 January 1933, Turner Papers.

of forcing the issue on rights to the Federation name (ironic as that may seem, since the name itself was at the heart of the current debate.).[266] A letter was even sent to Archbishop McNicholas of Cincinnati, Conrad's home. Recalling the bishop's presence at the meeting in November when Turner had presented the Federation to a bishops' committee, the layman expressed the hope that McNicholas would not (as had been reported) approve the new faction.[267] An attempt was also made to reach Bishop Schrembs in Cleveland and convince him to withdraw approval for the convention planned there. The effort was not successful[268]

One major issue in the struggle was, as always, finances. The treasurer of the Federation was from St. Louis and a Markoe supporter. Money was needed badly by both groups, especially for publicity. Turner decided to take a step he had been avoiding. He sought the active support of Archbishop Curley, which might force the treasurer to release funds. Secondly, he and the Washington group planned a rally in February to raise extra money.[269]

Curley had been receiving his own information on the controversy, largely through Father Gillard. The Josephite had sent him as far back as October a harsh analysis of all parties involved. The archbishop

---

[266]To secure legal advice, Turner wrote to C. S. Cuney, 21 January 1933, Turner Papers.

[267]Turner to Archbishop John T. McNicholas, 21 January 1933, Turner Papers.

[268]Turner to Mrs. Anita E. Lomax, 24 January 1933, Turner Papers.

[269]Clarke to Turner, 25 January 1933, Turner Papers.

was not particularly receptive, therefore, when Turner approached him. He was outraged at the publicity in the black press, which he considered unworthy of a Catholic organization. Father LaFarge's article in *America*, announcing a convention in Cleveland for the Midwestern group, had arrived at the same time as Turner's claims to the presidency. The archbishop pleaded that he had been left out of the Federation to this point and wished to remain so. "The parties who went to the fray, will have to fight it out, so far as I am concerned," he said.[270]

In a move which could have increased the archbishop's ire, Turner sent another essay to the black press about this time. In it he tried to repudiate the notion that the controversy was over whether the Federation should be interracial.

> We have always welcomed such members of the white group as desired to work with us, giving them sometimes as in [the] case of Reverend Markoe most important elective positions. This fact alone should qualify any persons, who seek to give the impression that our organization has not in the past encouraged fullest cooperation with the white group, as leading candidates for the Ananias Club.[271]

Rather, the real problem was two-fold: Markoe's refusal to obey constituted authority, and his assumption of extra-constitutional privileges (accusing Turner of anti-clericalism for vetoing them). He changed the name of the organ without approval, and his intention to dominate had been clear ever since. Then Turner introduced an accusation which had

---

[270]Curley to Turner, 4 February 1933, Turner Papers. For Gillard's comments on the controversy, see Gillard to Curley, 10 October 1932; Gillard to Curley, 22 December 1932, both in Gillard Papers. The article of LaFarge's to which Curley referred in his letter was "Catholic Negroes Take Stock," *America*, 4 February 1933, pp. 429-31.

[271]Turner, "The Catholic Federation Controversy Not a Question of Racial or Interracial Ideas," press release, 4 February 1933, Turner Papers.

not appeared before.

> The sole reason for the present disturbance is the inordinate desire of the good priest to put a stop to our progressive activity because he, himself, was afraid or otherwise hesitant in going through the whole program.[272]

Why did Markoe fear our methods? Turner asked. Because he did not wish to "wage battle in person." For example, Father Theobald offered to accompany the Federation committee to see the hierarchy, but Markoe never had. Indeed, when he realized that his reluctance to go the limit would be noticed, he decided to form an organization "behind which he could talk at liberty from a comfortably long range." The next comment was noteworthy. "The futility of such talk all of us and other people know too well."[273] Turner concluded by publicly advising Markoe that if he wished to do missionary and bi-racial work, he could start by converting "his own religious group" (the Jesuits). Obviously, they needed reform in some of their racial practices.[274]

The article indicated not only the personal element which had become characteristic of the controversy, but also the sometimes harsh tones of the publicity which surrounded it. If Curley saw the article, it could not have helped Turner's cause with him. The archbishop did agree at last to see Turner on February 11. Apparently this meeting produced no specific results. Turner followed it with a letter requesting particular actions from Curley; that he continue as spiritual director of the Turner group and that if possible he declare the Midwestern group

---

[272]Ibid.

[273]Ibid.

[274]Ibid.

illegal, including the Interracial Review. For the first time Turner indicated that if the Markoe group wished to start another organization, there would be no objection. All his group wanted, Turner declared, was to be "relieved of their further disturbing activity."[275] Our reason for being apprehensive, he noted, was that his organization did not wish to be controlled by the Jesuits or any other community. A postscript to the letter indicated it had the approval of Vice-President Clarke and Secretary Smith. Curley replied that he would need time to consider taking such a "pugilistic" attitude.[276]

Meanwhile the battle in the press continued. Markoe in an article in the Interracial Review for February applied the term "kingfishes" to black leaders who refused to share their authority with whites in an interracial rather than racial organization.[277] Smith replied in a letter subsequently published that the reference was obviously to Turner. "Here is the silly argument which we hear so frequently from ignorant whites: namely, that anything headed by Negroes is inferior to that which whites direct."[278] In any event, Smith continued, the solution to the present difficulty was not to attack others, but to show judicious and reasonable arguments.

---

[275] Turner to Curley, 21 February 1933, Turner Papers.

[276] Curley to Turner, 24 February 1933, Turner Papers.

[277] Markoe, " "Kingfish' Race Leaders," Interracial Review, February 1933, p. 29.

[278] "Markoe Refers to Dr. Turner as "Kingfish,' " Baltimore Afro-American, 4 February 1933.

Two other articles appeared which were so strong in their tone that they may possibly have decided the issue for Curley. They were written under the pen name Cora Grace Inman, and published in two successive issues of the Afro-American. The first, entitled "Pots, Kettles, Soap and Water Needed in Catholic Controversy," seemed the view of an outsider looking in on the issue. The author criticized the priests, including Father Gillard, for a recent article in the Colored Harvest, and congratulated the black leaders for their "intelligently objective" approach.[279]

The second article, "Open Letter to Catholics," appeared more the words of a member of the Federation. It was a public reply to LaFarge's recent article in America, "Catholic Negroes Take Stock." The author roundly criticized LaFarge for his article and for his recent involvement in Federation affairs. The identity of Cora Grace Inman was not clear, but her initials suggested at least to Gillard and Curley that she might be connected with Cardinal Gibbons Institute (possibly Constance Daniel, the assistant principal).[280]

Archbishop Curley mentioned the articles specifically when he wrote his final decision to Turner at the end of March. The issue had gone too far, in his judgment, for any reconciliation. Conrad had written asking the bishop to direct the Midwestern faction; Turner had

---

[279]Cora Grace Inman, "Pots, Kettles, Soap and Water Needed in Catholic Controversy," Baltimore Afro-American, 18 February 1933.

[280]Cora Grace Inman, "Open Letter to Catholics," Baltimore Afro-American, 25 February 1933. Curley expressed his suspicions about the true identity of Cora Grace Inman in a letter to Turner, 30 March 1933, Turner Papers.

requested supervision for the Eastern group. He would respectfully decline either offer, and had so informed Conrad.[281]

The only recourse Turner seemed to have left was the courts. He never used it. He did correspond with a constitutional lawyer, William Franklin Sands of Georgetown University. The reply Turner received was that while the constitution did not seem to warrant the action by which he had been removed, the president's next step (which is what Turner had asked about) should be to let those who had so acted "secede from the Federation." They could take the magazine, it seemed, but probably not the official title. In any event, Sands urged, do not fight any longer.

> . . . prove to the world by the calm and dignified bearing of your membership, under your guidance as a known and respected scientist, that your Federation is truly Catholic. . . .[282]

Whether Turner actually wanted to follow that advice is unclear. His group did not have the funds to publicize its position to any great extent. Members often complained that the two Jesuits had untold financial resources for doing battle.[283] In a final letter to Curley on the subject. Turner indicated that whether or not Conrad started a new organization, "I have no inclination whatever to run a competing circus along with them."[284]

---

[281]Curley to Turner, 30 March 1933, Turner Papers.

[282]William Franklin Sands to Turner, 21 March 1933, Turner Papers.

[283]Turner to Clarke, 14 March 1933, Turner Papers.

[284]Turner to Curley, 3 April 1933, Turner Papers.

To this end, Turner submitted his resignation to the executive committee on April 4, 1933. He listed as his reasons the desire to end the dissension which made any accomplishment of the Federation's aims impossible. The lack of proper means "to compete with unusual and abnormal situations" meant the group would have to enter an experimental phase again. This should not, however,

> . . . dampen our zeal nor cool our ardor to carry on for we have only scratched the ground in this great struggle to have the Negro see the Church in its fullness.[285]

The president's action was part of a larger decision by all the officers loyal to him. They had determined to submit their resignations to the group in the Midwest, along with the constitution and papers of incorporation, before any announcement from the latter's June executive meeting could be made. The Washington group hoped to make it clear by these acts that the Conrad group was beginning a new organization.[286]

Apparently Turner received so much response to this action that ten days later he wrote a form letter to his "friends," declaring that his resignation was not a withdrawal from the work to be done.[287] By June Turner was back in the role of president, with an executive meeting having been held and a convention planned for Washington in late August. That annual meeting shared some of the features of the earliest sessions,

---

[285]Turner to the executive committee, 4 April 1933, Turner Papers.

[286]H. M. Smith outlined the rationale for the resignations in Smith to Turner, 2 March 1933, Turner Papers.

[287]"It [the work] must look toward solidarity of Catholic Negroes, which must be accomplished through the unanimity of the thoughtful of the group." Turner to "Friends," 15 April 1933, Turner Papers.

held in Washington through the hospitality of St. Augustine's parish. In his annual address Turner repeated many of the points made so often in recent months about the "true" nature of the organization. He added a comparison of the Federation to other ethnic groups, the ancient Order of Hibernians, Polish Roman Catholic Union, Catholic Central Verein. What did they and the Federation have in common? ". . . to perpetuate and increase the national solidarity as an aid in advancing their civic and spiritual lives."[288] Then the president referred to an editorial in the February issue of the Interracial Review in which Markoe had argued that while immigrants had needed such organizations, the "already assimilated Negro" did not.[289] That, Turner replied, was the same as denying blacks all efforts at organizing. After mentioning some achievements of the Federation, he closed,

> . . . I do not wish to give the impression that the goal of our efforts has been reached. We have barely scratched the surface, but I hope they [accomplishments] will serve to convince any skeptic of the worthwhileness of these efforts [290]

The proceedings of the convention were published in an organ called the Voice, which became the new official publication. Later that year Turner once again stepped down from office, this time because of illness. G. A. Henderson and Eugene Clarke took over responsibility for the organization. Eventually, Henderson was elected president and Turner, honorary president. The group returned to the name Federated

---

[288]Turner, "Does the Roman Catholic Church Need a National Federation of Colored Communicants," address delivered at the ninth annual convention of the F.C.C., 27 August 1933, Turner Papers.

[289]"The Negro and the Immigrant," Interracial Review, February 1933, pp. 30-31.

[290]Turner, "Does the Roman Church."

Colored Catholics, and continued to hold meetings for several years. In 1952, the organization held its last function, a testimonial dinner for Dr. Turner.[291]

Attempts were made almost from the beginning of the split to effectuate a reunion of the two factions. The outlook seemed particularly promising in 1938, when Fr. William Walsh of St. Ignatius Church in Philadelphia served as mediator between Turner and Conrad. But the effort was unproductive.[292]

The Midwestern organization held its convention in Cleveland in September 1933, changing its name to the National Catholic Interracial Federation (the name opposed by Turner in New York). Archbishop McNicholas became its new spiritual director. Conrad made a trip to New Orleans during 1933 and considered it a likely prospect for the next convention. The city was not to be much more fortunate for him than it had been earlier for Turner, however, and invitations were not forthcoming.[293] No convention was held in 1934. Markoe's reappointment to the pastorate at his old church in St. Louis lessened his involvement in the organization. He had transferred ownership and operation of the

---

[291]W. B. Bruce, President, M. Bruce, Secretary, and F. T. Broadus, Chairman of Dinner Committee to Foster, 1952, Turner Papers, outlining plans for dinner, May 6, 1952. See also program for dinner, Turner Papers. Few records remain for the years 1940-1952, when it appears the organization was largely inactive.

[292]William J. Walsh to Turner, 6 April 1939, Turner Papers, in which Walsh complained that Turner had not answered his last letter, four months previous. When Turner finally did, he referred only to requests from Walsh for material on black history, not to the issue of reunion. See Turner to Walsh, 13 April 1939, Turner Papers.

[293]Markoe, "An Interracial Role," pp. 334, 337. Markoe noted that Conrad (like Turner) had only visited "his own people," and did not know the mentality of the priests there well enough.

Interracial Review to Father LaFarge in New York at the end of 1933. LaFarge's own interest in the Federation had begun to dwindle as well. Markoe attended a convention held in Cincinnati in 1935 at the insistence of LaFarge, who thought one of them should go.[294] Some of Conrad's efforts in 1938 and 1939 to reunite with the Eastern group may have been through a desire to regain vitality. In any event, LaFarge and Markoe had both turned in other directions. That, however, is another story.

---

[294] Ibid., p. 363. LaFarge was already printing the Interracial Review as a Catholic Interracial Council publication. The latter organization had been founded at a mass meeting sponsored by the Catholic Laymen's Union in New York on Pentecost Sunday, 1934. LaFarge and the Council took over publication of the Interracial Review as their official organ in October 1934. See Interracial Review, October 1934, p. 118. For some comments on attempts of the Midwestern group to reunite with their eastern counterpart, see minutes of the executive meeting, Federated Colored Catholics, 15 January 1939, Turner Papers.

Dr. Turner examining plants in his experimental Greenhouses, Hampton Institute

CHAPTER III

WILLIAM MORGAN MARKOE

William Morgan Markoe was born in St. Paul, Minnesota on May 11, 1892. He was one of seven children of Dr. James Cox and Mary Prince Markoe, and the descendant of several illustrious Americans.[1] In later life Markoe often used to tease that he had never finished a year of education, from grammar school through college. Whether it was literally true or not, he did maintain a dislike of studies, despite his many years on both sides of the desk.[2] After two years at St. Thomas College in Minnesota, Markoe entered St. Louis University in the fall of 1912.

He recalled in later life that his first impression of St. Louis was of a black city, since he had seen so few of that race in his early life.[3] During that first year young Markoe was initiated into the facts of segregation. Grand Boulevard divided the city's black and

___

[1] Markoe was reportedly the great great grandson of Abram Markoe, the founder of the Philadelphia City Cavalry in 1774, "for which troop he originated the first American flag having thirteen stripes." See <u>American Catholic Who's Who, 1948-49</u> (Grosse Pointe, Mich: Walter Romig, Publisher), p. 305. LaFarge also told Markoe after they met that they were cousins. LaFarge was a direct descendant of Benjamin Franklin, whose grandson had married a Markoe, William's great grand aunt, Margaret Markoe. See Markoe, "An Interracial Role," p. 141.

[2] Markoe, ibid., p. 2.

[3] Ibid, p. 1.

white sections, and he was told he should avoid the area "east of Grand Boulevard."[4] The Jesuit university exerted another influence, however, and the following year Markoe entered the order's novitiate at Florissant, Missouri. Located northwest of the city, it had been established by Belgian Jesuits in 1823, who came West from Baltimore to set up a seminary and Indian school in the region. Among their number was a young novice named Pierre de Smet and three young black slave couples, who were to run a farm for the priests at Florissant.[5]

When Markoe arrived nearly a century later, he was assigned the task of feeding the poor blacks from the Missouri River bottoms who came begging to the novitiate kitchen. Some of them were descendants of those early Jesuit slaves. This assignment plus a novitiate custom of taking long walks in the surrounding countryside proved a turning point in Markoe's life. He began to think about "spiritual food" for the blacks he met. He taught them prayers, and directed his walks toward their homes, in Anglum and Sandtown. By the end of that year he was talking with Austin Bork, a fellow novice, about dedicating his entire life to the black community.[6]

On September 8, 1915 Markoe made his perpetual vows as a Jesuit. For the next three seminary years he would have greater freedom

---

[4]Ibid., p. 2.

[5]William Barnaby Faherty, Dream by the River (St. Louis: Piraeus Publishers, 1973), pp. 26-7.

[6]Markoe, pp. 6-7. Markoe was urged to write his memoirs by several friends. Since he did not file his correspondence nor collect other private papers, these memoirs are the primary source of information on his early years.

to extend his new-found work. He organized a group of fellow seminarians, who set out in pairs to visit the black families in the surrounding area. "During my three years in the juniorate I walked an estimated 4,680 miles visiting and catechizing black families, often carrying heavy loads of food to them," Markoe recalled.[7] This was the first time the seminary had reached out to the blacks living nearby. Indeed, when some of the new converts began attending Mass at Holy Rosary Church (next to the seminary) the white parishioners complained.[8] Eventually two new churches were built, a crude log building at Sandtown and a somewhat finer frame structure at Anglum. The latter was made possible through the generosity of Markoe's aunt, Mrs. Michael Morgan, whose contributions to this work were to continue in later years. Priest instructors from the seminary came out to the churches each Sunday for Mass.

An added joy for William during this period was the entrance of his older brother, John, a West Point graduate, into the seminary at Florissant. Within months after his arrival, John, William, Austin Bork and Horace Frommelt signed a private pledge to serve the black community for the rest of their lives. William was later permitted to bind himself under vow to this promise. The original pledge read in part:

> We, the undersigned, resolve and determine . . . to give and dedicate our whole lives and all our energies, as far as we are able and it is not contrary to a pure spirit of

---

[7]Ibid., p. 8.

[8]Ibid., p. 9.

perfect indifference and obedience, for the work of the salvation of the Negroes in the United States . . .[9]

In the summer of 1918 William Markoe left for philosophy studies at Mt. St. Michael's Scholasticate in Spokane, Washington. He was there little less than a month when he met blacks of that city. The work began anew. Once more he organized the seminarians, this time into one of the first twelve units of the fledgling missionary organization, the Catholic Students' Mission Crusade. The aim of his unit? To work for the conversion of blacks, of course. Meanwhile, Loyola Press had published Markoe's "magnum opus" (required writing of each Jesuit seminarian), a biography of St. Peter Claver entitled "The Slave of the Negroes."[10]

A general methodology in this early apostolate began to emerge.

In instructing them [Negroes] for baptism we tried to
prepare them for the prejudice and discrimination that
they were likely to meet with from white Catholics within
the Church. . . . The problem was to instruct catechumens
so as to prepare them for the practice of the difficult virtue
of rejecting scandal of which the Negro convert could be the
potential victim. We would have to teach them that it is
not only wrong to give scandal, but it is also wrong to take
it. It is not only wrong to give poison, but also wrong
to swallow it.[11]

The consequences of discrimination filled Markoe with a disturbing but profound realization.

. . . if we hoped to lead the Negro into the Catholic
Church we would first have to convert the millions of
scandal-giving white Catholics.[12]

---

[9] Ibid., p. 12.

[10] Ibid., p. 16.

[11] Ibid., pp. 17-8.

[12] Ibid., p. 17.

Articles in America

To contribute his own part toward this conversion, Markoe began sending articles to America magazine, whose readership he knew was largely white and Catholic. His first effort was merely a letter commenting on the editorial of July 19, 1919, "Catholics and the Negro Question." Agreeing with its tone, Markoe related several stories about blacks he had known personally who were so scandalized by prejudice as to cease attendance at church services. His own suggestion for those engaged in work among blacks was to teach white Catholics in "common politeness if not in the fundamental maxim of Christianity, 'Love thy neighbor.' "[13]

In his first article in America, Markoe pleaded with his readers to try "Viewing the Negro Supernaturally." After reviewing the factual evidence that half or more of black Americans were unbaptized in any faith, he asked, why has our zeal been so lacking? He compared the black man to the Indian. The former lived in "peaceful docility, sociable, easily approached, speaking our own language" and the latter was a "roaming red savage." Yet we have preferred the latter.[14] (Markoe was to feel this even more strongly after spending the next two years on a Sioux reservation.) Why the preference?

---

[13]Markoe, letter to the editor, America, 9 August 1919, p. 451.

[14]Markoe, "Viewing the Negro Supernaturally," America, 19 June 1920, pp. 200-01.

Because blacks occupied a "unique social position" in our society--they were the outcasts, the "Pariahs of America."[15]

It was not his purpose to gain social equality for blacks, Markoe insisted. It was rather to point out their religious dependence on those who maintained outrageous concepts of them. For example, some insisted that if they were baptized, they would not persevere. This was to dismiss all fervent black Catholics, of which there were many, Markoe replied. Secondly, others viewed all blacks as liars and thieves. Again, this was an oversimplification of the real fact that there were bad members in all races. Finally, to those who would go so far as to describe the blacks as a bundle of the "most depraved and ferocious animal passions," Markoe could only retort that white men had already proved themselves quite as guilty of such conduct.[16]

The truth, Markoe went on, was that all Catholics must rise above their natural feelings and view only the "immortal soul of man. . . . The exterior may be crude and rough, but even from the dung-heap God can cause a beautiful flower to grow."[17] No Catholic should prevent that growth from occurring. Indeed,

> It looks more suspicious when some white Catholics discriminate beyond all excess against colored people in Catholic churches. When the Catholic Negro does fall away this is often the real cause. There must always be social

---

[15]Ibid., p. 201.

[16]Ibid., pp. 201-02.

[17]Ibid., p. 202.

grades among Catholics, but such distinctions do not exempt a higher caste from the law of charity in respect to a lower, much less are they a license for insult and injury.[18]

This initial article was followed by several others in late 1920 and early 1921, all written while Markoe was a student in Washington state. He spoke about "The New Race Problem," caused by the migration of blacks North during the first World War.[19] Here they hoped not only for better wages but improved political and social conditions as well. White people did not need to worry, Markoe quickly added, that the black man would seek self-improvement rashly. No, he would not "some dark night draw his razor and cut our throats."[20] Rather, he was organizing, publishing, educating his children. In this connection, Markoe mentioned the relatively new N.A.A.C.P.

> The organization and its publication are militant, by some called radical, brook no compromise, ask no favors, but demand full rights for American Negroes.[21]

Remarks such as this one were probably what prompted Markoe to say years later that his early *America* articles were quite mild, but at the time caused wide discussion. Indeed, the young seminarian was finally instructed to submit his writings to the assistant Jesuit

---

[18] Ibid.

[19] Markoe, "The New Race Problem," *America*, 9 October 1920, pp. 582-84.

[20] Ibid., p. 583

[21] Ibid., p. 584.

provincial, who was fortunately Matthew Germing, entirely sympathetic to the cause.[22]

It was through these articles that Markoe had his first contact with John LaFarge, who wrote from Ridge, Maryland, to complain that Markoe had never mentioned the Cardinal Gibbons Institute, the hoped-for "Catholic Tuskegee" then being established in Southern Maryland.[23]

Markoe's answer to the race problem was, of course, the Catholic Church. Now that blacks had migrated to the urban North, the Church with her vast facilities in every large city had a unique opportunity to meet the black man's needs, and solve the race problem permanently.

> I do not ask the recognition of the Negro in the social or profane world; but in religion he should not be denied his God-given heritage. Make the black man a child of God, a co-heir with Christ; having made him this, accept him as such, and the other tangled threads of this complicated problem will unravel themselves. Refuse him these rights and you reject the only real solution of a daily more perplexing racial conundrum.[24]

The real difficulty, he wrote, was that priests and nuns had not trained white people to "take a supernatural view of the Negro," and to "distinguish between their relations with colored people in the profane world and before God."[25]

---

[22]Markoe, "An Interracial Role," p. 18.

[23]Ibid.

[24]Markoe, "Solution to the Race Problem," *America*, 27 November 1920, p. 125.

[25]Ibid., p. 126.

Separate parishes were often not a feasible solution in the North. Besides, they were unCatholic, not established with lofty motives as ethnic parishes had been.[26] As for the social functions related to churches and schools, these should be seen as nonessential elements of the institution, Markoe insisted. If prestigious establishments such as West Point and Harvard could find a solution, surely Catholic parishes could. The most important thing was to begin now.[27]

Markoe readily admitted that the greatest resistance among Catholics was toward interracial education, even in the North where it was permitted by law. When sufficient numbers existed for separate schools, this was probably the only choice at times that would guarantee blacks a Catholic education. Where such numbers or funds did not exist, Markoe proposed a temporary compromise.

> If . . . the enforced granting of this inherent right to a colored Catholic threatened serious consequences, for example, the withdrawal of large numbers of white scholars, prudence would seem rather to dictate that the exclusion of the colored aspirant be tolerated, but not sanctioned, until such time when he can be received without detriment to the school as a whole.[28]

The compromise was tolerable only because work would begin immediately, according to Markoe's plan, in the development of new attitudes.

---

[26]Ibid. Of course, there were exceptions. Markoe mentioned the new black S.V.D. seminary at Bay St. Louis, Mississippi, approved by Rome.

[27]Ibid.

[28]Markoe, "Social Equality and Catholic Schools," America, 29 January 1921, p. 352.

>. . . the enlightening of our Catholic people must be
> the foundation stone of the part the Church is to play in the
> solution of the race problem.[29]

Such enlightenment should emphasize the "moral fitness" of all students, black and white, for entrance into Catholic schools, the freedom of choice inherent in all social relationships, and finally, the universality of the Church exemplified in interracial Catholic education.[30]

In the last of his articles from Spokane, Markoe asked his readers to consider "The Soul of the Colored Man." Reviewing his past articles, he repeated his conviction that viewing the black man supernaturally and according him his rights was the only feasible approach to the race question. Not only was it in keeping with Catholic tradition and the current positions of the Pope and hierarchy, but it faced the reality of present circumstances. Blacks were not about to disappear; their very presence had already caused riots in several major cities. For the Catholic to remain indifferent, he must ignore the fact that the Ku Klux Klan was anti-Catholic as well as anti-black, and that black leaders themselves (including black Catholics) were being educated in anti-Catholic institutions. The time was now, while blacks were ripe for an alternative to the segregated Protestant sects they had known.

Then Markoe discussed what he felt was the chief stumblingblock: miscegenation. Interracial marriage would not result automatically from interracial education, he insisted.

---

[29] Ibid.

[30] Ibid.

Indeed, we will rather prevent inter-marriage between the two races by admitting them both to Catholic schools where they can receive sound guidance and direction in matters pertaining to matrimony. There are already five or six million mulattoes in the country. If we are anxious that miscegenation should not get completely beyond control, we must convert the Negro to Christ and admit him to a moral and religious training. Marriage is recognized as a sacred and holy sacrament in the Catholic Church alone. It is a sound Catholic principle, moreover, that the marital tie should be solemnized preferably between parties approximating the same social rank and condition in life.[31]

For those Catholics who still felt reluctant, Markoe could only warn: ". . . the penalty of our injustice will be far more bitter. The wise man has no choice."[32]

These articles were accompanied by a lively discussion in the letters to the editor, Markoe often answering his critics personally. The latter objected largely to the "social equality" they felt interracial education would bring. To this charge Markoe replied repeatedly that Catholic schools were not primarily social but religious institutions, and that fusion of the races was indeed not the issue. The end of separatism could not justify the unjust means of denying black Catholics a religious education. Fusion was a risk that would have to be taken. Ultimately, however, it was not much of a risk. After all, Catholic schools had good discipline, they were not coeducational, and most marriages occurred after college. Moreover, "colored Catholic people *a fortiore* can be expected to have

---

[31]Markoe, "The Soul of the Colored Man," *America*, 5 March 1921, p. 475.

[32]Ibid.

the good sense and taste not to wish for fusion by marriage." Finally, if white Catholics did not marry persons of differing social ranks, why should they fear that blacks would "aspire" to marry them?[33]

After a summer at Campion College in Prairie du Chien, Wisconsin, Markoe was assigned to the Mission of St. Francis on the Sioux Rosebud reservation in South Dakota. During the two years he spent there as prefect of discipline in the Indian boys' school, the Jesuit reflected in much the same way as he had in his *America* articles.

> . . . the thought occurred to me how much more good the Jesuit Order could have done in the long run for the greater Glory of God if it had only directed more of its zeal, man power, and material assets to the evangelization of the American Negro. The Negro spoke our own language. He not only belonged to our own American culture but contributed much to its creation. . . . Our labors among the Indians have been most praiseworthy and heroic to constitute a glorious chapter in our annals; but why did we neglect the Negro![34]

Markoe personally found communication with the Indians much more difficult than with blacks.

> [I] experienced none of these handicaps in establishing a meeting of minds between [myself] and Negroes. [I was] practically never conscious of belonging to another race and, on the contrary, habitually felt that [I was] one of

---

[33] See letters to the editor, *America*, 15 January 1921, p. 308; 12 February 1921, pp. 406-07; 19 February 1924, p. 429. For responses pro and con to Markoe's articles, see letters to the editor, *America*, 18 December 1920, pp. 208-09; 8 January 1921, pp. 286-87; 15 January 1921, pp. 308-09; 22 January 1921, p. 333; 29 January 1921, p. 357.

[34] Markoe, "An Interracial Role," pp. 22-23.

them. This became more and more true as [I] sympathized more with their grievances and fought to alleviate them.[35]

He continued to write about blacks. A brief history of Catholic mission work among blacks in 1922 was published by Bodley Press, Inc. in a larger work entitled <u>Builders of the Nation</u>. He also began a collection of materials, largely clippings and notes, on the black race.[36] In September 1921, he published an article on "Catholics, the Negro, a Native Clergy" in <u>America</u>. Commenting that by then his previous articles had drawn negative response from some white priests in the South (even those in the black apostolate) the author declared that such reaction proved his point. Enlightenment among Catholics was truly needed. Blacks would never be converted until prejudice was overcome, even among some priests.

> I do not speak of a prejudice which forbids the Negro social equality and inter-marriage with whites. That phase of the problem is foreign to my present discussion nor does it of necessity enter into the religious aspect of the race question. I speak rather of that irrational, often ridiculous and childish prejudice manifested by many Catholics towards colored people in matters essentially religious.[37]

One manifestation of this prejudice was resistance to a native clergy. What Catholics forgot was that God called men to become priests, not mere man. Since no people had ever been converted without their

---

[35] Ibid., p. 24. As mentioned in an earlier chapter, Markoe habitually referred to himself by the editorial "we" in this work, converted here to the single pronoun.

[36] Ibid., pp. 23-24.

[37] Markoe, "Catholics, the Negro, a Native Clergy," <u>America</u>, 24 September 1921, pp. 535-36.

own clergy, God must be granting the vocations. It was prejudice which had prevented their fulfillment. Catholics would have to begin supporting such efforts as the new S.V.D. black seminary at Greenville, Mississippi. To say that black Catholics did not want their own priests would be the same as declaring that Irish wanted English priests, or the French preferred German clergy.[38]

Pursuing the subject of a native priesthood, Markoe next challenged questions of "Negro Morality and a Colored Clergy."

> I believe that the Negro before God is less guilty than the white man. Accordingly, I believe that the Negro is at least the white man's equal in morality.[39]

Markoe explained that when blacks were compared to white men in their "material guilt" (which could be seen), little difference could be found. The black man, unfortunately, had been portrayed as criminal for generations, as if it were in his blood.[40] Surely to say that the black man was immoral could not mean that the white man was perfect. If so, the latter would not need religion. Rather, the portrayal had varied. If newspapers had referred to every red-haired criminal by that characteristic, soon readers would have thought all red-headed men were criminals. "If any defenseless class of people is continually defamed, they will finally suffer an unsavory reputation," he observed.[41]

---

[38] Ibid., pp. 536-37.

[39] Markoe, "Negro Morality and a Colored Clergy," *America*, 12 November 1921, p. 79.

[40] Ibid., p. 80.

[41] Ibid. The reference to red-readed men came from a black newspaper which made the same point.

Seminaries were not for perfect men, but for those who wished to attempt a virtuous life. Here Markoe quoted an earlier America comment that if black Africans could be martyrs in Uganda, black Americans could be priests in this country.[42]

Perhaps feeling that some readers by this time were prepared to act on behalf of blacks, Markoe wrote some practical suggestions on "Catholic Aid for the Negro." Quoting Harding's famous phrase that "the black man should seek to be, and should be encouraged to be, the best possible black man and not the best possible imitation of a white man," the author pleaded for the Church to make that possible.[43] Among the practical steps to be taken he listed:

(1) general missions to the black people, which flourish where assistance is provided;

(2) native clergy, through the admission of black applicants to existing novitiates and seminaries, and the support of such separate endeavors as the S.V.D. seminary;

(3) contributions to the Catholic Board for Mission Work Among the Colored People;

(4) establishment of a national laymen's league for the conversion of blacks.

The last suggestion anticipated Markoe's White Friends of Colored Catholics and Claver Clubs, and LaFarge's Catholic Interracial Councils.[44]

---

[42] Ibid.

[43] Markoe, "Catholic Aid for the Negro," America, 18 February 1922, p. 417.

[44] Ibid., pp. 418-19. Actually, the White Friends of Colored Catholics proposed the idea for their establishment to Markoe, who accepted it.

A discussion of higher education among blacks compared Catholic and non-Catholic efforts in the field. Statistics revealed that nearly all blacks were being educated by the state, sects, or private philanthropy. "I know of no young colored man or woman," Markoe commented, "who graduated from a 'white' Catholic college, university, or convent last year."[45] Whereas non-Catholic sects had erected numerous separate schools where necessary, the Catholic Church had only a few normal schools for girls and Xavier College in New Orleans.[46] For a people who sought higher education as much as blacks did, the Church could hold its youth only by fulfilling that need.

The April 15, 1922 article on "Negro Virtue" repeated many of the arguments contained in "Negro Morality and a Colored Clergy." This time Markoe was answering a reader, who had commented in the letters to the editor: "It is utterly impossible to make them understand what decency and purity mean."[47] The priest's reply was simple: you do not know "them." The priests and sisters who do (including myself) are aware not only of their virtue, but of the steadfastness of black Catholics under great hardship. No white Catholic had needed that kind of loyalty to his Church.

---

[45]Markoe, "Negro Higher Education," *America*, 1 April 1922, p. 559.

[46]Ibid. It may have been to this comment that LaFarge later referred when he complained that Markoe had never mentioned the work of the Cardinal Gibbons Institute.

[47]Markoe, "Negro Virtue," *America*, 15 April 1922, p. 606. The original letter to the editor appeared in *America*, 18 February 1922.

Obviously Markoe by now had decided that his contribution to work among blacks during this period would be the written word. The articles to America continued on a regular basis. In June he wrote on the mission crusade and black education. Referring to his earlier discussion of black higher education, he reminded his readers once again that black Catholics must either have schools of their own or admission to white ones. Examining the cause for refusing black students, he cited a peculiar convention accepted by parents, teachers and students. Teachers generally blamed parental or student pressure for existing policies. How strange, Markoe noted, when the school should be molding its students instead. Then the scholastic appealed to the students themselves. They should become guardians of the welfare of black Catholic students, and use their newly organized Catholic Students' Mission Crusade to promote black Catholic education. As a source of encouragement, Markoe quoted Archbishop Ireland, who had insisted on an open policy in parochial schools in 1892. Failure of the C.S.M.C. to promote the same end would make all their other missionary efforts--collecting stamps and tin foil, for example--of no real value.[48]

On September 9, the feast of St. Peter Claver, Markoe wrote of "The Need of Another Claver."[49] Reviewing the vast accomplishments of the saint in South America, Markoe lamented that his spirit must be

---

[48]Markoe, "The Mission Crusade and Negro Education," America, 3 June 1922, pp. 154-56.

[49]Markoe, "The Need of Another Claver," America, 9 September 1922, pp. 486-88.

dead in the United States, where so few labored on behalf of blacks, often under grave obstacles. Then he suggested a solution which he and his brother John were to take up successfully several years later: the creation of Claver Clubs in each parish, to aid black missions in their work.

In 1923 Markoe shifted his emphasis to the political realm. Speaking of the crisis in the Near East, and also of the current Indian and Japanese criticism of Caucasian supremacy, he warned his readers of the potentially damaging effect of such thought on blacks. Although he had been loyal to his country from the beginning, and still generally followed the conservative leadership of Tuskegee, the black man now heard new voices in the more militant Afro-American press. These new leaders often aligned themselves with the non-white world in its struggle for racial equality.[50] The scholastic mentioned the N.A.A.C.P. as the focus of this new emphasis. If its leaders were to be kept from succumbing to the influence of alien powers with whom they identified, it could only be because they had been granted full justice in their own country.

Markoe's February article, on "The Catholic Church and Slavery," was apparently prompted by the probing challenge of a non-Catholic black man on the Church's past position.[51] The Jesuit began by

---

[50]Markoe, "The Importance of Negro Patriotism," America, 27 January 1923, p. 345.

[51]Markoe, "The Catholic Church and Slavery," America, 12 February 1923, pp. 415-17. In a letter, J. M. Buddy of Minneapolis to Turner, 25 March 1933, Turner Papers, the former indicates that he had written to Markoe in 1923 about the Catholic Church's involvement in the slavery issue and that the Jesuit had responded in an America article, probably the one above. The letter itself is now barely readable.

admitting that the slavery issue, while dead, still "rankled" in the minds of some intelligent blacks, who saw the Reformation as primarily responsible for emancipation. The truth, Markoe claimed, was that slavery spread <u>after</u> the sixteenth century, and that the Catholic Church was most responsible for its demise. Wherever she existed she had worked to eradicate all evil, elevating the life of the slave, and in some instances prompting his emancipation. Why had she not condemned slavery outright? Such a question

> . . . rather indicates ignorance of a comprehensive ethical aspect of slavery or a lack of appreciation of the times and conditions with which the Church had to deal. To have condemned all forms of slavery absolutely in the days of Constantine might have caused an upheaval far more disastrous than the evil of slavery. . . . Nor was the Church categorically obliged to condemn slavery unequivocally from the moral standpoint. As there are justifiable reasons for which a man must forfeit his life, so there may be reasons in the course of justice by which one could lawfully be reduced to a limited degree of slavery. The Church, however, in all its long history has never pretended to defend unmitigated slavery . . .[52]

Markoe defended Bishop Las Casas, an early South American prelate sometimes accused of introducing slavery into the New World. The bishop <u>found</u> slavery when he arrived, Markoe argued, and while he did suggest the use of black slave labor, it was as an alternative to Indians, whom Las Casas considered less fit for work in the metal mines. The suggestion had been an illogical one, which Las Casas later admitted. What was important, Markoe concluded, was to realize that Las Casas was not the Church. She had always defended the slave, ransomed him, comforted him. Because of her

---

[52]Markoe, p. 416.

influence, even freed slaves had been better off in Catholic countries than elsewhere. The Church did not tolerate caste distinctions; in her sphere all were equal.[53]

In his last essay published before leaving the reservation, the scholastic compared racial and religious prejudice. The Catholic suffered from discrimination much as the black man did, because ignorant non-Catholics felt they were adequately informed on the Church. In reality they had often gained their facts from professional bigots, and Catholics themselves were too ashamed of their faith to defend it. The same ignorance prevailed about the blacks, often promoted by groups such as the Ku Klux Klan. Oddly, blacks and Catholics were also prejudiced against one another, only confounding their difficulties. Indeed, how much total discrimination would be alleviated if only Catholics would listen to interracial commissions, and blacks would invite Catholics to speak at their meetings.[54]

Catechetical Work in St. Louis

In the summer of 1923 Markoe returned to St. Louis University for theology studies preparatory to ordination. Here he found the company once again of his two sisters, both nuns at the Visitation Academy, and his co-workers of earlier days, Austin Bork and Charles Owens. The latter had been waiting anxiously to share with Markoe a new field of endeavor, the black neighborhoods surrounding St. Louis

___

[53]Ibid., p. 417.

[54]Markoe, "Race and Religious Prejudice," _America_, 12 May 1923, pp. 77-78.

University. Markoe set out to visit the poorer blacks east of Grand Avenue, most of them recently arrived from the South. Bork took the somewhat more settled, wealthier neighborhoods west of Grand Avenue. Markoe described these first visits:

> Connecting the front of a street with the rear there were passages called "gangways." . . . Before long [I was] acquainted with just about every gangway between Grand Avenue and the River on all the streets. The tenements swarmed with families . . . [I] climbed hundreds of rickety stairs knocking on every door on every floor to meet the people. The living conditions were abominable and woefully substandard.[55]

The adults were reached through their children, and religion introduced only after relationships had been established.

> And, as heretofore, we found that these people never knew that they could be Catholics. They thought the Catholic Church was a white man's Church. This illusion of theirs spoke volumes concerning our neglect of the Negro.[56]

The young scholastics set up a mission center in a small chapel behind St. Joseph's Church, formerly a Jesuit German parish from which most of the white people had moved. Once again, other scholastics were organized as catechists, along with college students of the city. In his memoirs, Markoe recalled an incident typical of the period. A Christmas party was planned at St. Joseph's Church, only to be cancelled by the pastor, along with all work among blacks at the parish, only two days before Christmas. Ingeniously, Markoe and Bork obtained permission to hold the party at nearby St. Patrick's, and

---

[55]Markoe, "An Interracial Role," p. 28. The material for this early St. Louis apostolate is taken also almost entirely from these memoirs.

[56]Ibid., p. 29.

informed their black friends that plans had been changed merely to accommodate the crowds in a larger hall.[57]

Austin Bork also opened a center for blacks west of Grand Avenue, in the chapel of the Helpers of the Holy Souls, an order of nuns who also served as catechists in the new work. A third center was begun at St. Elizabeth's Church, the official black parish of the city. Markoe's description of St. Elizabeth's, a Jesuit parish of which he was soon to become pastor, is interesting.

> The Church, school, and rectory constituted one old delapidated [sic] building and withall made a rather poor image of the zeal for the salvation of St. Louis' thousands of Negroes on the part of the great Archdiocese of St. Louis and the great Missionary Jesuit Order. The Negro parishioners were poor and discouraged and were denied access to all so-called "white" Catholic grade schools, high schools, the St. Louis University, all Catholic hospitals and were unwelcome or segregated in the "white" Catholic Churches.[58]

During their visits to black families, the scholastics had noticed one other Catholic church in the area, the old German St. Nicholas parish. Since it appeared nearly abandoned, they boldly rang the rectory doorbell and asked the pastor's permission to use the facilities. Apparently the school had been sold to a furniture company and the elderly pastor, soon to retire, had no objection to the use of the church, since the people had all gone. Markoe reflected:

> What did Father Adrian mean when he said the people were all gone? Are not Negroes people? . . . Is a good shepherd responsible only for the sheep in the fold and not for those wandering and straying outside it?[59]

---

[57]Ibid., pp. 32-33.

[58]Ibid., p. 36.

[59]Ibid., p. 38.

The statistics for these efforts were impressive: nine months after Markoe had returned to St. Louis, there were 200 new black Catholic converts.

The *America* articles continued as well, written now in the context of the new mission work. Where Markoe found the time is itself amazing, since he was also a fulltime theology student at this point. "Claver Clubs for Colored People" appeared in August 1923, elaborating on an earlier suggestion that the Catholic Students' Mission Crusade or other Catholic organizations take up the work of supporting the black missions. *Our Colored Missions* (the publication of the Commission for Catholic Mission Work among the Negroes and Indians) could be the official organ, and subscription drives one of the projects. Once again, Markoe emphasized the mood of the times. Blacks were migrating in large numbers to Northern cities where the Catholic Church was strong. In this one way Claver Clubs could be different from other mission organizations. Its members could meet their "natives" in person and serve as missionaries themselves.[60]

In October Markoe entered a plea for the development of black Catholic leaders. He divided contemporary black leadership into three camps: the radical labor leaders such as Claude McKay, the conservative Tuskegee school headed by Booker T. Washington, with R. Moton as its spokesman, and the "progressive middle course" of W. E. B. DuBois

---

[60]Markoe, "Claver Clubs for Colored People," *America*, 4 August 1923, pp. 368-69.

and the N.A.A.C.P.⁶¹ Unfortunately, all these men, indeed most black leaders, were graduates of non-Catholic institutions. Many had imbibed a "materialistic philosophy and code of ethics."⁶² For this reason, the education of blacks in Catholic universities was essential. Some institutions had begun to lower racial barriers, but not nearly enough to meet the need for black Catholic leaders, now.

His work among blacks east of Grand Avenue, many of them recent immigrants from the South, gave Markoe an appreciation of that great movement in the twenties. He wrote in February 1924 of its significance. After citing several relevant statistics, he discussed the question of motivation. The South claimed that the boll weevil and Northern labor agents had drawn blacks North, while the black man himself spoke of better treatment. Markoe quoted the Chicago *Defender*: the question was not "where they are going" but "what they are leaving."⁶³ The lesson for the South at least was clear; if it did not treat the black man any better, it must suffer his loss, Markoe warned.

This discussion of migration was followed by an article on the Church's role in this new movement. Obviously if blacks had left the South to avoid discriminatory treatment, they would hardly tolerate it in a Northern Catholic church. No, the Church must be truly *catholic*. Otherwise, she was no different from the Protestant

---

[61]Markoe, "The Importance of Negro Leadership," *America*, 13 October 1923, p. 605.

[62]Ibid.

[63]Markoe, "A Great Migration," *America*, 9 February 1924, p. 397.

churches whose separatism had cost them so many black members. Markoe repeated his experience among so many blacks--they did not yet believe the Catholic Church was open to them. This uncertainty had been caused by the indifference and hostility of white Catholics toward blacks. Indeed, in many places blacks were still denied two basic religious rights, to worship and education under Catholic auspices. The C.S.M.C. could alleviate part of this problem, particularly seminary units, by letting school authorities know that the students did not support racial barriers. Irish Catholics too could make a contribution by eradicating all impression that they as a group were peculiarly opposed to blacks in the Church.[64]

The new catechetical centers had afforded an opportunity to put Markoe's Claver Club idea into operation. He described the work at the various centers, performed as Claver Club activities, and called for the creation of a thousand such clubs across the country. "Each Claver Club is a little inter-racial commission in daily practical operation," he wrote. All that was required for membership was three or more persons and one subscription to Our Colored Missions.[65]

In his last article (May) for 1924, Markoe invited his white readers to note the great progress which the black race had made in the United States. Against great odds its members had proven themselves

---

[64]Markoe, "The Negro and Catholicism," America, 23 February 1924, pp. 449-50.

[65]Markoe, "Claver Clubs in Operation," America, 5 April 1924, pp. 590-92.

not essentially lazy or incapable.[66] They still faced great handicaps, of course, especially in education—a fact which caused lethargy in many blacks at fourteen or fifteen years of age. Still, they numbered several scientists and cultural artists, had contributed greatly to agriculture, and owned not inconsiderable wealth. They had their own press, and were advancing politically and socially. All this should convince white Catholics of the importance of black conversion. Markoe concluded his argument with congratulations to the Cardinal Gibbons Institute and other such efforts in the field of black Catholic education.[67]

The classes at the catechetical centers soon led to the conversion of a number of black children to Catholicism. The black Catholic school in St. Elizabeth's parish was too small to accommodate these new Catholics. Besides, St. Elizabeth's was located in a well established black neighborhood, and the new converts were largely children of poor black families east of Grand. Therefore, Markoe arranged to rent the second floor of old St. Nicholas School, now the property of a furniture company. Before leaving for the summer at Lake Beulah, Wisconsin with the other scholastics, he also arranged for two Blessed Sacrament sisters as teachers in the new school. Later he commented wryly that all these arrangements were made without any

---

[66] Markoe, "The Negro's Progress," *America*, 24 May 1924, pp. 127-28.

[67] Ibid., p. 128. Such mention might have been prompted by LaFarge's earlier complaint that Markoe had neglected the Cardinal Gibbons Institute.

real authority; indeed, most of his work was extracurricular and unknown to his superiors.[68]

The building for this new adventure was in a state of grave disrepair. Unfortunately, the new sister-teachers saw it in just that state. Their greatest fear, however, was not the poor facilities, but a lack of students in the fall. Markoe set about organizing a cleanup of the premises and a publicity campaign in the neighborhood. When the first day of school arrived, the scholastics and nuns had only old boxes to sit on as they waited for their pupils. To the sisters' amazement, 500 children appeared to enroll the first day, in a school with no desks, no blackboards, no books.

> They [the sisters] wanted to know what was our magic. . . . I told her [Sister Pius] our magic was simply love for these wonderful people.
> . . . To think that people so ignorant, so poverty stricken, from such poor backgrounds, could have such respect and love for these Sisters was in itself a mystery and a sermon. I used to ask myself how many generations of these people have come and gone in the city of St. Louis without ever having known a Scholastic, a Seminarian, a Nun, or a Priest? Whose fault was this? How eager they were to embrace the faith once they were exposed to it![69]

Obviously, some pupils had to be turned away. Four lay teachers were hired, among them Mrs. Badeau, the mother-in-law of Roy Wilkins, later National Director of the N.A.A.C.P. Markoe obtained second-hand desks from the school board, appealed for funds, and rented the first floor of the building as well. Once the

---

[68]Markoe, "An Interracial Role," pp. 42-43. The school itself was to function under Father Adrian's name, as retired pastor of St. Nicholas.

[69]Ibid., p. 49.

scholastic had gained the support of Dr. Frederick P. Kenkel, National Director of the Central Verein, even Archbishop Glennon seemed to show an interest. He asked Kenkel to head a Peter Claver Association for the education of poor black children. This organization, however, did not prove a lasting one[70]

Now that St. Nicholas was in operating condition, Markoe began (in his own words) "to look for a new world to conquer."[71] An old Irish church, St. Malachy's, looked like a logical prospect. Once again, the scholastics asked for the use of what seemed an abandoned parish. The pastor insisted that his remaining parishioners (twelve men who attended Mass elsewhere) should vote on the matter. The result was telling. Father Rogers reported that

> . . . his men had met and had unanimously passed a resolution to the effect that rather than have the "niggers" use the St. Malachy plant they would prefer to see it turned into a pickle factory.[72]

Meanwhile, Markoe was continuing his articles in *America*, along with talks to promote the black apostolate among his fellow Jesuits. Apparently some women from Louisville, interested in the Claver Club idea, visited St. Louis to learn about them firsthand. Markoe described the Louisville Claver Clubs in an *America* article of January 1925. Interestingly, one of the original members was Dr. Turner's acquaintance from the National Catholic War Council, Colonel P. H. Callahan.[73] Markoe's description of the clubs is significant: "These

---

[70]Ibid., pp. 53-54.

[71]Ibid., p. 54.

[72]Ibid., p. 56.

[73]Markoe, "How Help the Negro?" *America*, 3 January 1925, p. 271.

clubs were to be interracial in character and their purpose was to promote interracial justice and charity."[74] He emphasized that the clubs had a "sociological aspect," in that both in St. Louis and in Kentucky they were affiliated with the Inter-Racial Commission. By cooperating on a religious level, they solved problems not only in the Church, but the larger race problem itself.[75] Although each club was autonomous, Markoe did issue diplomas to each and encouraged city and diocesan-wide coordinating committees for greater impact, as well as cooperation with local clergy.[76] (All this, of course, sounds reminiscent of the Detroit regulations of the later Federated Colored Catholics.) Markoe was to regret that time did not permit him to promote the clubs more fully. "If the Claver Club idea could have been implemented," he later wrote," it would have anticipated our present Catholic Interracial Councils by many years."[77]

Besides the Claver Clubs, Markoe promoted a second organization for his helpers, the Knights of Peter Claver and its Ladies' Auxiliary, because "Negroes were inclined to join fraternal organizations."[78] This effort took on a clandestine air when the group met in the cafeteria of St. Louis University at night, an institution whose facilities had never before been opened to blacks. The Knights

---

[74]Markoe, "An Interracial Role," p. 61.
[75]Markoe, "How Help the Negro?" p. 272.
[76]Ibid.
[77]Markoe, "An Interracial Role," p. 61.
[78]Ibid., p. 58.

eventually moved elsewhere, since the cafeteria was under the president's room![79] Unfortunately, the strange administrative arrangement for black Catholics in St. Louis interfered with this project. Father Lynam of St. Elizabeth's Church objected to any black fraternal organization other than his own parish's Knights of America. He had the authority to do so, since in theory all black Catholics in the city were members of his, "the" black Catholic, parish.

Before leaving for Lake Beulah once again, Markoe published one more article in *America*--his last--in May 1925. In it he emphasized that blacks assisted the needy of their own race.[80] After citing numerous personal examples of this fact, Markoe reminded his readers that the black man saved the city and state a huge expense by caring for his own children and aged. White people should be more conscious of this, he commented, when they saw white beggars, for example, on the streets. The black man had taken in his own.

On the way to Lake Beulah in the summer of 1925, Markoe stopped in Chicago to see his brother John, then teaching mathematics at the University of Detroit. Both men, with their love of work in the black community, decided to visit Fr. Joseph Eckert, known for his work at St. Elizabeth's (black) parish in Chicago. The pastor himself answered the door. The scholastics introduced themselves and explained their reason for visiting. Eckert somehow missed the name, for part way through the ensuing conversation he began to complain of the

---

[79] Ibid., p. 59.

[80] Markoe, "The Negro Helps His Own," *America*, 2 May 1925, pp. 56-57.

difficulties to his work created by the articles of "some fool Jesuit" named Markoe in *America* magazine. How could the Church convert the black man when a Catholic magazine presented the Church as racist?[81] Markoe awkwardly but honestly repeated his identity, then tried to explain that his purpose had been to attract blacks to the Church, not to its scandal-giving members. In addition, the author was convinced most of his readers were white intelligent Catholics, who needed to hear such things. Markoe described the situation as

> the first of many verbal battles I had with Fr. Eckert through succeeding years.
> . . . Generally speaking Fr. Eckert was an ultra conservative in regard to race relations. He was a man of great personal kindness and zeal, but gave the impression that he was satisfied with the status quo in respect to Negro civil rights.[82]

Father Eckert's name, of course, was to appear regularly in Federation affairs. Indeed, several months after this conversation with Markoe, the priest attended the first annual convention of the Federated Colored Catholics in Washington, D.C.

Even the few months at Lake Beulah had by now become too long a period away from the black apostolate, so Markoe helped Fr. John Henry with his mission to black children in Milwaukee at every opportunity. One great joy for William on returning to St. Louis for the last year of study before ordination was the presence of his brother John under the same roof again. St. Nicholas School opened for its second year, and although the sisters still looked to Markoe for

---

[81] Markoe, "An Interracial Role," pp. 61-63.

[82] Ibid., pp. 63-64.

guidance, newly ordained Fr. Charles Owens accepted most of the responsibility. This left Markoe free for more concentrated study during this important year.

As the day of ordination drew near, however, a peculiar problem arose. Both Austin Bork and Markoe wished to send invitations to their black friends, but were forbidden to do so by the seminary rector. Finally, Father Germing, then acting provincial superior, intervened on behalf of the scholastics. Their newfound black friends attended the ceremony on June 16, 1926.[83]

After the summer once again at Lake Beulah, Markoe stopped in Chicago to see Father Eckert. He was pleased to find that the S.V.D. pastor was still receptive, despite the verbal battle of the previous year. In fact, Eckert gladly permitted Markoe to preach at St. Elizabeth's, pronouncing the latter a potentially fine speaker. Markoe had learned by then that Archbishop Glennon was to hand over St. Nicholas parish (in which the new black school was located) to the S.V.D. fathers. Eckert informed the Jesuit that Father Holkens would be the new pastor. When Markoe returned to St. Louis he visited Holkens, introduced him at all the Sunday Masses and gave him the remaining funds for the school. Unfortunately, Holkens was used to stable parishes, and thought the new school merely a "nuisance."[84] Holkens was eventually transferred and his successors proved better able to continue the work Markoe had begun.

---

[83]Ibid., pp. 69-70.

[84]Ibid., p. 75.

The school term 1926-27 was the last for Markoe at St. Louis University. Since St. Nicholas was now in other hands, he could devote more time to his studies. In the spring, however, he did deliver a speech to the faculty of the medical school on "The Negro's Viewpoint." He sent a copy to Father LaFarge at America for publication, but it was never printed. In fact, no future articles were. For some strange reason Markoe had lost what he considered his "national forum."[85] Not until the St. Elizabeth Chronicle was he to have the opportunity to write on race relations again.

What Markoe told the medical faculty that spring was that white men, despite their personal feelings, must become aware of how the black man thinks and feels. Then he proceeded to outline his own interpretation of the black mind. The black man, he said, thought that the white man was entirely responsible not only for the race problem of the past, but for its continuance in the present. The root of the race question, Markoe went on, was the white man's undue horror of miscegenation. Although the black man also opposed such unions, he wished to take a more reasonable approach to the difficulty. He saw the white man's solution as keeping the black man in his "place," which was equivalent to keeping him "down," whether by ridicule, patronizing airs, or rank abuse. The black man, on the other hand, asked only a just opportunity to advance himself, knowing full well that if he preferred lighter-skinned women, there were plenty within his own race to choose

---

[85]Ibid., p. 87. Indeed, "The Negro's Viewpoint" was not published until the second issue of the St. Elizabeth's Chronicle in 1928.

from. Markoe concluded by advising his listeners that the answer was "for white people to learn and apply correct principles in dealing with the situation."[86]

Two major themes emerged in this address which Markoe would repeat again and again in succeeding years. The first was that the root of the race problem lay in the white man's horror of miscegenation. The second was the necessity of seeing the black point of view. Indeed, Markoe later prided himself on feeling more a black man in thought than a white man. He shunned the companionship of his own, seeking instead the homes of his black friends and parishioners.[87]

Pastor of St. Elizabeth's

As the end of the school year approached, Markoe nervously awaited his first assignment. Once again, Father Germing sensed the apostolic bent of the young priest and sent him to St. Elizabeth's parish for the summer. When the Jesuit pastor there expressed a desire to get away for a few months, Markoe was left temporarily in charge.

> So [I] found [myself] in a flash the lord of all [I] surveyed. The entire Negro population of St. Louis was my flock.[88]

---

[86]Markoe, "The Negro's Viewpoint," St. Elizabeth's Chronicle, April 1928, p. 3.

[87]Rev. Claude Heithaus confirmed this attitude in an interview, St. Louis, June 1973. It will emerge to some extent in Markoe's writings. Heithaus recalled Markoe not having "time" for socializing with white people, so immersed was he in his black apostolate.

[88]Markoe, "An Interracial Role," p. 90.

Even the "rival" presence of St. Nicholas' did not dim Markoe's enthusiasm.

> There were more than enough Negroes for all. Moreover, [I] always maintained that every pastor in the city should feel responsible for all people of whatever color living within the confines of his parish.[89]

William Markoe was to remain at St. Elizabeth's for fourteen years, with only brief interludes elsewhere. Recalling later that Fathers Edward C. Kramer and Vincent Dever objected strenuously to segregated parishes, Markoe justified his own situation.

> In accepting the pastorate of St. Elizabeth's Negro Church [I] justified [my] doing so from the beginning by resolving to make the parish and the city of St. Louis a base of operations nationally for the promotion of interrcial justice and charity throughout the United States.[90]

It must be added that one of the priest's greatest joys was being present when the word came from Cardinal Ritter in 1950 to dissolve St. Elizabeth's as a Jim Crow parish. Another significant fact should be mentioned here. The problem of caring for blacks could have been solved through the conversion of older, nearly abandoned churches such as those Markoe had used as a catechist into parishes intended to serve the people of the area, then largely black. This was being done in other major Northern cities. It was what Markoe had hoped for in St. Louis, but Archbishop Glennon refused this path. He felt the parishes belonged to those who had originally lived there, whether they used them or not.[91]

---

[89] Ibid.

[90] Ibid., p. 91.

[91] Ibid., pp. 98-99, 590.

Soon after his arrival at St. Elizabeth's, Markoe's parish was struck by the great tornado of 1927. The new pastor went to white churches to preach on interracial justice and gain financial aid for his people. It was a practice he was to continue as new projects arose in succeeding years. Soon Markoe was dreaming of a new church plant, to be built on property available further west of Grand Avenue, in the white Visitation parish. He moved the annual parish banquet to the new People's Finance Building, obtained Fr. Stephen Theobald as guest speaker, and persuaded the archbishop to sign the deed of trust on the land in time to announce it at the dinner.

Money, of course, was plentiful in 1928, as the building campaign was launched. Soon contributions from poor blacks and interested white Catholics totalled over $10,000. The accompanying publicity generated another kind of response, however. Father Collins of Visitation parish and the Home Protective Association of the area visited Markoe to protest the establishment of a black parish so far west. Markoe replied that if Collins wished to take responsibility for the blacks in his parish, the Jesuit would drop his plans immediately. Instead, the Home Protective Association planned a meeting at Visitation, with all the pastors of the area's parishes present. Markoe meanwhile contacted his brother John and another scholastic who agreed to attend the meeting disguised as reporters. The independent Catholic Herald stood ready to print their story. Unaware that anyone was taking notes the white pastors spoke out at the meeting, openly criticizing the archbishop as well as others involved. When the entire story came out in the Catholic Herald the next Sunday, sold at the white churches whose pastors had attended the meeting, Markoe knew he had won. Father Collins left town on vacation, and the Jesuit proceeded with his plans.[92]

In the spring of 1928, John Markoe and his fellow "reporter," Laurence Barry, suggested a monthly parish bulletin for St. Elizabeth's, which they agreed to edit. In March 1928, the first issue of the St. Elizabeth's Chronicle was published. From the beginning, William Markoe envisioned this effort as much larger than his parish boundaries.

> . . . it dawned on me that in the Chronicle we had a vehicle for the promotion of interracial justice and charity. In the very first issue we published as its permanent slogan: "Justice and Charity for All."[93]

It is significant that the articles were directed toward white readers, and that it was sent to all black parishes, with accompanying requests that black Catholics send in news of events in their locality.

The first issue outlined in some detail the plans for a new St. Elizabeth's, emphasizing that all blacks of the city would be asked to contribute, since so many had already profited in sending their children to St. Nicholas or St. Elizabeth schools. Markoe also explained the purpose of the Chronicle: to present a Catholic solution to the race problem.

---

[92] Ibid., pp. 103-107.

[93] Ibid., p. 109

... Negroes have a great deal to learn about the eternal principles of right and wrong as enumerated by that undying Church which Christ built upon a rock. If colored people better realized the power, more or less dormant, in the Catholic Church slowly to crush and smooth out uneven and unfair conditions arising from the close juxataposition of two great races, they would make greater haste better to understand and make an ally of that power.[94]

In September Markoe was ordered to report for his year of tertianship in Cleveland. Austin Bork would replace him as temporary pastor.[95] Brother John and Laurence Barry would continue publishing the St. Elizabeth's Chronicle. Needless to say, the change from bustling St. Elizabeth's to placid St. Stanislaus Seminary in Cleveland was an adjustment for Markoe. He found some refuge in the friendship of Fr. Thomas E. McKenney who welcomed the young Jesuit's assistance at Blessed Sacrament (a black parish). Apparently, however, the tension of adjustment proved too great in the beginning. In the midst of the thirty day retreat which began the tertianship, Markoe became so ill he had to return to St. Elizabeth's to recuperate. After several weeks of relaxation, he returned to complete the prescribed year.[96]

---

[94]Markoe, "The St. Elizabeth's Chronicle," St. Elizabeth's Chronicle, March 1928, p. 7.

[95]Markoe's contributions to the St. Elizabeth's Chronicle from May through August consisted of reprinted articles from America. See Markoe, "Race and Religious Prejudice," May 1928, p. 3; "The Negro's Progress," June 1928, p. 3; "The Negro Helps His Own," July 1928, p. 3; "The Catholic Church and Slavery," August 1928, p. 3. Jesuit tertianship is the third year of novitiate, required of Jesuits as a means of spiritual renewal after several years of religious profession.

[96]Markoe, "An Interracial Role," pp. 119-21.

During the Lenten season of 1929 Markoe was sent back to St. Elizabeth's to preach. Bork asked him to help with a musical comedy to be performed by young people of the parish. Markoe enlisted the capable advice of Fr. Daniel Lord who lent his support not only that year, but in many succeeding ones. A significant fact about these shows was that they were probably the first theatrical events in St. Louis attended by integrated audiences. Markoe had been warned against setting such a precedent, but he merely sold the tickets regardless of race and let people choose their own seats. The result was a truly mixed audience.

> [I] discovered over years of experience that the less legislation in regard to segregation the less trouble. [My] rule was to let people naturally take care of themselves, give them freedom of choice and there would be no trouble.[97]

The annual event generated much needed funds and publicity, of course, for the parish building campaign.

Upon his return to St. Louis from tertianship, Markoe was assigned as permanent pastor to St. Elizabeth's. Since none of the debt had been paid during his absence, he set about raising money. The stock market crash hit in October, destroying nearly every source of revenue.[98] Meanwhile another event occurred, however, which was to set Markoe on

---

[97]Ibid., p. 124.

[98]Especially devastating were the financial losses of John S. Leahy, who had owned the property the parish purchased. Leahy was the archbishop's lawyer and had a brother who was a Jesuit priest. He had promised Markoe a $1000 plate dinner to which Leahy would invite fifty men. It had been postponed until the October Markoe returned, which in the light of the imminent crash proved to be too late. See Markoe, "An Interracial Role," pp. 96, 101, 126-27.

a different course for several years. He heard of a forthcoming annual convention of the Federated Colored Catholics in Baltimore. Apparently he had been unaware of its existence until 1929. William Prater had contributed an article to the June issue of the Chronicle on the organization and one in the September issue announcing the convention. Perhaps these had provided Markoe with an introduction to the group.[99]

Editor for the Federation

When Markoe arrived in Baltimore for the convention, he stopped in to see the Josephite Fathers whose headquarters were there. He soon received the distinct impression the order was suspicious of Turner, and convinced that the Federation wanted to abolish all segregated parishes (which was the case with most Josephite churches). "They even seemed to fear he [Turner] might lead the Catholic Negroes into schism," Markoe recalled.[100]

The Jesuit, however, had an entirely different opinion once he saw the Federation in action. He sincerely felt that it was not radical, but reactionary, a Jim Crow organization.

> The Josephites might have given me a warmer welcome if they knew then that [I] personally [was] going to be the instrument for the complete abolition of the Federated Colored Catholics of the United States . . . my reason for bringing about the dissolution of the Federation would be because it itself was a segregated Jim Crow organization in its basic make up and modus operandi.

---

[99]Prater, "The Federated Colored Catholics of the United States," St. Elizabeth's Chronicle, June 1927, p. 17. Also Prater, "Federated Colored to Convene," pp. 13-14.

[100]Markoe, "An Interracial Role," p. 130.

> . . . At this first convention that [I] attended I was
> really infiltrating the organization, because I was a
> white man. [I] didn't like the self imposed segregation
> that [I] saw, and liked it less that no one, neither the
> "radical" and "dangerous" Dr. Turner nor Fr. LaFarge
> took umbrage at it or even manifested an awareness of it![101]

Markoe was to retain this feeling throughout his association. Indeed, he claimed later that he offered the Chronicle to the F.C.C. as a method by which he could further infiltrate it, and eventually change its direction.[102]

None of this, of course, appeared in the magazine's first issues as the new Federation organ. They spoke only of promoting the organization, published its constitution and history, and even contained an editorial in the June 1930 issue entitled "Just Watch Us Grow."[103] It was not until the July 1930 number that Markoe first gave a hint of his own views, commenting on the June executive committee meeting in an article entitled "Our Jim Crow Federation." As pointed out in earlier chapters, the article did not really criticize the Federation, but did hint that "others" were criticizing, perhaps because the name "Federated Colored Catholics" was a misnomer. Markoe tried to introduce his own as the "true" aims of the organization:

---

[101] Ibid., pp. 130, 131.

[102] Ibid., p. 131.

[103] "Why the Chronicle," p. 15; "Federated Colored Catholics-Constitution, 1929," Chronicle, November 1929, pp. 27-29; Smith, "An Outline History," p. 305; "Just Watch Us Grow," Chronicle, June 1930, pp. 132-33.

> The inter-racial aspect is not our chief motive, because
> our chief motive must always be the love of God and a
> supernatural desire "to restore all things in Christ."[104]

He also hinted broadly that there were already too many white members in the Federation, as in the N.A.A.C.P. and Urban League (he had begun himself serving on the St. Louis Urban League that same year), for it to be considered a separatist group. That Markoe was promoting a bi-racial effort is clearly obvious in the article.

Meanwhile in St. Louis he had other tasks before him. The church and school were still in need of renovation, and the property purchased with such expectation had a debt still lingering. The second musical comedy in the spring brought some funds and its own lessons in interracial cooperation. During the matinee performances for Catholic school children, Markoe talked to the white youngsters and their teachers about interracial justice and the need for black Catholic education. His work as chairman of the industrial committee of the city's Urban League made him an arbitrator in several strikes involving black workers.

Despite all these concerns, Markoe set out in the spring on a promotional tour for the <u>Chronicle</u> and Federation. It was the same year (see Chapter II) that Turner was ill, Clarke and Conrad otherwise occupied, and the two priests left with much of the organization's work. The trip Markoe embarked upon was rather extensive: New York, Buffalo, Washington, D.C., Ridge, Maryland (the location of Cardinal Gibbons Institute), Philadelphia, Pittsburgh, Cleveland, Cincinnati,

---

[104]Markoe, "Jim Crow," p. 150.

Columbus, Toledo, Detroit, Chicago. Several cities proved particularly important. In Philadelphia Markoe established the <u>Chronicle</u> committee which was later to cause such controversy over its official status in the Federation. When Markoe arrived in New York, John LaFarge received him with great warmth and enthusiasm. Their cooperation, of course, was to leave its lasting influence on the future of the Federation. Markoe himself later described their relationship.

> We made a strange pair, not too compatible. He was a scholar and genius in many fields. I was neither in any field. He was what I called a "safety first man," I was rather rash and reckless. He was ultra prudent. I considered prudence, as an alibi for neglect, not always a virtue but sometimes a sin! He seemed always to enjoy the confidence of his superiors. I seemed always to make my superiors somewhat nervous and doubtful. Fr. LaFarge was older. I was almost of another generation. He was an Ivy Leaguer from Harvard, I always disliked all schools, especially any Ivy League school. As regards race relations, in spite of his great interest and the notable contributions he made in behalf of interracial justice, I always felt that Fr. LaFarge was a white man who sincerely wanted to help the Negro, but was not quite black enough himself. In fact he often gave me credit for arousing his interest in the race problem nationally.
> . . . I believe it true at this stage in Fr. LaFarge's career, as I knew him, he was rather conservative in regard to race and race relations. He was still prudently feeling his way and with the passage of years he flowered into the great champion of interracial justice that he became. This liberal growth continued until his participation in the great historic march on Washington [1963], in his old age. . . [105]

LaFarge arranged for Markoe to visit the Cardinal Gibbons Institute at Ridge, where the younger Jesuit met Victor and Constance Daniel, the administrators. He was soon aware of a growing rift between the Daniels and Father LaFarge, which Markoe defined as a

---

[105]Markoe, "An Interracial Role," pp. 141, 143.

difference in philosophy. The Daniels, educated West Indian blacks, espoused the liberal educational theories of W. E. B. DuBois, whereas LaFarge admired Booker T. Washington. He had already in fact described his efforts at Cardinal Gibbons to Markoe as an attempt to create a Catholic Tuskegee. The editor did not take sides in the debate, which apparently at this point had not openly surfaced between the two parties involved. He was, however, aware from the complaints the Daniels made to him that all was not well at the Institute.[106]

This trip also took Markoe to Detroit, where he helped with plans for the upcoming F.C.C. convention there. His reception in nearly every city was rewarding:

> In practically all these cities [I was] feted as a champion of the cause of Catholicism among Negroes and of the rights of Negroes within the Church, especially by Catholic Negroes.[107]

What was probably of greater significance, however, was the real purpose of the visits. Besides promoting the Chronicle, Markoe had a second goal: "to inculcate among the members the idea of making the Federation more interracial in character and more militant in opposing segregation and unjust discrimination in the Church."[108]

---

[106]Ibid., p. 143. This debate will be handled in greater detail in Chapter 4. If affected the Federation both because LaFarge's interest in that organization lasted about as long as the Institute did, and because Constance Daniel apparently became one of LaFarge's most outspoken public critics during the Federation controversy.

[107]Ibid., pp. 138-39. Indeed, Markoe has many quotations in his memoirs which indicate an enthusiastic response to his visits in every city.

[108]Ibid., p. 138.

Upon his return to St. Louis Markoe once again took up the many activities of his parish. He made one important addition to the <u>Chronicle</u> staff, Hazel McDaniel Teabeau, an educated young black woman who worked from that time on closely with Markoe on all Federation matters. Dr. and Mrs. Teabeau had many friends among black intellectuals of the country, and Markoe always saw his new assistant as one of the most progressive and aggressive blacks he had known.[109]

Later in the year Markoe was invited to speak to the annual convention of the Knights of Peter Claver in Oklahoma. His address apparently shocked his largely Southern black audience, who were unused to having a white priest speak so bluntly about discrimination in the Church. After the talk appeared in the <u>Claverite</u>, Markoe received several critical reactions from priests in the South. His reply to them was similar to that given Father Eckert earlier: the black man needed to hear such things from Catholic priests. Later the same organization in a Lafayette, Louisiana parish invited Markoe there. His experience was strange, for the lay people asked him to their homes by indirect means, never through the pastor. Markoe began to wonder whether visiting black homes was expected of the Southern parish priest. In any event, he later felt that neither Conrad nor Turner had understood New Orleans; perhaps he was convinced that he alone had experienced both sides of Louisiana Catholic life.[110]

In late August Fr. Emil G. Brunner wrote to Markoe from New Orleans. It is not clear whether the letter was prompted by Markoe's

---

[109]Ibid., pp. 150-51.

[110]Ibid., pp. 151-52; 165-66.

recent trip to Louisiana, or merely by a current issue of the Chronicle which Brunner had seen. The Josephite began by admitting that he had read Markoe's earlier articles in America and judged the author a zealous but imprudent man. When he had heard that Markoe contributed the Chronicle to the Federated Colored Catholics, the Josephite was only more convinced of his original impression. Brunner felt that Turner and C. Marcellus Dorsey (at one time printer of the F.C.C. organ) were Catholics in name only.

> Our experience with them has taught us that in any trouble (and they are capable of raising plenty of it) they are first race men--and only as an after thought--Catholics. No matter what may be the issue between you and them, they pass their final judgment upon it from the stand point of what they think your attitude is to the Race--and to their God-given destiny to lead the Race as they see fit. I can assure you that when troubles arise, and I have every confidence they will, they will not hesitate to pass judgment upon you as they have, times out of memory, upon the Josephites.[111]

Brunner took exception to a recent review of the Gillard book in the Chronicle and also to a comment by Markoe on the luxurious quality of the Josephites' new administrative headquarters. Finally, he explained that the Josephites were forced to accept slanderous remarks about their unwillingness to accept black candidates because they refused to point a finger at the Southern bishops who would not place black priests.

Thus began a correspondence which was to continue sporadically over the next few months. In it Markoe attempted to convince the Josephite of the true value of the Federation and Chronicle, while the

---

[111] E. G. Brunner to Markoe, 28 August 1930, Gillard Papers.

latter cautioned against promising blacks too much too soon. Brunner sent all his correspondence to Gillard for his information and commentary. In one of these letters Markoe outlined his hopes for the Federation.

> We seek to organize the Negro . . . and thus give him a greater share in the active life of the Church, improve his brand of Catholicity, put him on the map so as to attract to him the dormant attention of our white Catholic laity as to arouse the latter to a greater interest in affording better opportunities to the Catholic Negro for the salvation of his souls and in the conversion of the non-Catholic Negro who is ready for the Harvest.[112]

Later in the same letter he admitted that his purpose might be different from that of the original Federation. Nonetheless, it was the direction which the members should now pursue. Markoe urged the Josephites to support the work.

> . . . I believe that the program of the Federation properly understood offers the only practical solution for America's race problem and the conversion of the Negro. If this result was not seen or intended by the Federation in its initial stages, we by now guiding and helping the Federation can make it mean that.[113]

Brunner read the speech which Markoe delivered to the Knights of Peter Claver in Oklahoma. His reaction was that while blacks had the right to hope for integrated churches someday, it was unwise to arouse that hope now. Others had done so, and then been unable to fulfill it. He had wisely refrained.[114]

---

[112]Markoe to Brunner, 20 September 1930, Gillard Papers.

[113]Ibid.

[114]Brunner to Markoe, 22 September 1930, Gillard Papers.

While Markoe admitted that Brunner was operating in a more deeply Southern atmosphere, he maintained that the climate in St. Louis was not far removed from the South. All circumstances aside, however, the principle should remain the same.

> To my mind the reason that there are so few colored Catholics today, and the greatest obstacle to the conversion of the race as a whole is the uncatholicity of Catholics. . . . This uncatholicity manifests itself in a lack of charity, a lack of justice, and in a failure to apply correct Christian principles in the case of interracial relations. . . . when Catholics in a wholesale fashion and habitually fail in these respects, and consequently become obsessed with false principles of conduct, then in practice, at least, they are beginning, to put it mildly, to border on the verge of heresy.[115]

As for Brunner's objection that facing racial prejudice so squarely was impractical, Markoe replied that it was an eminently workable solution.

> Now in this matter of being on the Negro's side rather than on the white man's side, for the sake of justice and because it is right (and because taking it all in all the Negro is in the right and the white man is in the wrong) we have a practical program which we priests who are engaged in the work can carry out. We may not be able to batter down the prejudice of a nation, but we can eliminate the curse from ourselves, be colored rather than white, and convert the race, which will judge the Church more by what we do than by the conduct of priests at large.[116]

From this position Markoe felt there could be no departure. It was simply a matter of Christian morality.

> My policy is deliberately to preach to colored people that there is hope for them to have absolute equality with white people in the enjoyment of the good things

---

[115]Markoe to Brunner, 24 September 1930, Gillard Papers.

[116]Ibid.

which Christ came to give us all. Not to hold out this hope to them would be not to preach to them the Gospel of Jesus Christ.[117]

Such exchanges obviously reveal an incompatibility that never was resolved. Brunner maintained his conviction, in turn conveyed to Gillard, that Markoe was a demagogue and Turner not to be trusted.[118] Nearly two years later, when Fr. L. J. Welbers wrote to Gillard for advice on the Federation, the latter urged him not to write for the Chronicle or trust its officials, Markoe, LaFarge, or Turner.[119] Part of this was due to Gillard's own experiences, but some may have also been prompted by his knowledge of this correspondence. Later, Gillard wrote Markoe himself to insist that none of his articles be reprinted in the Chronicle, whose editorial policies the Josephite disapproved.[120] Markoe later referred to criticisms of Turner which he had heard from various clergy. Undoubtedly part of that was in this series of correspondence. Unfortunately, Markoe too never won the full cooperation of the Josephites.

In September he attended the F.C.C. convention in Detroit, where the new regulations of the organization were drawn. An

---

[117] Ibid.

[118] Brunner to Gillard, 22 September 1930, Gillard Papers. Also Brunner to Gillard, 9 December 1931; on Brunner's opinion of Turner see Brunner to Markoe, 22 September 1930. One positive outcome of these letters, however, was that Brunner became convinced that the society could no longer afford to protect the Southern bishops, but must lay the blame at their doors. See Brunner to Gillard, 11 September 1930, Gillard Papers.

[119] Welbers to Gillard, 30 April 1932; Gillard to Welbers, 5 May 1932, both in Gillard Papers.

[120] Gillard to Markoe, 29 June 1932, Gillard Papers.

interesting incident occurred there which clarifies our understanding of Markoe's relationship to the race question. The Jesuit had learned that a certain Dr. Rupert C. L. Markoe, a black physician, resided in Detroit. His elderly father from St. Croix was then visiting him. Markoe took John LaFarge with him to visit the father and son, who bore the Markoe name because they were descendants of slaves of the old Markoe plantation on St. Croix. The Jesuit had always been aware of this fact in his ancestry.

> . . . historically my family was more Southern than Mississippi or Alabama or Louisiana. Our family for generations lived close to the equator on the Island of St. Croix where they owned large estates and hundreds of slaves. This was precisely one real reason why I was interested in interracial justice and felt, like my brother John, that we owed some restitution to the Negro race. Markoe wealth had come from the blood, the sweat, the tears of Negro slaves.[121]

Upon his return to St. Louis, Markoe lent his support to the conversion of the old St. Mary's Infirmary in St. Louis into the first black Catholic hospital in the United States. His own more personal contribution was to insist upon going there whenever he needed hospital treatment. He would be, of course, the only white patient there, which was his own small way of trying to integrate the institution![122]

---

[121]Markoe, "An Interracial Role," pp. 159-60. A former black parishioner of St. Elizabeth's informed me that Markoe had nursed a hope all his life, especially after learning of this doctor by the same name, that he too had a drop of black blood in him. Interview with Antoinette Robinson, St. Louis, June 1973.

[122]Markoe, "An Interracial Role," p. 164.

With all the traveling which Markoe had been doing, he soon began to hear warnings from his provincial, Father Germing, to "mind the store" at home. The reaction did not surprise Markoe much. He later remarked that not one superior had ever really encouraged him in his work, and several were obviously "jittery" about it. His brother John and Laurence Kenny provided the greatest support.

> [I was] often told [I was] ahead of [my] time. [I] could not understand how that was possible when [I was] nearly two thousand years behind Christ who implicitly preached everything [I] preached.[123]

As the year 1931 progressed a group of white Catholic men approached Markoe to request that they be permitted, while remaining a part of their own parishes, to integrate into the activities of St. Elizabeth's. This was the origin of the White Friends of Colored Catholics. Several prominent white Catholic organizations of St. Louis at this period also became resolutely involved in work in the black community.

Meanwhile, of course, the large task of preparing for the 1931 Federation convention in St. Louis had to be organized. Committees were set up in the parish, which was to serve as host. When the archbishop refused permission for the opening Mass to be celebrated in the cathedral, Markoe turned to friends at St. Louis University. The college chapel was obtained, along with university facilities for a Sunday night session, a dance in the gymnasium and a hall for priest-guests of the convention.[124]

---

[123]Ibid., p. 174.

[124]Ibid., pp. 187-89.

The convention events have already been described in some detail. Markoe thought it was significant that the message containing the Papal Blessing had omitted the word "colored" from the organization's title. He felt the meeting itself had been beneficial to the Federation, who had received good publicity, the parish, which had gained greater respect in St. Louis and the Jesuit scholastics who attended, many of them learning valuable lessons in racial justice. In fact, the convention had proved so favorable from his own viewpoint that Markoe referred to the organization as an <u>interracial</u> one in his first editorial after the meeting.[125]

Despite the success surrounding his Federation activities in 1931, Father Markoe's pastoral life had been thrown into chaos, a fact largely unknown to anyone around him. A few days before the convention Fr. David Hamilton appeared in the rectory at St. Elizabeth's and quietly announced that he was the new pastor. A shocked Markoe consulted with Father Germing, his superior, who confirmed the appointment with some embarrassment. He explained that he could not appoint Hamilton as an assistant, since he was three years older than Markoe. The latter realized the fallacy of that argument, since he had already buried several older assistants! Hamilton himself tried to relieve the situation somewhat, especially in view of the forthcoming convention, by suggesting that he announce his new position at a later date. Thus the strange drama began in which Markoe deferred to Hamilton in private, and Hamilton to Markoe in

---

[125]"The Convention," pp. 631-32.

public.[126] Markoe never did learn the true reason for his demotion. Hamilton later admitted that he had been sent to "reform" the parish, but could find nothing to improve. He did not assume his status as pastor publicly until nearly one year later. By then Markoe had become so deeply involved in Federation affairs that relief from pastoral duties was almost a welcome necessity.

In the meantime, however, Markoe's parochial activities continued to grow, each one marked by an increasing interracial emphasis. In the latter months of 1931 the White Friends of Colored Catholics staged a comedy in a white parish before an interracial audience. The evening closed with an interracial dance in the white parish hall, undoubtedly a shocking event to many St. Louisans. The seventh annual parish banquet was also marked by interracial attendance, with Daniel Lord the keynote speaker and Stephen Theobald the guest of honor. Father Theobald died the following June, and when Markoe left to deliver the funeral sermon, he took several black friends of Theobald with him. They stayed with Markoe's brother and sister-in-law in St. Paul, a move which the Jesuit admitted made his family a bit nervous at the time. The funeral sermon reflected Markoe's own concept of the priestly role:

> . . . . the good priest even while in the flesh has already died in advance to live only for Christ. His consecrated life of self-sacrifice, of purity, of sub mission to authority, and of detachment from the things so prized by the world render his death less violent

---

[126]Markoe, "An Interracial Role," pp. 208-208.

> since it becomes merely a more complete fulfillment of his desire to give himself wholly to God and to possess God alone in Whom is all good![127]

Stephen Theobald's death was a great loss to the cause of a black clergy, Markoe declared.

> His death removed a noble living exponent of the practicality, advisability, and usefullness of a Negro priesthood in the United States.[128]

In that same month of June 1932, Markoe had begun yet another project in racial justice, the "Interracial Hour" over WEW, the university station. The programs gave many white persons the opportunity, he felt, to listen to black speakers in an anonymous atmosphere. Though Markoe promoted the idea in the Chronicle, the only place to follow suit was New York City.

Campaign for Interracialism

At the June executive committee meeting of the Federation, final plans had been drawn for the fall convention in New York City. It was at that same meeting that Secretary Smith revealed requests from Chicago members for a new organization title. The recommendation was passed to Father Dever's constitution committee for consideration. Markoe, present at the meeting, later wrote an editorial (as mentioned in chapters I and II) referring to the Federation as a "National Catholic Inter-Racial Organization."[129] That issue of the

---

[127]Ibid., pp. 222-23.

[128]Ibid., p. 219.

[129]"A National Catholic Inter-Racial Organization," pp. 177-78.

Chronicle (September), along with the preceding one were published from New York rather than St. Louis. LaFarge had asked Markoe to come to New York two months in advance of the convention, to aid in its preparation. Hazel McDaniel Teabeau accompanied Markoe. Ironically, they spoke at that time to George K. Hunton, at LaFarge's request, on the operation of the Chronicle. It was Hunton two years later who became editor in the New York office of the Interracial Review.

Father Markoe, now free of pastoral duties (Father Hamilton finally "announced" himself during Markoe's absence), and Mrs. Teabeau prepared programs and invitations for the convention. They spent endless hours promoting the Federation and its convention in speeches and side trips to nearby cities. There was an added purpose in their efforts.

> In all these activities [I] kept preaching and urging more and more that in the very nature of the case the Federation should officially become and declare itself to be an interracial organization. [I] did this as an individual in keeping with [my] Catholic principles governing [my] thought on race relations.[130]

Markoe even visited "key members" in Washington to present his "interracial" rather than "racial" ideas. He traveled to a pilgrimage at Torresdale, Pennsylvania, where many Federation members were gathered, to enlist a few more followers. Mrs. Teabeau had been

---

[130]Markoe, "An Interracial Role," p. 228.

convinced of the idea, too, and she set out to contact her Harlem friends with the new message of interracialism.[131]

When Markoe defined the purpose of the Federation in interracial terms for the convention program, he drew the first sharp reaction from Turner. Upon arrival at the convention, the president approached Markoe with objections to the priest's description. Later Markoe recalled the incident as one which revealed a new side to Turner's character. Up to that time, Markoe had felt that most criticism of Turner (especially from white priests) had been motivated by prejudice. But had that really been the case?

> Now [I] detected a side to his character that caused [me] to wonder. Today [I] would explain it in modern terminology by saying I detected a little bit of the Black Muslim in him. He betrayed a deep seated dislike for and distrust of white people, especially a white like myself who was getting too big for his breeches and beginning to put him in the shade. [I] did not blame Dr. Turner for having a certain animosity for white people and maybe a little extra for white priests; I had some myself, but [I] knew such animosity could not harmonize with the ideals and objectives of the Federation. To succeed the Federation could not display this kind of animosity.[132]

In his memoirs Markoe went on to define the argument between Turner and himself, which eventually destroyed Federation unity.

> [I] insisted that any Catholic organization having as its objective the promotion of better race relations

---

[131] Ibid., pp. 228-29. How much Turner may have known of Markoe's visit to Washington, D.C., is unclear. If he did at all, it may have prompted his later charges that Markoe was turning Federation members against him deliberately. Markoe himself always counted Mrs. Teabeau's support as indicative of his position as that of progressive blacks, which he considered her to be. See Markoe, "An Interracial Role," p. 235.

[132] Ibid., pp. 229-30.

> had to be interracial or it would itself be un-Catholic. Dr. Turner seemed to disagree with me that the objective of the Federation was to promote better race relations. Rather he seemed to think that the purpose of the Federation was to fight for Negroes' rights within the Church by fighting the whites in the Church. This idea was the opposite of promoting better race relations as a means of attaining for the Negro what was due him within the Church in keeping with the basic meaning of Catholicism and justice.[133]

There seems little doubt, therefore, that Markoe had embarked upon a course which he knew would be controversial, but considered necessary nonetheless. Indeed, he described the events of the New York convention as "revolutionary history . . . made in the field of Catholic race relations."[134] While the ordinary schedule of the meetings proceeded, he began campaigning quietly among the delegates.

> My lobbying was all directed toward having the delegates adopt a new name for the organization which would eliminate any racial aspect such as "colored." Secondly, to rewrite the constitution as far as necessary to adopt it to the fact that we had become a Catholic organization and were no longer a racial group.[135]

It would not be that difficult, of course, to control changes in the constitution, since Markoe had replaced Dever as chairman of the revision committee. The guarantee of success lay, however, in gaining Father LaFarge's support, for he controlled the New York delegation. This last was guaranteed when LaFarge delivered an emotionally charged speech to the assembly on the necessity of interracial cooperation. Few, indeed, had ever seen the gentle Jesuit so

---

[133] Ibid., pp. 230-31.

[134] Ibid., p. 234.

[135] Ibid., p. 235.

vehement.[136] The result, of course, was that the convention voted, after some resistance in the closed executive session, in favor of an entirely new name and constitution for the organization. The National Catholic Federation for the Promotion of Better Race Relations had been born. As Markoe left New York his friend LaFarge suggested a new name for the magazine which the editor considered quite appropriate, the Interracial Review.

The ensuing debate between Markoe and Turner has been described in detail in chapter II. From Markoe's view, the battle had already been won fairly in New York. Turner, though reluctant, had added his vote of unanimity to the changes. The black press at first seemed supportive in their reviews of the convention. Markoe, now free of pastoral obligations, had volunteered his services as a national field agent as well as editor. All seemed well as the new Interracial Review was readied for the presses. Then a sharp reaction arrived from Turner, and criticisms appeared in the Afro-American. Markoe saw these as violations of the trust displayed by all parties in New York. In addition, he felt personally wronged for all the time, effort and money he had poured into an organ that was legally the Jesuits', though lent with great generosity to the Federation cause. Finally, he felt that Turner's stance was totally contrary to all that he as a priest had sought to accomplish in his years in the black apostolate.

---

[136]Ibid., pp. 235-36. Unfortunately, this speech does not seem to have been preserved.

> In the last analysis more was involved than racial versus interracial. It was clearly a case of un-Catholic versus Catholic. Catholicity essentially means an all-embracing union of the members of the human race willing to be united; it essentially means interracial union. Un-Catholicity means disunion and chaos. Our Federation could not afford to be less Catholic than the National Association for the Advancement of Colored People or the National Urban League or the future Committee on Racial Equality. We could not afford to put an emphasis on color as being essential to the nature of our organization, as is "Black" to the title and nature of Black Muslims today.[137]

The meeting which Eugene Clarke urgently called in November to moderate the differences between the two men was to Markoe the real "rump" session in the debate.

> . . . he [Turner] evidently felt he could hold some kind of a meeting in Washington and in some way nullify what was done in New York. Putting it bluntly he determined to double cross me and the convention [138]

Markoe's description of that meeting has already been quoted. Although he later regretted the personal animosity displayed there, the priest was convinced that Turner was responsible for the disruptions in Federation unity. When Markoe arrived in New York after this Washington session, he consulted with LaFarge. What they decided is not certain, but the basic agreement of the two Jesuits on interracial principles had already been established at the convention.

Markoe did indeed have the support not only of the New York Federation, but the Chicago and St. Louis chapters as well. Shortly

---

[137]Ibid., pp. 238-39.

[138]Ibid., p. 247.

after changing the magazine's title, he began receiving positive letters to the Interracial Review, which were printed in succeeding months.[139] The Chicago chapter invited him as guest speaker to their symposium on "Race Prejudice! What Can Catholicism Do?" The Jesuit so impressed his audience that Chicago lawyer C. Augustine Skinner wrote Turner a firm rebuke of his presidential actions, and later defended Markoe publicly in the press. The speech which Markoe delivered in Chicago was later published as an editorial in the December 1932 Interracial Review. In it the Jesuit roundly criticized educators, pastors and other white Catholic leaders who often cited the prejudice of white lay Catholics as primarily responsible for their inability to admit blacks to Catholic institutions.

> In alleging prejudice as a justification for the denying of opportunities, so necessary for salvation, it is usually referred to as something which is at least made to appear as an almost necessary part of a white man's make-up and being. Educators, pastors, and rectors of seminaries usually will regret the existence of prejudice, but at the same time emphasize the undeniable fact of its existence. That is the way white people are and we must all face the fact and not indulge in Utopian theorizing as to how things should be—facts are facts! Some people even attach a certain honorable respectability to prejudice. It is a mark of taste, good breeding, culture. If it develops in conversation that an individual is without the ordinary prejudice against Negroes, he is considered a little odd or peculiar and jokingly might be referred to as a "nigger lover." Such a one may even be deemed out of order![140]

---

[139]Letters to the editor, Interracial Review, December 1932, p. 249; March 1933, p. 59.

[140]"Prejudice Outlawed," Interracial Review, December 1932, p. 244. Though moderate by contemporary standards, the speech clearly reflects those attitudes which made Markoe a popular spokesman for black rights in the Church in his day.

The truth, Markoe went on, was that prejudice was a sin. It became as ridiculous, therefore, to bar a black man from a seminary of prejudiced students, as to tell him he could not enter because the students were all pick-pockets!

> But the truth is that the vast majority of our white Catholic people in America are <u>not</u> prejudiced against the Negro. God has given them consciences and the Holy Ghost enlightens them. What they need chiefly are greater opportunities to put into practice their Catholic principles and instincts as regards race relations.[141]

For those who were guilty of prejudice, the solution should be the same as for any other sinful fault.

> The sin of race prejudice must be eliminated by means of the confessional, the pulpit, the press, the class room, the home, and in general God's grace as dispensed through His Church, which certainly must include some effort at proper guidance and instruction.[142]

While the blacks who heard this talk in Chicago applauded it, Cardinal Mundelein of that city had a different reaction. He informed the Jesuit provincial in St. Louis that Markoe was never again to speak in his diocese.[143] Markoe, however, felt that the black Catholics present had understood the reason for his strong message.

> . . . the Negroes in Chicago who received [my] talk with such acclaim knew [I was] speaking for the benefit of the many white people present. They delighted in hearing white people enlightened honestly by a white speaker. They

---

[141]Ibid., p. 245.

[142]Ibid.

[143]Markoe, "An Interracial Role," p. 261.

have more difficulty in doing it themselves because as Negroes they already have one strike against them in prejudicial white minds.[144]

Thus the Jesuit who in his controversy with Turner was being so severely attacked in the Afro-American as a racist was winning the applause of black Catholics in the Midwest, and even some censure as a "radical" priest! Surely from Markoe's own perspective the new Federation born in the New York convention could not have been proceeding more surely along the path of true interracial cooperation. Its principles had become, in his estimation, the only ones which could guarantee a viable solution to the race problem. There had been one hundred chapters represented at the convention, many for which Markoe felt the Chronicle and he personally were responsible. Even the Jesuit Superior General had sent an encouraging letter about the convention proceedings. The response to the radio programs and the new Interracial Review format had been heartening. What Markoe actually felt about arranging the "rump" session which ousted Turner in Chicago has not been preserved. What is clear, however, is that he saw it as the inevitable solution to a perplexing problem. He later emphasized the representative nature of the body which met there, convinced as he was that the majority truly favored an interracial approach. Although it appears that LaFarge removed himself

---

[144]Ibid. His speeches to all black audiences, on the other hand, were more subdued, because he felt they needed more to hear about the Church's benefits, since they were often asked to defend her against criticism. He spoke on those occasions about the Church's "record" on slavery, in a similar vein to his earlier article on the same subject in America. See Markoe, "An Interracial Role," pp. 261-71, which contain a speech delivered in Kansas City to an all black Catholic audience at this period.

largely from the entire controversy, he did send Markoe a telegram during the Chicago meeting. Markoe later wrote the older Jesuit that the actions taken in Chicago were made necessary by the circumstances. Markoe also complained that Mundelein and Eckert had been particularly resistant to the proceedings.[145]

If Markoe had any regret, it was that George Conrad was elected president in Turner's place. Archbishop McNicholas had sent Conrad a letter of congratulations upon his election, emphasizing the need for "prudence" in solving the race problem. Markoe wrote

> I believe this letter contributed much to Mr. Conrad's failure as a president of, and the ultimate dissolution of, the Federation. He was too "prudent" before being told to be extra prudent. . . . Mr. Conrad was a fine man. Today, however, the leaders of the Negro revolution would classify him as an "Uncle Tom." And that was what the Archbishop wanted him to be.[146]

Despite his hesitations about the president, Markoe set about immediately arranging the fall convention. Its success would be vital to the future of the new Midwestern faction. He contacted his old friend Fr. Thomas McKenney in Cleveland, who agreed to serve as host. An official letter of invitation soon arrived from Bishop Joseph Schrembs.

Markoe's editorial in the *Interracial Review* during this period reflected the methodology on interracial justice which he was then employing. He wrote in the January issue that it was foolish to presume that blacks could solve the race problem themselves. In the first place, the problem was not within one race or the other, but

---

[145]Markoe to LaFarge, 27 December 1932, LaFarge Papers.

[146]Markoe, "An Interracial Role," p. 288.

rather between them. A person might as easily tell a prisoner to solve his problem of confinement. "It is necessarily a question of interracial justice, understanding, and cooperation.'[147] Secondly, if the burden rested with one race more than the other, it was surely with the white man,

> . . . who creates the difficulty which is inappropriately called "the Negro problem." It should more accurately be called the problem of the white man's injustice towards the Negro.[148]

In this same issue a second editorial reviewed the history of Catholic involvement in the race problem. As with many of his talks to black Catholic audiences, Markoe quoted papal condemnations of slavery, and the official effort toward emancipation. The emphasis upon the Church rather than individuals within it was somewhat reminiscent of earlier Federation documents. If the Catholic Church in America seemed negligent, Markoe declared, it was probably due to her youth and lack of influence. When America were as Catholic as other nations, blacks would experience the full benefit of Catholic interracial justice.[149]

In February Markoe scored another contention of the Turner faction, that the black Catholic needed an organization similar to the Catholic ethnic groups which had been so prominent at an earlier period (Ancient Order of Hibernians, Turnverein, etc.). The black man was

---

[147]"Solving Our Own "Problem'," Interracial Review, January 1933, p. 8.

[148]Ibid., p. 9.

[149]"The Church Still Lives," Interracial Review, January 1933, p. 9.

just the opposite of the immigrant, Markoe argued. The black man knew the language and culture of America as well as any "native." Indeed, to separate him as a special group was to turn back the clock, for he was already assimilated.

> Consequently how any Negro leader can so far betray his cause and further sanction this outrage of differentiation even in the sphere of religion and on a national scale is beyond our limited powers of comprehension. . . . The Negro is not different, never had to be assimilated, because from the beginning he helped create American civilization and culture. His only difference is his fading accident of color. In the case of the immigrant one idea of nationalistic organizations was to hasten and make smooth the process of assimilation. In the case of the already assimilated Negro a national organization strictly racial in character will only confirm and help make permanent the heresy of non-assimilability.[150]

The answer was rather for the black man to organize in his Catholicity with white Catholics (since the problem was one of relationship) and present to the world the Catholic interracial ideal.

In a signed article in the same issue, Markoe bluntly criticized Turner in a more personal way. Without using names, he spoke of "that type of Negro leader who would prefer to be a 'kingfish' in a Negro organization than a respected human being in an interracial group."[151] Few missed the obvious target of his attack. The priest insisted that such men were responsible for a proliferation of substandard hospitals, churches, and other institutions, all kept alive by their desire for

---

[150]"The Negro and the Immigrant," pp. 30-31.

[151]Markoe, "Kingfish' Race Leaders," p. 29.

authority. It was they who perpetuated racism itself by acknowledging that the black man was different and should be treated thus.

> Negro achievement is much to be desired, but it is only by selfrespect and the lessening of prejudice through interracial co-operation and good will that it can be accomplished. It was interracial action that freed the slaves, and every mile-stone of Negro progress since the Civil War has been blazed along the highway of interracial co-operation. Each rung in the ladder of Negro achievement has been some phase of interracial action. The really capable and high principled Negro leader welcomes white collaboration on an interracial basis because he knows he can measure up to usual white standards of competence.[152]

This statement succinctly defines Markoe's own raison d'etre. He was thoroughly convinced that interaction between the races, specifically interracial cooperation on an equal basis, was the only means by which racial justice would at last be achieved.

National Catholic Interracial Federation

In June 1933 the Midwestern faction met in executive session and accepted the resignations of those officers who did not support the changes. Turner's resignation was not acknowledged as such, since the group had already declared his office vacant in December, and elected Conrad to fill it. In his own words, Markoe felt that Turner with his friends had "picked up his marbles" and gone home, refusing to play the game. At least one goal of the Washington group was achieved by their resignations. Markoe did later refer to the new Federation as a "complete break with the past" rather than a

---

[152]Ibid.

continuation of it.153 Archbishop McNicholas of Cincinnati assumed the position of Spiritual Director, thus shifting the center of the Federation to the Midwest. Conrad defined the new purposes of the organization, now called the National Catholic Interracial Federation, at the same June meeting.

> He declared its purpose was to effect cooperation and proper adjustments in regard to racial differences within and without the Church, and to protect the rights and privileges of Negroes within the Catholic Church.154

John LaFarge had preferred to remain rather silent during the Federation's most controversial period. Apparently he did not attend either the meeting at Clarke's home in Washington nor the December session in Chicago. He did continue to write his column, "Doing the Truth," for the Interracial Review, and also an article for America supportive of the changes in the Federation.155 He sent his regrets in June for not being able to attend the executive session in Cleveland. His absence from so many Federation meetings was unusual, and Markoe later speculated on the reasons.

153Markoe, "An Interracial Role," pp. 300, 305. In his later years, Markoe still maintained that no one had sought to rid the Federation of Turner: "No one in the whole organization, to [my] knowledge, desired to see Dr. Turner or any of his intimates, either leave the organization, or even cease functioning as officers. In New York the Federation had overwhelmingly reelected Dr. Turner president, and his close friends to other offices. All that the delegates desired to do in New York was to give him and the other officers a better, and more Catholic, instrument to work with more effectively." (p. 302)

154Ibid., p. 306.

155LaFarge, "Catholic Negroes Take Stock," pp. 429-31.

... about this time it seemed to me he began slowly drifting away from the Federation. One of the reasons for his former great interest in the Federation (as the F.C.C.) was that it was something of a semi-official sponsor of the Cardinal Gibbons Institute, a favorite project initiated by Fr. LaFarge, largely because of his interest in the Rural Life Movement. With the evolution and development of the Federation nationally as a militant interracial group he may have felt it was losing sight of, and interest in, the Cardinal Gibbons Institute. This was to some extent true. Many Federation chapters were not particularly interested in what today would be called a more or less de facto segregated agricultural school for Negroes in the South.

Another reason possibly for a loss of enthusiasm for the National Catholic Interracial Federation on the part of Fr. LaFarge may have been he felt it was in its new form pretty much my creation, and he would let me paddle my own canoe. Or he may have felt [I] moved in and stole it from him. [I] know for a fact he always felt I was somewhat lacking in prudence in my crusading for interracial justice. He was not the only one who in this respect doubted my wisdom! . . . My whole modus operandi was different from his . . .

Possible all these speculations might be wrong. . . . We must remember, too, that Fr. LaFarge was a very busy man with many irons in the fire. I had only one![156]

---

[156]Markoe, "An Interracial Role," pp. 310-11. The real differences between Markoe and LaFarge, seen perhaps only in approach here, were to surface only later at a meeting of the Jesuit Institute of Social Order in Chicago in late 1946. Markoe found the discussion there on race relations quite dissatisfactory. He described one reason later in his memoirs: "One was Fr. LaFarge's insistence at the panel discussion that the race problem was not a moral question but purely economic. Having been preaching for years on the immorality of racism, this was too much for me to swallow. In talking this point over with others later I was told by some who claimed they had read everything Father LaFarge had ever written on the race question and that in all his writings they had never found a condemnation of racism from his pen on the score of its immorality. [I] cannot vouch for this [myself] because I have never had the courage or perseverance to plough through all his writings on the race question. I have always found him hard to read." (pp. 446-47) Markoe found the entire conference so dissatisfactory that he later embodied his objections in an article for the I.S.O. Bulletin. Although his remarks were moderated by others' editing, they still proved quite controversial once published. In the ensuing debate, Markoe remarked in a letter to Fr. Francis J. Corley, editor of the Bulletin, that he, Markoe, also took issue with LaFarge's position that every effort should be made not to embarrass Jesuits in the South, but rather to

On July 31 Markoe arrived in Cleveland to set up convention headquarters. He had nearly a month in which to prepare the details of the program and promote attendance. The Midwestern faction had now enough N.C.W.C. support that Miss Bresette, so prominent in past conventions, spent two days in Cleveland arranging the industrial conference for September 2. The day featured discussions on F.D.R.'s new National Recovery Administration, its effect on blacks in the light of the social justice encyclicals of Pope Leo XIII and Pope Pius XI.[157] Despite the fact that Conrad had indicated to Curley that the National Catholic Interracial Federation would be a new organization, its convention was featured as the ninth annual Federation meeting. Invitations were sent to all chapters, with the presumption that if they did not respond to the contrary, they were now members of the new organization. A solemn high Mass was celebrated at the cathedral on Sunday morning, and Bishop McNicholas later spoke to the assembled delegates. He advocated a revolutionary crusade of prayer for interracial justice, urged the members to put religion before the elimination of prejudice, and promoted new black schools, churches and institutions. His message clearly disappointed Markoe, who guessed its impact on those present.[158] The third day's sessions were devoted to answering the question, "How Can Better Race Relations Be Promoted?" Father Eckert attended this

---

keep them as much as possible on the "bandwagon" of racial justice. See Markoe to Corley, 29 January 1947, quoted in full in his memoirs, pp. 458-65.

[157]Ibid., p. 316.

[158]Ibid., p. 329.

convention and Markoe attempted to gain from him an invitation to hold the next convention in Chicago. None was forthcoming, and the meeting adjourned without setting a time and place for the following year. As mentioned earlier, no meeting was held in 1934 as a consequence, since Conrad's hopes for an invitation from New Orleans also were unrewarded.

Another event of equal importance occurred near the end of 1933. The new Jesuit provincial, Father Horine, informed Markoe that he would have to submit all future articles for the Interracial Review to a board of Jesuit censors. As with so many other orders, the reasons for this command were apparently never clarified. Markoe felt that time considerations alone would make such a procedure impossible. He had been operating the magazine with little assistance, and could barely meet deadlines each month. The specter of anti-black censorship was also galling. Markoe contacted LaFarge in New York and arranged for the magazine's transfer. Later LaFarge was to refer to this move in his autobiography as a financial necessity. Markoe always insisted, however, that LaFarge had never known the true reason.[159]

In the summer of 1934 Markoe was reappointed pastor of St. Elizabeth's Church. Since he was no longer editor of the magazine, or a national officer in the Federation, his involvement in its activities waned considerably. Upon learning that the organization would hold its 1935 convention in the home city of its president and

---

[159]Ibid., pp. 340-41. See also LaFarge, The Manner Is Ordinary (New York: Harcourt, Brace and Co., 1954), p. 339.

spiritual director, Cincinnati, he decided that others could well handle the responsibility of the meetings. Since his two parish assistants at that time were older men, Markoe focused his attention once more on St. Elizabeth's. The parish school had been closed, the young people's activities had ceased, and the parish itself was poor. The pastor had much work ahead of him.[160]

Meanwhile in 1934 members of Father LaFarge's Catholic Laymen's Union (some of them also Federation members) had organized the Catholic Interracial Council. The group did not affiliate with the Federation, but took over the Interracial Review as its organ. When the fall of 1935 arrived, LaFarge urgently requested Markoe to attend the Federation convention in Cincinnati. Apparently Markoe was not impressed with the convention, for he left the meetings convinced that Conrad like his predecessor was not adept at planning successful sessions.[161] This seems to have been the Jesuit's last contact with the organization. Markoe's ultimate estimate was that the decline of the Midwestern Federation had been both the cause and the result of the birth of the Catholic Interracial Council. Events in St. Louis (the transfer of the Interracial Review, his reappointment as pastor)

---

[160]Markoe, "An Interracial Role," p. 346.

[161]Ibid., p. 363. Markoe commented that while Conrad was a good man, he was "not one to organize a convention. Neither had Dr. Turner been one to organize a successful convention. The conventions held during his regime that amounted to anything were organized for him. He would merely appear on the scene at the last minute to take the center of the stage. He did not have as winning a personality as Mr. Conrad."

> . . . plus the zeal of Fr. LaFarge and his men combined with their skepticism concerning the future of the Federation under prevailing conditions, including the rather weak leadership of Mr. George W. B. Conrad, were the chief factors in the development of the first Catholic Interracial Council in New York City [162]

William Markoe remained at St. Elizabeth's until 1941. A recent historian of St. Louis Catholicism summarized the impact of those years.

> Much of the history of the Negro Catholics in St. Louis during the late twenties and early thirties revolved around the name of tough-fibred William Markoe.
> . . . In a way it might be said that Fr. Markoe worked all his life to liquidate his own position as pastor. More and more he realized that the concept of a distinct Negro parish was both anachronistic and un-Christian. Negro Catholics should have received a welcome in any parish. According to the law of the Church they should have worshipped in the parish where they lived. Quite often, of course, these mere arbitrary territorial alignments did not build on or result in a natural community; but that was the way the Church authorities had wanted it. The idea of "separate but equal"—a "Jim Crow" type of Church arrangement—might correspond to the transitional exigencies of American life. It denied basic Christian and American beliefs. It would have to end some day.[163]

All of Markoe's work at St. Elizabeth's was carried out, of course, within this general framework of the St. Louis archdiocese at that period. Of that atmosphere the same historian, William Barnaby Faherty, recently wrote:

> The amazing growth of the Catholic Church in St. Louis was an exclusively white growth. The vast majority of Negroes moving into the city of St. Louis in the twentieth century were Protestants. The Church seemed unconcerned about them religiously or socially. The Catholic Negroes were, for the most part, descendants

---

[162]Ibid., p. 361.

[163]Faherty, pp. 169, 171.

of slaves of Creole families who had grown up in an
atmosphere of Catholic ceremonial. Their parish remained
city-wide and segregated, they formed a small minority
both among their fellow Catholics and among their
fellow Negroes.[164]

Of John Cardinal Glennon, archbishop from 1903-1946, Faherty recalled that when the prelate was asked by the apostolic delegate around 1920 for a report of Negro Catholic activity in St. Louis, two major facts emerged. First, Glennon felt that blacks were seeking equality in the churches, on which he commented

> . . . this is impractical for the present at least in a city such as St. Louis which is by sentiment and tradition a southern city, and where consequently putting in operation the demands of the colored Catholics would lead to much disturbance.[165]

Secondly, the archbishop reported that blacks generally thought too much of their rights and not enough of their obligations. In most instances white people supported their churches and schools.[166] Faherty continued, "Glennon would live by this viewpoint until his death many years later, and so he missed one of the greatest opportunities of his lifetime."[167]

Faherty also offers one telling insight into Glennon which may be a key as to the real limitations within which Markoe operated. The historian concludes his portrait of Glennon with these words.

---

[164] Ibid., p. 155.

[165] John Cardinal Glennon to Cardinal Fumasoni-Biondi, 18 February 1927, quoted in Faherty, p. 155.

[166] Ibid.

[167] Ibid.

> Whatever the biographer will finally conclude as to
> Glennon the man, Glennon's episcopacy shone brightly
> for twenty years. The last twenty were less brilliant,
> but still impressive.[168]

Unfortunately, the second twenty years were those under which Markoe tried to bring Catholicism to St. Louis blacks.

In the summer of 1941 Markoe was assigned to Mankato, Minnesota, "a town in which not a single Negro lived." [169] After a brief stay he went to Denver, where he once again worked in the black community from 1942-48. For the next three years he preached as a member of the midwestern Jesuit mission band, traveling from city to city. In 1951 he was assigned to teach theology at Marquette University in Milwaukee, where he continued to preach the message of interracial justice. He retired there in 1966 and died on December 6, 1969. His life is perhaps best summarized in the title he chose for his memoirs, "An Interracial Role."

---

[168] Ibid., p. 184.

[169] Markoe, "An Interracial Role," p. 398. Markoe was uncertain of the reason for the transfer. Faherty commented only that with the advent of World War II, the work among blacks in St. Louis took a new turn, and new faces and ideas were needed. See Faherty, p. 172.

CHAPTER IV

JOHN LAFARGE

To write of John LaFarge is to write of many men. He was a lover of sacred art, music and liturgy, at home in many languages, a man of peace. His life was spent in the causes of racial justice, the renewal of rural life, greater ecumenical understanding. Those who remember him can envision a Jesuit on horseback in Southern Maryland, a bespectacled journalist whose articles were published here and abroad, but in all an untiring friend of the famous and the forgotten. Such breadth of talent was partly born in him. He was the tenth child of John and Margaret Mason Perry LaFarge, born at Newport, Rhode Island on February 13, 1880.[1] His father was a well known painter and muralist, who first learned his art in the studio of William Morris Hunt, alongside William and Henry James. Young John's first memories of his father were his return from the South Seas with Henry Adams in 1891. The elder LaFarge's companionship with famous people brought son John into contact early with stimulating and varied personalities, which compensated somewhat for his father's own frequent absence from home. Margaret Perry LaFarge was

---

[1]Most of the material on LaFarge's early life is taken from his autobiography, <u>The Manner Is Ordinary</u>.

the granddaughter of Oliver Hazard Perry, and the great-great granddaughter of Benjamin Franklin. Born an Episcopalian, Mrs. LaFarge converted to the Catholic faith after her marriage.

In his earliest years John LaFarge lived in Newport with his mother, while his father worked in New York on a mural of the Ascension for the church of that name, returning to Newport at infrequent intervals. Young John attended Newport's public schools and imbibed the town's atmosphere at every opportunity. He read voraciously, and even as a boy knew some of the city's more prominent intellectuals. The wealthy New York "palace-builders" who came to Newport in the gay nineties fascinated his older brothers and sisters more than young John.[2] He recalled later that his own reputation for intelligence had already begun.

> I was very much disturbed by the fact, that I seemed to be considered a prodigy. . . . The only comfort was that the boys and girls my own age never taunted with the prodigy business, simply took me for granted for better or worse.[3]

At about the age of twelve John LaFarge quietly realized that he wished to become a priest. He later confessed that little in his early upbringing could have led him to that decision, except the gift of two books from clerical friends, a Latin missal and Cardinal Manning's The Eternal Priesthood.[4] During his second year in high school John developed appendicitis and had to discontinue his

---

[2] Ibid., pp. 40-44.

[3] Ibid., pp. 47-48.

[4] Ibid., p. 49.

studies. In 1895 the family was reunited with the father in New York, where John completed high school. There he met two Jesuit friends of his father, Fr. John Prendergast and Dr. Herman J. Heuser, who left their own mark on his future vocation.

Passing over Georgetown and Columbia Universities, LaFarge finally chose Harvard for further study. His choice of studies was influenced by Theodore Roosevelt, then police commissioner of New York and a good friend of brother Grant LaFarge. "T. R." suggested that John pursue Greek and Latin, in light of his intellectual preferences and plans. The young LaFarge gratefully accepted the advice.[5] Fifty years later his strongest memories of Harvard were George Santanyana's Wednesday evening lectures (which the young Catholic stopped attending because of the professor's bias against the Faith), Charles T. ("Copey") Copeland's English course, further training in piano and organ (for which he had talent) and Professor Ashley's course on medieval agricultural economics. Though the last seemed highly impractical at the time, LaFarge later used its principles in dealing with the social problems of rural communities.[6] One interesting insight into the young man's personality comes from his recollection that two professorial friends advised him that he was too introspective, one that he should seek the "common crowd." Since he "never got around to it," his naturally weak physical constitution often suffered throughout his Harvard years. He regularly

---

[5]Ibid., p. 59.

[6]Ibid., pp. 62-64, 70.

visited Fr. Thomas Gasson, the rector of Boston College, for advice and confession. It was the latter who suggested upon John's graduation that he continue his studies at Innsbruck. Once more "T. R." influenced John's academic career, convincing the older LaFarge and brother Bancel that Innsbruck was a good choice.

Innsbruck

In July 1901 John LaFarge sailed for Germany, where he began studies as a lay theology student at Innsbruck. The university itself was in frequent tumult from the conflicting interests of German and Italian-Austrian students. In these controversies, LaFarge later wrote, he had glimpsed the beginning of movements that would one day produce Hitler and Mussolini. At the time, however, his far more personal concern was sheer homesickness, living as he did in his own apartment rather than the seminary community. After the Christmas of 1901 LaFarge could stand the strain no longer, and entered the seminary to be "at home." It seemed to be the perfect cure.

> Once within the seminary walls, I found myself, in every sense of the word.
> . . . I groaned a bit over some of the primitive features of the life (no heat, toilet facilities), but began to thrive and enjoyed during those four years a health I had never known before.[7]

LaFarge received a solid grounding in theology from the Jesuit faculty at Innsbruck, but regretted that the only subject still absent from his curriculum was scholastic philosophy. Study in Europe provided, of course, the opportunity for travel, at that time quite cheap.

---

[7]Ibid., pp. 91, 93.

In the summer of 1902 John's mother and sister visited him for a tour through Germany. The following Easter the three again met in Rome, where the young seminarian saw both Pope Leo XIII and the future Pope Benedict XV. With no summer session to attend in 1903, John visited Paris with his mother and sister, and then England to see Henry James. After a brief period at home in Newport in the summer of 1904, John returned to Innsbruck for his final year. In January 1905, he made a retreat in which he decided to become a religious priest. The retreat master, a good Jesuit, advised the young man to join that order. After a trip to Rome for an audience with Pius X and a conference with the English Assistancy of the Society of Jesus, LaFarge's plans were complete. He was to be ordained at Innsbruck first (July 26, 1905) and then return to the United States to enter the Jesuits as a priest.[8]

"The Manner Is Ordinary"

The title of John LaFarge's autobiography is a summation of that line from the Jesuit rule which most deeply impressed his life: ". . . the manner of living as to external things is ordinary . . ." And thus his existence became when he entered the novitiate of the Society at Poughkeepsie, New York on November 13, 1905. Since he had already been ordained, LaFarge received some ministerial experience by saying Mass for the staff and patients at the Hudson River State mental hospital, and occasionally for cadets at West Point.[9]

---

[8]Ibid., pp. 123-25.

[9]Ibid., p. 133.

After his two years of novitiate LaFarge was assigned in 1907 to Canisius College in Buffalo, New York. He found the institution in turmoil, for the former German Jesuit mission was being transferred to the New York-Maryland province of the Society and arguments were raging over the use of German in the school. It came as a relief, therefore, when LaFarge was ordered to Loyola College in Baltimore for the second semester. At the end of that school year he received a long awaited opportunity for two years of study in scholastic philosophy at Woodstock College in Maryland. During his second year there LaFarge was asked to help translate a long German article for the Catholic Encyclopedia. His health had begun to fail again. In the fall of 1910 his father became gravely ill, and the months before the elder LaFarge's death on November 14, 1910 were an additional strain on the son. He returned to Woodstock after the funeral in a state of total exhaustion. His superior confronted him with the obvious fact that a life of study was physically draining on LaFarge. He was urged to try a pastoral assignment. LaFarge went for brief periods to St. Thomas Manor in Charles County, Maryland and St. Joseph's Church in Willing's Alley, Philadelphia, where he did indeed rest awhile. But his next destination was hardly calculated to give relaxation to a sick man: for eight months he worked at the hospital and penal institutions on Blackwell's Island, at one point serving as the only priest on the island. "Innsbruck and Woodstock were schools of knowledge," LaFarge reminisced, but "Blackwell's Island was a school of life and death."[10]

---

[10]Ibid., p. 152.

Southern Maryland

John LaFarge had ended his formal academic career. On September 13, 1911, he embarked on a pastoral assignment which was to last for fifteen years and profoundly affect the remainder of his life. He boarded a train for Washington, and from there sailed by steamer to the Leonardtown Wharf in St. Mary's County, Maryland, to be the new assistant pastor of St. Aloysius Church in Leonardtown. Few priests have ever ministered in Southern Maryland with a greater sense of its Catholic heritage, nor few Jesuits with a keener interest in the Society's history there. Much of this became apparent in LaFarge's preparations for Maryland's tercentennial celebration in 1934, but all that belongs to a later story. He admitted that the territory presented new challenges. Gone was the intellectual atmosphere which he had known most of his life. The people themselves, with a long history in the region, differed greatly from the ethnic groups he had met in parishes elsewhere. The blacks of Southern Maryland were almost a new experience, since the only others he had ministered to were on Blackwell's Island. In a manner that was to become typical of him, LaFarge studied the area carefully, particularly its people. He learned not merely from books and maps, however, but from his missionary rounds. These trips in Southern Maryland in the early twentieth century were no small feat. LaFarge's particular role was to develop the outlying areas of the parish, which he could reach only by circumventing, on horseback, the surrounding waterways and swamps. LaFarge himself described the task in those days.

> The missions covered an enormous territory when you considered the slow and difficult transportation of those days. With one exception, the roads from Leonardtown to Mechanicsville were mere dirt roads, impassable in winter and anything but easy in summer, so that much travel in olden days was by water. The missionary often spent several days on the road, and slept in the homes of parishioners who traditionally offered him the best of their hospitality. Many of the better old manor or plantation residences kept a special "priest's room."[11]

Such physical labor did leave a man some time to himself. Someone such as LaFarge could still become lost in thought.

> The long drives offered a chance to meditate, to think out sermons, plan lessons for instructing adults and children, or if you were of a literary mind you could think out an article. During those journeyings I began to ponder about the possible application of the social doctrine of the Church, of which I had heard so much during my Innsbruck years, to the problems of the world in which I was then living. I wondered whether some of the hardest nuts of a social kind might not be cracked if we really took earnestly the Church's social teaching and applied it to the human relations that I saw around me. Although things went along fairly calmly under a patriarchal form of life, those relations would become a source of discord and bitterness as soon as the place was opened up to the outside world. The young Negroes of the County whose fathers and mothers had been content to do odd jobs for present or former landlords, to help out on the tobacco farm or to do some work around the fishing boats, would feel very differently when they were obliged to seek occupations in the city and would run up against the stiff walls of racial discrimination. I wondered, too--the question haunted me--whether the Church might not speak definitely about the rural economy, whether a message could be obtained from the Church itself to enable the people to feel more pride in their land and more interest in keeping the integrity of their Catholic homes. These thoughts were pretty vague, yet they began to take some shape in my mind.[12]

Although the black Catholics LaFarge met were often in a depressed economic condition, he was impressed by their pride: ". . . they

---

[11] Ibid., p. 156.

[12] Ibid., pp. 168-69.

wore their proprietorship proudly and seldom complained that they did not share some of the religious advantages of their white brethren," he later wrote.[13]

LaFarge saw three major problems in the Counties, schooling, the condition of blacks, and the "rural life problem." The Xaverian Brothers had just opened a school for boys in Leonardtown, to which the Jesuit superior had suggested that an agricultural school be added. The move was not made then, but LaFarge would later embody the idea in the Cardinal Gibbons Institute.

In September 1915, John LaFarge was transferred to St. Inigoes Manor, St. Mary's City, Maryland. His knowledge of Polish was needed for ministering to a new community of Slavs at St. James in Ridge. What the new assistant noted equally well, however, was the great needs of black Catholics. He soon learned the history of these people, some of whom were descendants of former slaves of the Jesuit Fathers themselves. Two other priests lived at the St. Inigoes Manor, Fr. Brent Matthews, the superior, who ministered at St. George and St. Nicholas missions, and Fr. Abraham Emerick, responsible for St. Ignatius, St. Michael's at Ridge and St. George's Island. Prior to LaFarge's arrival, an incident had occurred at St. Michael's in Ridge, under Father Tynan as pastor. The white organist apparently refused to play after the black one; ultimately the black people were sent to St. Peter Claver Hall nearby for Mass. The latter had been built earlier for organizational functions. The two parishes have remained separate to this day. LaFarge understood

---

[13]Ibid., p. 163.

quickly the temper of race relations in the region, complicated by the frustrations of English Catholics as a rural, poor minority among their wealthier Protestant neighbors. He later commented on the missionary problem this presented.

> The plain fact was that the interests, spiritual or temporal, of the Negro in that region could never be handled in any rational and Christian manner save by men of imagination, energy, and a certain imperviousness to the terrific claims of timidity and human respect. No easy formula existed in the past; none exists today, and in all probability there will be none in the future. No matter how tactful and apologetic the pastor might be, he was told that he was moving the Negro "out of his place" the moment he treated him as a human being. He came in conflict at once with an age-old tradition by which Negroes were not to be considered as persons in their own right but only as persons subject to another's right, as servants.
> . . . The trouble was and still is in such communities that this minority [of prejudiced people] so easily takes the lead and sways a large number of people who are fundamentally well disposed but are simply unable to face any strong form of marked disapproval.[14]

In the difficulty at St. Michael's was foreshadowed the deep questions that would soon have to be faced, not only in worship but in education.

> . . . the Negroes in southern Maryland, and throughout the nation, came deeply to resent any attitude on the part of white co-religionists which would seize upon the establishment of "special works" for the Negro as an excuse for excluding them from places of worship attended by the whites, or would assign to them an unequal status in such places of worship if admitted.
> . . . Without adequate schools, the Faith would perish, and the folks themselves would be defrauded of their legitimate development.[15]

---

[14]Ibid., p. 191.

[15]Ibid., p. 193.

Ridge Schools

In the fall of 1916 LaFarge began saying Mass on alternative Sundays at St. James, for the Slavs, other white and black Catholics in the area. This was virgin territory, and he held services in a simple hall built for catechetical instruction, to which a sacristy was added eventually, with a priest's room above it. The latter was a common feature of the mission church, because Jesuits traveling on horseback often stayed overnight at the outposts they served. Land had to be cleared around the building and a barn raised for the priest's horse. That same year LaFarge began a school for the white children, under the direction of two young laywomen. The following January he opened one for the black students nearby, with a black laywoman in charge. In September 1917, John LaFarge left Ridge for one year's tertianship at St. Andrew-on-Hudson at Poughkeepsie, New York. The year's peace was interrupted only by the opportunity to preach the funeral of Mother Francis Xavier Cabrini, later canonized an American saint.[16]

Though LaFarge's health had improved little during these years, his superiors were impressed by his work in the Counties. He returned to Ridge in June 1918, to begin a period he later called

---

[16]Ibid., p. 198. Mother Frances Xavier Cabrini, foundress of the Missionary Sisters of the Sacred Heart, was born in Italy in 1850. She emigrated to the United States, became a naturalized citizen, and worked with her nuns in charitable efforts for many years. She became the first American saint. See New Catholic Encyclopedia, s.v. "St. Frances Xavier Cabrini," by A. M. Melville.

"the hardest years of my life."[17] The black school had continued in his absence, under the able dedication of Mrs. Jenny Beale, and financial support from the Blessed Sacrament Sisters and Father Kramer of the Board of Colored Missions. But the two lay teachers at the white school had had to leave, with no replacements. In September, however, LaFarge did find four Missionary Servants of the Blessed Trinity who agreed to open a white school at St. Michael's in Ridge. To support these educational endeavors LaFarge begged funds from friends in New York and Washington, D.C., a task he found distasteful. It had its advantages, though. "The necessity for obtaining funds forced me to come out of my shell . . ." he later admitted, "to think over problems with a wider perspective, and to study the unusual history of the place where I was working."[18]

One result of these efforts was a lecture before the Catholic Club of New York City on Catholicism in Southern Maryland. Another was the first article LaFarge ever wrote for _America_ magazine on blacks. In December 1921, "Full Measure for the Negro" appeared.

---

[17]LaFarge, _The Manner_, p. 199. "The years 1918 to 1922 were years of struggle, in many respects the hardest years of my life, certainly those in which I felt most helpless and abandoned by everything human. . . . I felt deep revulsion at having to seek outside aid for my work. I could appeal to plenty of friends and relatives. . . . But it was extremely disagreeable to me to pass the hat and talk money to people . . ."

[18]Ibid.

> Whatever we can give the Negro, it is certainly plain that the colored people of this country have so far not secured for themselves the most valuable elements in our white man's civilization.[19]

Their heritage, LaFarge had learned, was a system of tenancy, credit and vote-bartering. Even their religion had been more emotional than helpful. LaFarge put his emphasis on education. While it was true that a few blacks had achieved considerable academic success, society was dependent upon a broader foundation.

> . . . the very best in our civilization is not the striking accomplishments of a few, it is rather the habits and principles by which a man's nature is developed, individually, into a fully rounded character, and socially so that it be adjusted and perfected in the most important human relationships. Given these essentials, the fine fruits of civilization will follow in due course.[20]

Drawing upon his current experience in Ridge, LaFarge called for physical, intellectual and moral training of black Catholics, in rural areas and large cities. The domestic life of the rural black, he continued, should have a material base in land ownership, an economic base in agricultural and industrial training and a spiritual base in strong marriages. LaFarge's sentiments were those of the Southern University Race Commission, which he quoted: "The solution of all human problems rests upon rightly directed education."[21] Since Christianity had taught the world for centuries, hers should be the voice speaking to black Americans. Apparently LaFarge was also

---

[19]LaFarge, "Full Measure for the Negro," *America*, 17 December 1921, p. 197.

[20]Ibid.

[21]Ibid., p. 198.

aware of some efforts to organize black Catholics, for he referred in the article to the good inherent in such a step.[22]

Whether this comment had been related to Turner's early committee work is not clear, but LaFarge did mention the black scientist in his next *America* article. He quoted Turner's remarks to the Catholic Men's Council Convention in Washington, D.C., about the race problem as an issue not of the black man's capacity, but of the white man's attitude.[23] Now was the time, LaFarge insisted, to do as Senator David I. Walsh had suggested at the same convention; "take the Negro by the hand, and lead him into his rightful inheritance."[24] Others had already begun. Catholics could not afford to miss this opportunity, for the Church alone possessed the key to a spontaneous and natural development of blacks. She as the mother of civilization could best interpret it to her children. "A hundred agencies may claim the Negro's activity and enthusiasm, but the Catholic Church alone can reach his mind and heart," LaFarge wrote.[25] That she had already done so was obvious in hundreds of black Catholic homes in Southern Maryland. How was the Church to achieve this result elsewhere? Through Catholic leaders among the black race.

---

[22]Ibid., "The possibilities for good, not merely for the Negro himself, but for the Church at large, of a solid union of all American colored Catholics, such as is now contemplated by the National Council of Catholic Men, is not to be overlooked."

[23]LaFarge, "The Immediate Negro Problem," *America*, 24 December 1921, p. 221.

[24]Ibid.,

[25]Ibid., p. 222.

> . . . however we may view the matter, the colored man is
> deeply influenced by those of his own race. The Negro alone,
> with rare exceptions, can fully understand the Negro, and
> obtain from him full confidence. The ears that are deaf,
> through suspicion or indifference, to the most earnest
> exhortations of the white man, will respond at once to the
> simple, but intensely sympathetic tones of even a rambling,
> unlettered speaker of their own race.
> . . . by leaders we mean men and women who will lead;
> not those who will shine like stars in a summer sky, but
> practical folk, who will get down to business, and tell their
> colored brethren what they have to do to lead a sensible,
> profitable Christian life; who will show them in a prac-
> tical manner how to do it, and instruct them in direct
> language that they can understand.[26]

Such practicality, LaFarge went on, could be found in the training of Tuskegee and Hampton Institutes. The Catholic Church should build just such institutions of her own. LaFarge made this point, of course, while planning the Cardinal Gibbons Institute, which he was often later to call a Catholic Tuskegee. More will be written on that subject later.

The issue of black Catholic leaders raised the obvious question of a native clergy. LaFarge viewed this as an undeniable need, but believed it would follow, not precede the development of a strong laity.

> . . . in the writer's humble opinion, the immediate
> problem, the gist and pith of all the rather academic
> discussion in these two papers, is that of the training
> of colored Catholic lay leaders. Accomplish this
> immediate task, and I believe that the more difficult
> problem of the colored clergy will solve itself as a
> matter of course.[27]

---

[26]Ibid. LaFarge referred to one discouraged Catholic leader, possibly Turner, who complained that non-Catholics had been the only ones to organize his race.

[27]Ibid.

The emphasis on education apparent in these articles, and inherent in LaFarge's pastoral activity, stemmed largely from his view of the mission apostolate. (It should be kept in mind, of course, that the Jesuit work in the Maryland Counties and black Catholic work throughout the country were seen as missionary endeavors.) To LaFarge the heart of every Catholic mission had always been its school. Indeed, the heart of the Catholic Faith itself was a deposit of truth. LaFarge reflected on this view in later years.

> I was occasionally asked why I was so persistent in trying to start the Ridge schools in view of all the difficulties connected with them. My answer is simple. It is because the Church is not complete without its schools . . . especially if one considered the very nature of our Faith. The Faith for us is a deposit, entrusted by the Eternal Son of God to human hands at the foundation of His Church, to be passed on intact until the end of time, yet forever growing in meaning with the development of the human race.[28]

The white school at St. Michael's suffered in its first years, since the Missionary Servants of the Blessed Trinity (not really religious sisters but misfits from other communities) proved entirely unsatisfactory. After much heartache and embarrassment, LaFarge dismissed the teachers in 1920. For the next two years young laywomen shouldered the burden until the Sisters of St. Joseph arrived in 1922. In the fall of 1924 the Oblate Sisters of Providence opened a consolidated black school at St. Peter Claver in Ridge. These academic advances had caused LaFarge to neglect another small mission in the woods, St. Nicholas, which was three-fourths black and one-fourth white. The parishioners had always worshipped together, sharing

---

[28]LaFarge, The Manner, pp. 203-204.

much the same interest on preserving a strong family life. In them
LaFarge could watch, however, many of the changes he knew were coming to
Southern Maryland. As black and white lost their traditional economic
interdependence, he wondered, how would they continue to relate to one
another? Would they opt eventually for a total separation? LaFarge hoped
not.

> . . . would they realize that they were still bound
> by a common interest . . . more cultural and civic and
> spiritual . . . somehow they would be <u>obliged</u> to discover
> a common working basis, if they were both to survive.
> The Cardinal Gibbons Institute, secondary school for
> Negroes which I helped to establish at Ridge, was
> an attempt to reach such a common basis.[29]

The Cardinal Gibbons Institute

In 1916 the state of Maryland provided funds for the establishment of an industrial school for blacks in Southern Maryland. Jesuit Fathers Matthews, Emerick and LaFarge gathered those interested in such a project at St. Peter Claver's Hall on a Sunday in November. They proposed that such a school be a Catholic one, a counterpart of the St. Mary's Industrial School for white boys in Baltimore, directed by the Xaverian Brothers. "It was conceived definitely as a reform school," LaFarge recalled in his autobiography.[30] With the support of those present at the meeting, the priests approached Cardinal Gibbons, who approved the plan and donated $8,000 for the purchase of property. A site was selected directly across from St. Peter

---

[29] Ibid., p. 207

[30] Ibid., p. 209. Material for this background is taken from LaFarge's autobiography as well as a history LaFarge wrote for Horace B. McKenna, "Colored Catholics in St. Mary's County," <u>Woodstock Letters</u> 79 (February 1950): 55-78.

Claver Church, the old "Pembroke Farm" on Smith's Creek, and the title vested in a corporation known as the St. Peter Claver's Institute. The war intervened and nothing more was attempted for its duration. With Cardinal Gibbons' death in 1921, new possibilities were explored. LaFarge consulted Dr. Turner, Eugene Clarke and several people at the National Catholic Welfare Conference, including Fr. R. A. McGowan, Miss Mary Lynch and Miss Agnes Regan. The black educators urged that the aims of the Institute be expanded, pointing out that Protestant education among blacks aimed much higher than reform schools. The personnel at N.C.W.C. recommended Arthur C. Monahan of their Education division, an expert on black education in the South. Monahan suggested not only a general scholastic program, but one broader than that of an agricultural institution. He advised a coeducational student body, a black principal and an effort to enlist widespread popular support. On October 25, 1921, a meeting was held at N.C.W.C. headquarters with Fathers Matthews, Casey, LaFarge and the newly appointed Archbishop Curley of Baltimore. Plans were laid for a national school to be directed by a lay board. The school would be open to Catholic and Protestant black students, and administered by an all-black faculty. These plans were approved by Archbishop Curley on February 6, 1922. The first board meeting, held at N.C.W.C. headquarters on April 25, 1922, included a cross section of clerical, lay, black, white, Protestant and Catholic members. The official chairman of the board was Archbishop Curley, with Admiral William S. Benson, ret., as vice-chairman. (Thomas W. Turner was an original member of that board, and as mentioned earlier was even offered the post of first principal.) The board hired Victor H. Daniel as the school's principal and his wife, Constance E. H. Daniel, as assistant principal.

Although land had been purchased six years earlier, the property had not been developed further. The Supreme Board of the Knights of Columbus voted at Montreal in September 1923 to assess each member five cents, donating the total of $38,000 to the Institute for the erection of its first building. Auxiliary organizations of the Institute were soon established in several locations, and as mentioned in chapter II, the Federation supported the school as a special project. Indeed, LaFarge wrote in later years of the Institute as the "first national Catholic project for the Negro in the United States," and as giving meaning, even birth, to the Federation.[31] What is equally significant is that he saw this endeavor later as the spearhead of the entire interracial movement in the United States.[32] On October 26, 1924 the first building of the Cardinal Gibbons Institute was dedicated and the first school year launched. There were twenty-eight students, some boarding and some day pupils. In the same year Victor Daniel began agricultural conferences with farmers in the surrounding community, which led eventually to an extensive program of home improvement, agricultural fairs and exhibits, education in health and sanitation and occasional night classes for adults.

---

[31]LaFarge, The Manner, p. 212. As mentioned in chapter III, Markoe viewed LaFarge's interest in the Federation as intimately tied to his work for the Institute. In an article for the November 1929 issue of the Chronicle, LaFarge had said, "Out of their work for the Institute has come the work of the Federation itself. . . ." (p. 7)

[32]McKenna, p. 72.

These additional programs were part of the initial plan of the Institute, which LaFarge viewed as a Catholic Tuskegee, as well as an American version of the Danish folk schools. The latter were based on the philosophy that children are best educated through education of the community.[33] This community work continued even after the Institute was forced to close in 1933.

When LaFarge left Southern Maryland to join the staff of America in 1926, he retained membership in the Institute's Board of Trustees and therefore an active voice in the school's affairs. Although the pastor of St. Peter Claver's Church was the official chaplain of the Institute, LaFarge remained the liaison between Jesuit superiors and the school.[34] Funds were provided by the General Education Board, the Julius Rosenwald Fund, the state of Maryland and the American Catholic Home Mission Board.[35] Initial expenses were high,

---

[33]LaFarge; "A Catholic Folk School," America, 8 June 1927, pp. 233-34.

[34]LaFarge to Superior General Vladimir Ledochowski, 26 December 1931; LaFarge to Edward C. Phillips, 6 June 1933; LaFarge to Emile Mattern, 20 July 1933; Phillips to LaFarge, 11 December 1933; LaFarge to Phillips, 15 December 1933; LaFarge to Phillips, 22 March 1934;, Phillips to LaFarge, 26 February 1934; LaFarge to Phillips, 29 March 1934; LaFarge to Ledechowski, 20 February 1934; LaFarge, "Memorandum on the Cardinal Gibbons Institute at Ridge, Md.," 20 May 1934; Phillips to LaFarge, 5 June 1934; LaFarge to Phillips, 10 June 1934; LaFarge to Phillips, 15 September 1934; LaFarge to Phillips, 11 November 1934; LaFarge to Phillips, 18 December 1934; Phillips to LaFarge, 21 December 1934; LaFarge to Phillips, 23 December 1934;, Phillips to LaFarge, 1 January 1935; LaFarge to Phillips, 6 January 1935; LaFarge to Phillips, 12 January 1935; Phillips to LaFarge, 15 January 1935; LaFarge to Phillips, 17 January 1935; Phillips to LaFarge, 24 May 1935; LaFarge, memorandum on Cardinal Gibbons Institute, 12 September 1935. All the above are among the LaFarge Papers.

[35]LaFarge, "The Cardinal Gibbons Institute," Commonweal, 17 February 1932, p. 434.

however, and when LaFarge came to New York he established a fund raising committee there. His brother, O. H. P. LaFarge, vice-president of General Motors Acceptance Corporation, served as chairman, replacing Admiral Benson. O. H. P. LaFarge gathered his New York friends together, transferred the existing funds to New York, and stimulated interest there in the new school. But he became ill, and John LaFarge had to assume his post.[36] This new position tied him to the Institute's affairs even more closely, but distance was a disadvantage. The depression made it impossible to do more than meet current operating expenses. The original debts remained. Arthur C. Monahan, secretary of the board, resigned. There is strong evidence of incompatibility between Monahan as direct overseer of the Institute and the Daniels as its administrators.[37] On September 30, 1931 George K. Hunton, a New York attorney and friend of the LaFarge family, replaced Monahan. The following year he signed an agreement with the Institute and the Blessed Sacrament Sisters to establish a New York public relations office. The funds were supplied largely by the Sisters, who were to receive the bulk of the publicity. The move, however, did centralize financial activities for the Institute in New York City.[38] Despite all efforts, however, the school's debts

---

[36]LaFarge, memorandum on Cardinal Gibbons Institute, 12 September 1935.

[37]Victor Daniel to Board of Trustees, Cardinal Gibbons Institute, 1 August 1928, LaFarge Papers.

[38]LaFarge, The Manner, p. 214. Also contract between George K. Hunton and the Blessed Sacrament Sisters and Cardinal Gibbons Institute, September 1932, LaFarge Papers.

remained. On December 31, 1933 it was forced to close. Archbishop Curley insisted that it not be opened again until all debts were paid. The Daniels were dismissed and a white social worker in the area, Mrs. Helena M. Graydon, administered the plant and carried on whatever community work was possible.

LaFarge, convinced that Archbishop Curley would never reopen the Institute for its original purpose, began a tireless campaign to establish it as a Jesuit work. Despite his efforts LaFarge succeeded only in placing a Jesuit there for a short period, during which little progress was made on the debt.[39] In January 1935 the school owed between $12,000 and $13,000 plus notes at the bank and mortgages on property. LaFarge arranged for a grant from the Friedsam Foundation for $6,500, provided the trustees of the Institute would pledge the remainder. They did so only after Archbishop Curley agreed to underwrite the amount.[40] All these delicate negotiations did not resolve the issue. Ultimately the board, unable to meet its pledges, sold the Institute property to the archdiocese for far less than its worth, and the debts were repaid. Fr. Horace B. McKenna, by then pastor of St. Peter Claver's parish across from the Institute, reopened the school in 1936, as a black Catholic secondary school. In that form it attained stable footing, especially after Nathan Pitts

---

[39] For Curley's insistence that the debt be paid, see Phillips to LaFarge, 5 June 1934. Also, on LaFarge's efforts see LaFarge to Phillips, 15 September 1934; LaFarge to Phillips, 23 December 1934; Phillips to LaFarge, 1 January 1935; LaFarge to Phillips, 6 January 1935; all in LaFarge Papers.

[40] LaFarge, Memo, 12 September 1935.

was hired as principal, along with an all-black faculty, in 1938.[41]

The reasons for the Institute's failure were many. The coming of the depression was a major factor. The pioneer character of the school may have been another. Conditions at Cardinal Gibbons were nearly primitive at first. The Daniels lived on the property with a family of seven children. Victor Daniel was principal, instructor, and often plumber, carpenter, excavator and janitor as well. It is easy to forget that the Institute was also a farm, and eventually a center for rural life instruction in the area. So it had been intended. Yet Daniel became so ill that at one point his wife had to assume the role of administrator. There is every indication that her husband suffered from exhaustion and a nervous breakdown.[42] Besides the physical problems, the Daniels were in frequent disagreement with Arthur Monahan. They grew to realize an ideological difference, as Markoe had noticed, with LaFarge as well. Finally, they found themselves in a peculiar situation when they sided with Turner during the Federation controversy. If the articles in the

---

[41] Interview with Horace B. McKenna, Washington, D.C., November 1974. LaFarge had listed the Institute as reopening in 1936 in his autobiography (p. 214), but listed the date as 1938 in McKenna, p. 72. After discussing the matter with Father McKenna, it appears the truth (insofar as he could remember) is that he tried himself to teach all courses in 1936, and hired Mr. Pitts in 1938.

[42] For evidence of the physical hardships attached to life at the Institute, see Victor Daniel to Board of Trustees, 1 August 1928, LaFarge Papers. For references to Daniel's illness, see Constance Daniel to LaFarge, n.d., LaFarge Papers. Also Turner to LaFarge, 19 March 1932, Turner Papers.

Afro-American by Cora Grace Inman were truly Constance Daniel's, the relationship of this couple with LaFarge and the Institute must have been much strained near the end.[43]

The character of Cardinal Gibbons Institute as a national Catholic secondary school for blacks had been intended to draw attention and support from as broad a base as possible. But the depression, lack of knowledge or interest in black Catholic education (especially rural) and its location away from urban Catholic centers in the North did not make this vision feasible. Markoe once remarked that even Midwestern members of the Federation found little to inspire them in a Jim Crow Southern industrial school (see chapter III). Though this was not the portrait LaFarge had intended, he too realized the difficulty of negotiating support in New York for a school in Southern Maryland. He also admitted later that a drive on the part of some people to provide a completely agricultural education had not helped, and that the establishment of Patuxent Naval Air Station during the war would have ended the need for such an effort anyway.[44]

---

[43]There was some publicity at the time of the closing of the Institute to the effect that such a move was not necessary. Apparently the Daniels resisted the decision at first. See "Gibbons Institute Trustee Accused of Insincerity," Baltimore Afro-American, 23 December 1933; "Would Reopen Gibbons Institute Just to Get State Funds," Afro-American, 30 December 1933; "Gibbons Institute Head Still at 'Farmhouse'," Afro-American, January 1934. The Daniels were still complaining about the closing three years later. See "Race Prejudice Keeps Colored Priests Out," Afro-American, 14 November 1936; Victor Daniel, letter to the editor, Afro-American, 21 November 1936. It seems the Daniels also sought additional compensation after they had left the Institute. See Phillips to LaFarge, 5 June 1934, LaFarge Papers.

[44]LaFarge, The Manner, p. 215

The thrust toward a national base had affected Archbishop Curley's attitude as well. He soon saw the project as being in the archdiocese, but not of it. LaFarge realized that Curley was not about to assume more than nominal responsibility, even as chairman of the board. Even the board itself eventually sought new leadership. LaFarge used this as a major argument for transferring the Institute to Jesuit hands, but to no avail.[45]

Finally, the affairs of the Federated Colored Catholics may have indirectly affected Cardinal Gibbons Institute. The school was in the throes of financial difficulty in 1933, the same year as the split in Federation membership. While this event may have had little financial effect on the Institute, the same individual—Archbishop Curley—was the final authority in both cases. Each was an interracial effort, and each in trouble. Curley, it seems evident, was uncomfortable with both prospects. Whether his decision to withdraw from Federation affairs prompted him to do much the same with Cardinal Gibbons (although he could not avoid the final fiscal responsibility) is not clear. The coincidence of events is at least worth mentioning. Curley did later write to LaFarge on another matter involving an interracial commitment:

> I have never had much inclination to be a "joiner," but now I keep off Committees altogether.[46]

---

[45]LaFarge to Phillips, 22 March 1934; LaFarge, "Memo," 20 May 1934 (sent to Superior General Ledechowski), both in LaFarge Papers. LaFarge was most open in his comments on Curley's attitude, which is helpful in the light of the Archbishop's handling of the Federation controversy during this same period.

[46]Curley to LaFarge, 3 January 1944, LaFarge Papers.

The failure of Cardinal Gibbons Institute was a great disappointment to LaFarge, but it never dimmed his fondest memories of those years. The Institute was his first and perhaps his most beloved interracial effort. He later viewed this school as the birthplace of the Catholic interracial movement in the United States. Specialized as it had been in the secondary training of black students, under an all-black faculty, in a rural setting, its purpose was to serve as a model that could be duplicated throughout the nation.[47] What was more, its board of directors, as well as support, was to come from a diverse group of people, cutting across racial, religious and sectional lines. It was the training ground for all future interracial work.

> Men and women connected with the Institute were destined to play a very important part in the launching of the new program. The program was destined to teach to the public the age-old lessons of the Church on the dignity of man and the natural equality of all men as children of God and brothers in Christ.
> . . . In the griefs of the Institute the interracial movement was born. Such is the age-old line of Christian history.[48]

In some respects this fact was literally true. The core of men who founded the Catholic Interracial Council were drawn from the Board of Trustees of the Cardinal Gibbons Institute. Although he realized that the Institute had taxed his energy, time and even professional

---

[47]LaFarge, "The Meaning of Cardinal Gibbons Institute," Chronicle, November 1929, p. 7.

[48]McKenna, pp. 72, 74.

development, LaFarge also knew that it was a concrete symbol of his faith in the black community and the rural life he had first met in Southern Maryland.[49]

America and the Federation

In the midst of his educational endeavors at Ridge, LaFarge received word that his mother was very ill. She died at Newport on May 2, 1925. On the day of her funeral LaFarge had a phone call in Newport asking him to report to Fr. Wilfrid Parsons, editor at *America* magazine in New York. Parsons explained there that he wished LaFarge to join the staff. The latter requested some time to settle affairs in Ridge; one year later, on July 22, 1926, he assumed his new post. Thus he began a career which was to make the LaFarge name synonymous not only with *America* magazine, but ultimately with Catholic journalism throughout the country. Indeed, some would say later that his life began at forty-six.[50] Shortly after LaFarge's

---

[49]LaFarge's interest in rural life was based at least in part on his conviction that the nation, the Church and the black man must found their strength in the land. LaFarge, "Why Rural-Life Education?" *Chronicle*, December 1929, pp. 21-22.-". . . no nation can survive if uprooted from the soil . . ."-"The colored race, as a group, must retain and hold onto the land if it is not to perish." See also LaFarge, "Doing the Truth," *Chronicle*, January 1932, pp. 4-5. "Any race, if its major part does not own the land, will perish . . . the colored population of this country should, as far as possible, live on their own land . . . furthermore that a sizable proportion of the group should actually get their living through agriculture, from the land that they themselves own and live upon."—LaFarge also had greater faith in Catholic social advances in the country than in the city. See LaFarge, "The Cardinal Gibbons Institute," p. 433: ". . . the country in the long run is more remedial than the city."

[50]"John LaFarge, S.J. (1880-1963),"*America*, 7 December 1963, p. 725.

arrival in New York, he began a series of articles on blacks in the North. He drew heavily on his Southern Maryland experience, emphasizing that black migration made the "Negro problem" as pressing in Northern cities as it was in the rural South. His warnings to the Church along this line are similar to Markoe's words in the same magazine six years earlier.[51] To ignore the issue as too explosive, LaFarge argued, was not only imprudent, unjust and unreasonable, but simply impossible. The black man's welfare was tied to too many other vital issues: home missions, American education, social justice and economic problems[52]

LaFarge's solution arose from his own experience. He had come to see "the Negro" not as a classification, but as a human being.

> The colored man not only is, but feels himself to be an ordinary human being like the rest of us. Once he has been fortunate enough to enjoy normal conditions of life and education, the fact that he is radically different from anyone else in town does not occur to him. He realizes, of course, that there are certain racial traits attaching to his group; but that there is any such profound, far-reaching difference as to constitute practically a new species "Homo" appears to him an artificial sentiment, based on previous conditions which no longer concern him, or on images aroused in other people's minds, which he can with difficulty comprehend.[53]

The only way to understand the black man's own self-image was through personal contact with him. This contact, for LaFarge, was

---

[51] Markoe, "Viewing the Negro," pp. 200-202; "The New Race Problem," pp. 582-84; "A Solution to the New Race Problem," pp. 125-26. See chapter III for complete discussion.

[52] LaFarge, "The Catholic's Voice in Negro Guidance," *America*, 23 October 1926, pp. 32-33.

[53] Ibid., p. 33.

the heart of all interracial work, for it meant a meeting of minds, where the solution to all human problems lay. Let no one believe that such contact was easy, for LaFarge himself had discovered that such knowledge comes slowly.

> You may live, talk, work and play with people for years, yet know next to nothing of their real interior make-up, simply because you have not met them on the plane that is fitted for the exchange of the best that is in you and in them. . . . But the contact of mind with mind, whether that mind be learned or simple, on the basis of our fellowship as human beings in God's service, bound to observe to the full His precepts of justice and charity, is the prerequisite for the adjustment of all human misunderstandings. When the mind in both instances are trained somewhat above the ordinary, so as to discuss causes, effects, conditions and remedies with a large and dispassionate vision, then the upward path has been begun.[54]

Since intellectual contact was central to LaFarge's approach, he stressed meetings between the leaders of both races. The educated subscribers to America may have influenced this emphasis somewhat, but the method was later applied repeatedly in LaFarge's interracial activities.[55]

Another hallmark of work among blacks to LaFarge was its missionary character. In "The Blue Horizon" he asked, why do these activities receive so little support? First, they lack appeal as anything different from ordinary parish work. Secondly, they suffer the weight of prejudice against blacks. The average white Catholic had

---

[54]Ibid., pp. 33-34.

[55]The Cardinal Gibbons Institute, Catholic Laymen's Union, Catholic Interracial Council and even the Federation, as LaFarge saw the latter, were all meant to build an interracial core of leaders who could spread their understanding of the race problem to the Catholic and American public.

difficulty seeing the effects of poverty on mission work. What was needed most was well trained personnel, from the educated and cultured classes, too, LaFarge emphasized. A few black men were also qualified for the priesthood and should be granted the opportunity to pursue their vocations.

The third in this series of articles was a further analysis of the black missions, in language which revealed LaFarge's association with the newly formed Federated Colored Catholics. He quoted the words of Kelly Miller at a recent Federation meeting, in which he urged the Catholic Church to emphasize its universality, "its most passionate claim to ascendancy."[56] Miller was only one among several non-Catholic leaders who saw the validity of the Church, LaFarge continued. They would judge the Church, however, by the treatment she accorded her present black Catholics. That only a few blacks were educated enough to judge the Church was unimportant. The voice of that few was critical.

> For if the conversion of the colored race is ever to go beyond the isolated cases of individuals; if it is ever to partake of a widespread general movement, then it can only occur through the cooperation of the leaders, mentally and morally, of their own people.[57]

LaFarge listed two major difficulties which black Catholics faced at present. One was the dangerous influences on their children from non-Catholic sources. The claims of black parents to a Catholic

---

[56]LaFarge, "The Crux of the Mission Problem," *America*, 6 November 1926, p. 80.

[57]Ibid.

education were legitimate and urgent, not matters of special privilege. Although white Catholics might not be responsible for the wrongs of the past, they were obliged to learn through personal contact with educated black Catholics about their claims to basic human rights in the Church. The second difficulty in the black apostolate was the legitimate grievances of Northern blacks about discrimination in the Church. Perhaps, LaFarge stressed, black Catholics would have to be counselled in patience, but with a frank admission that injustice did exist. The major grievances were discrimination in churches, in education on every level and the lack of interest among Northern Catholics in black activities, such as the Urban League or Tuskegee Institute. That LaFarge was drawing upon ideas gained in Federation contacts seemed evident in the last paragraphs of the article. For he warned that ignoring these grievances would only force blacks toward greater racial solidarity based purely on material needs, an argument used by the Federation in its letter to the bishops in that same year. The choice was between principle or expediency, LaFarge concluded, and in that the Church really had no choice. "We may counsel patience with wrongs, but our religion forbids us ever wholly to acquiesce in them."[58]

In the last of this series, the Jesuit described a place which had become familiar to him in the country, "Hard Corner," a spot where the "chaff and trash of rural idleness will gravitate."[59] Although

---

[58]Ibid., p. 81.

[59]LaFarge, "Hard Corner," America, 11 November 1926, p. 109.

ambitious members of the rural community migrate to the cities, they take their bad "Hard Corner" habits with them. The Church was beginning to see this phenomenon appear in the North, where Catholicism could deal with the results, but not its rural source. Few Catholic efforts had been made to help rural blacks envision a better life. Hampton, Tuskegee and Rock Castle Institutes had shown the way. Finally, Cardinal Gibbons Institute had appeared as a Catholic contribution. Its purpose was to provide character training "toward a well-ordered home life" as a major element in education. LaFarge emphasized home life because he felt that it was the heart of all social reconstruction. Character training in strong family ties could be useful in the city or country. LaFarge's experience, however, had made him especially conscious of the needs among rural blacks as they migrated to cities. "Hard Corners" were symbols of what happened in the absence of character training, and could become indictments of the Church's indifference.

> The position in which the colored Catholic finds himself in this country is a challenge to our Catholic manhood: to our mentality, our wisdom and our missionary spirit. On our response to that challenge will depend the judgment of posterity as to the genuineness of our Catholicism.[60]

The Federation influences mentioned were the result of LaFarge's growing association with Turner and the other members. LaFarge addressed the first Federated Colored Catholics convention, and reported on the second one in *America*. He compared the Federation delegates to the

---

[60]Ibid., p. 111. See also LaFarge, The Manner, p. 230:-"The work in St. Mary's County had helped me to realize how closely the life of families and thereby the salvation of souls was affected by welfare and adjustment within the rural community. I became painfully aware of the gap between the city and the country, which in many respects is greater in the United States than it is abroad."

early Christians who had met from Antioch, Rome and Alexandria to share experiences. It was a natural answer to a long felt need. After describing several highlights of the meeting, LaFarge listed the address of the official magazine, the Council Review, thereby offering an opportunity for readers to inquire.[61] A few months later LaFarge was busily preparing to host a Federation convention in New York. Apparently he was also entertaining doubts about the Federation's future, for he wrote to Turner requesting a meeting before the convention. He had conducted a recent study of Catholic organizations, learning thereby some of the keys to success in such enterprises. He did not hold much hope for the Federation unless some changes were effected soon. As mentioned in chapter II, no concrete actions appear forthcoming from these comments, although they may have served as background for LaFarge's later proposals. His concerns were in keeping with his role in the Federation at this point, for he had composed its convention resolutions, advised Turner on the letter to the bishops and prepared guest lists for the upcoming convention.[62]

LaFarge reported on the New York meeting in America, calling it the first broad meeting of black Catholics in their two hundred year-history.[63] How ironic, he pointed out, that immigrant white

---

[61] LaFarge, "The Federation of Colored Catholics," America, 1 January 1927, p. 284.

[62] LaFarge to Turner, 3 October 1926; LaFarge to Turner, 27 July 1927; LaFarge to Turner, 23 August 1927, all in Turner Papers.

[63] LaFarge, "After Two Centuries," America, 1 October 1927, p. 584. This statement was incorrect, since the Afro-American Catholic Congresses (see Chapter I) had preceded the Federation by more than thirty years.

Catholics so new to this country had so many flourishing societies! LaFarge described the convention as free from rancor or local grievances, even though many had experienced discrimination on the journey there. He mentioned also the establishment of a new interracial committee (which worked then with the N.C.W.C. in developing the Industrial Relations day at future conventions). LaFarge, however, had been impressed by something more basic than these activities.

> . . . most striking of all, as it seemed to an observer, was the fact that here was a group of Catholic laymen seeking and praying for just those spiritual advantages which their white brethren so often disregard . . .[64]

Among the greatest of these advantages was education. The Federation had pledged itself to help unite all black Catholic efforts in that direction. Once again LaFarge urged his readers to see the validity of these desires. He quoted the words of Alain Locke:

> The choice is not between one way for the Negro and another way for the rest, but between American institutions frustrated on the one hand and American ideals progressively fulfilled and realized on the other.[65]

In 1928 LaFarge published his first book, The Jesuits in Modern Times, a composite of reflections on the Jesuit spirit while on mission in Southern Maryland.[66] LaFarge posed the question, what characterizes the apostolate of Jesuits? He answered,

> . . . the Society is characterized not by preference shown to any one given form of action, but rather by the choice in every direction of those works, "other things being equal,"

---

[64]Ibid.

[65]Ibid., p. 585.

[66]LaFarge, The Jesuits in Modern Times (New York: America Press, 1928), p. 1.

which will benefit the greatest number of men with the most solid and lasting results.[67]

In a new country such as ours, society benefited most from work performed on the "outposts," rather than the settled regions. LaFarge saw four such major "outposts."

>1. Men are forgetful or ignorant of the truth.
>2. Social and economic disorder combine with physical obstacles to hinder the spread of God's kingdom in North America.
>3. A vast world of other races and tongues lies at our doors, in the West Indies and Far East, to whom the visible Church and her institutions are unknown.
>4. The Church is also faced with a supreme struggle to ensure the Christian education of youth in the United States and her possessions.[68]

LaFarge reduced all the tasks above to a single one, education. Without it, all other efforts would fail. Furthermore, the foundation of all such education was not the elementary school, but the college.

> . . . the work of education is particularly the work of the outposts of the Kingdom of God. All other activities, all other problems, are reducible sooner or later to a question of education. Moreover, all matters of primary or elementary education depends in their assumptions on higher education, particularly on the work of the colleges. The Catholic college is the very heart of the Church's apostolate. Behind it are ranged all the forces for good, all the courage and loyalty that the Church can muster. Opposed to it is every influence that tends to weaken and dissolve not only religion but our country, our liberty and our homes.[69]

This conviction provides an insight into all LaFarge's future work in the black community: his development of educated black leaders in the Catholic Laymen's Union, his emphasis on rapport between

---

[67]Ibid., p. 61.

[68]Ibid., pp. 65-66.

[69]Ibid., p. 84.

educated black and white leaders about the problems of blacks, their effort in turn to educate other white laity, through the Federation, the Catholic Interracial Council, the Clergy Conference on Negro Welfare, the Catholic Students' Mission Crusade and a host of other groups. The keynote always was education.[70]

LaFarge was involved, of course, in many social movements during this period. At the behest of Wilfrid Parsons of America, he helped to found the Catholic Rural Life Conference and faithfully attended its annual meetings. His interest in the renewal of liturgical worship was linked to these social concerns. He was a charter member, too, of the Catholic Association for International Peace. These concerns were reflected in his column, "With Scrip and Staff," first published in America under the by-line, "The Pilgrim," on December 4, 1926.

> The Pilgrim is not a wanderer. His path is rambling, and sometimes his way is cloudy. . . . Nevertheless there is a Goal. The road, wherever it leads, is the Homeward Road, in Patriam. To the peace of the Father's House in eternity, to the fullness of Catholic life in time, as the preparation for that Home, tend all Catholic events and activities. The lessons drawn by the Pilgrim from what he may note and comment upon by the wayside . . . are all lessons in the great art of the Homeward Voyage, that may be some guide to others. . . .[71]

---

[70] Thomas Harte, Catholic Organizations Promoting Negro-White Race Relations in the United States (New York: Paulist Press, 1947), pp. 26, 28. Harte himself quotes LaFarge, The Race Question and the Negro (New York: Longmans Green and Co., 1944), p. 256, in which he stresses education.

[71] LaFarge, "With Scrip and Staff," America, 4 December 1926, p. 185.

Although LaFarge's social involvement was encouraged at America, it did not meet with approval everywhere. Before the publication of the encyclical Quadrigesimo Anno in 1931, he later admitted, many people felt such problems were not religious issues. In addition, there was the "plain, hard work" involved in studying and "doing the truth" where so little guidance was available. LaFarge, however, felt the problems could not wait.

> I was convinced that the problem of social disorder which had betrayed the Old World would, if neglected, prove an abundant seed-ground for Communism even here in the United States.
> . . . The idea of a world revolution would appeal, I felt, to certain elements of the American mind: to those who felt themselves disinherited, and particularly to the discontented minority groups, the American proletariat, whether they were rural workers or racial and religious minorities.
> . . . The task, as I saw it, was one of getting to work early on the problem of social reconstruction. That meant a fundamental renewal of religious life in its totality, and particularly in its communal aspect, the renewal of communal religious worship as it was practiced in the earlier ages of the Church and was recommended by the leading liturgical scholars of the present time. Furthermore, it meant putting our shoulders to the wheel in working out the remedy for some of our grave domestic social disorders whether in the economic or the racial areas. At the same time we had an obligation to study the causes of international conflict and the obstacles to world peace.[72]

Two events affecting LaFarge's interracial work occurred in 1928, one positive and one negative. Victor Daniel wrote the Board of Trustees of the Cardinal Gibbons Institute in August, answering charges that he and his wife had not been open to suggestions. He

---

[72]LaFarge, The Manner, pp. 246, 248. Among LaFarge's many concerns must also be listed black history, the history of Southern Maryland, and Maryland's tercentennial celebration in 1934. See, for example, LaFarge, "The Unknown Field of Negro History," America, 21 July 1928, pp. 349-50; "Eucharistic Honor in Colonial Maryland," America, 22 September 1928; The Manner, chapter thirteen.

enclosed twenty pages of instructions he had been given and his response to them. The letter was a foretaste of greater troubles to come.[73] On the other hand, LaFarge proudly described in *America* of the same month the first annual retreat of the Catholic Laymen's Retreat Union, that organization which was the future basis of the first Catholic Interracial Council.[74]

LaFarge did not attend the fourth annual Federation convention in Cincinnati, because he was ill. He later mentioned it only briefly in a review of "American Catholic Life in 1928," emphasizing the first joint meeting of the Federation and the Catholic Conference on Industrial Problems.[75] In December 1928 LaFarge found himself in the minority as a Catholic priest, when he attended the National Interracial Conference in Washington, D.C. He reflected later on why the Church did not do more for blacks. Often Catholics felt they would interfere with non-Catholic work, an impression LaFarge had found dispelled at the conference. Indeed, the Jesuit felt some speakers were hinting at the need for something more than ideals, something the Church could offer. A few Catholics would still argue, of course, that American social institutions were too "crystalized" for the Church to affect them. Nonsense, LaFarge insisted; crystals could and have often been dissolved. Being a Catholic minority was

---

[73]Victor Daniel to the Board of Trustees, 1 August 1928, LaFarge Papers.

[74]LaFarge, "With Scrip and Staff," *America*, 18 August 1928, p. 451.

[75]LaFarge, "American Catholic Life in 1928," *America*, 5 January 1929, p. 306.

not the problem, LaFarge continued, quoting a conference speaker, Herbert A. Miller: ". . . new ideas come down from the class to the mass."[76] (That statement would seem the epitome of LaFarge's own view.) LaFarge continued the thought himself.

> It is the minority in any case which ultimately settles things. The only true difficulty in realizing Catholic ideals is simply that of sufficient spiritual caliber to form such an effective minority. The real work will be done always by men and women who will devote to the task their personal service.[77]

Priests and religious had been the first such dedicated individuals. Now the laymen were beginning to contribute their part. Perhaps LaFarge had in mind his newly formed Catholic Laymen's Retreat Union.

By the time of the fifth annual Federation convention in Baltimore, LaFarge was offering his services and suggestions. Among other things he wrote Turner about his intention to recommend to the assembled delegates that they form groups to discuss social questions, and also begin making retreats. The Jesuit wrote several letters of introduction for Turner, who was planning a trip abroad (see Chapter II). In September LaFarge's address to the Baltimore convention was reported favorably in an N.C.W.C. news release.

> One of the most comforting addresses of the meeting was that of the Rev. John LaFarge, S.J. . . . The discussions of the day, Fr. LaFarge said, could be summed up in the phrase, "We seek justice."

---

[76]LaFarge, "Opportunity for the Negro," *America*, 2 February 1929, p. 407.

[77]Ibid. He concluded on an interesting note. Mentioning the silver jubilee of Monsignor Olds at St. Augustine's parish in Washington, D.C., LaFarge called it "one of the most harmonious and progressive colored congregations in this country." (p. 407)

. . . "With the authentic teaching of the Church as
a basis, and the cooperation of those who have made
these matters a study," continued Fr. LaFarge, "our
colored Catholics should be able to reach some consensus
of opinion on matters concerning which they are now
divided; such as the best economic opportunities
for colored young men and women. . . "[78]

LaFarge himself reported on the entire convention in *America*, describing its keynote as confidence.

The greatest difficulty that the colored man faces
in his daily life in this country is uncertainty. Fear,
which is the child of uncertainty, is at the root of most
racial troubles.
. . . the Federation encourages confidence of the Negro
in himself, both by mutual encouragement for the members
of the race who are working to help their brethren spiritually and temporally, and as well as by increased confidence in the small group of Catholic colored men and women
who have enjoyed more than the ordinary education, and
both as practical Catholics and as unselfish laborious
workers are trying to open doors of greater opportunity
for the Catholic Negro in America.[79]

LaFarge also summarized his own address, as one which stressed the Church's social teachings as a power containing definite ideas, a value placed on individual human worth and the importance of charity. The latter, he insisted, was necessary for even a minimal social justice. The Federation's efforts to end discrimination were a means toward a positive end.

. . . it may be described as a sentiment of the
Federation . . . that the abandonment of the policy of
mere acquiescence and acceptance of objectively unfair
conditions should be final . . . adoption of some
constructive effort . . .[80]

---

[78]N.C.W.C. news release, "Industrial Relations Conference at Federated Colored Catholics Convention," 3 September 1929, LaFarge Papers.

[79]LaFarge, "Colored Catholics Discuss Their Situation," *America*, 14 September 1929, p. 544.

[80]Ibid., p. 546.

Another important event at the Baltimore convention, of course, was the introduction of William Markoe and the Chronicle to the Federation. LaFarge had at least been aware of Markoe's work earlier, as he described it in America of April 1929.[81] (He had also written Markoe at the time of the latter's articles in America. See Chapter III.) The Federation provided a basis, however, for continuous cooperation between the two priests. Almost immediately after the convention LaFarge sent some notes to Markoe for his private use on the question of black priests. In them he insisted that the basic argument for a native clergy should not be that they would be more effective, but rather that all groups should enjoy all seven sacraments of the Church. This approach avoided the question of effectiveness and took the issue out of the realm of race. "The real strength of the truly Catholic position," LaFarge argued, "is in its ignoring of race."[82]

LaFarge contributed to the Chronicle almost immediately, although he did not begin his regular column, "Doing the Truth," until 1931. In his first Chronicle article he discussed the Cardinal Gibbons Institute, assuring his readers that it was not a separatist project.

> It is simply to provide a specialized help on definite lines which simply cannot be given by any other Catholic institution, because the Institute is of its very nature

---

[81]LaFarge, "With Scrip and Staff," America, 27 April 1929, p. 67.

[82]LaFarge, "Notes on the Question of the Negro Priesthood," 1 October 1929, LaFarge Papers.

> a community work growing right from the people, with the people, for the people.[83]

His description of its aims was a concise summary of LaFarge's rural philosophy.

> . . . the Institute aims to provide our youth with every possible means of gaining an intelligent and practical economic foothold on the land, in the belief that the possession and the intelligent use of the land by any group of people is the surest guarantee of their economic permanence and their eventual economic triumph.[84]

This emphasis on land ownership was expanded in LaFarge's second article for the Chronicle. "No nation can survive if uprooted from the soil," he declared.[85] Ancient Rome and modern England had proved that. One reason for the success of urban Jews was their emphasis on land ownership. Secondly, the Church's own source of population had always been the country, which had supplied her city parishes. The black race, too, must learn this lesson.

> Moreover, it is not merely a question of bare ownership, but of utilizing an opportunity which is really the basic economic opportunity of human life . . . a root should be retained on the land by the colored race in this country.[86]

Dr. Turner became ill while in Europe at the end of 1929, and Eugene Clarke and George Conrad were burdened by professional responsibilities, leaving Markoe the most active Federation officer (see Chapter II). It was during Markoe's tour of several cities to promote

---

[83]LaFarge, "The Meaning of Cardinal Gibbons Institute," p. 7.

[84]Ibid., pp. 7-8.

[85]LaFarge, "Why Rural-Life Education?" p. 21.

[86]Ibid., pp. 21-22.

the Federation that he discovered a growing division between the Daniels at Cardinal Gibbons Institute and LaFarge, who might have been unconscious of it. Later Markoe described it as a clash between the philosophies of W. E. B. DuBois (the Daniels) and Booker T. Washington (LaFarge).[87] Meanwhile LaFarge himself had begun corresponding with the Josephite author, John T. Gillard. The latter published his study of <u>The Catholic Church and the American Negro</u> in 1929. Archbishop Curley (as Gillard's bishop) requested LaFarge to write the foreword.[88] After reviewing the manuscript, however, LaFarge wrote that his own misgivings would prevent him from doing so. Subsequently, he sent a detailed list of comments, positive and negative, which Curley forwarded to Gillard. The latter had apparently already revised portions, and sent the final copy to LaFarge, with a comment that the entire work might prove "irritating" to some. LaFarge's response was telling, in the light of his later noninvolvement in the Federation controversy. "In the long run," he wrote to Gillard, "pacific methods appear to accomplish more in the work for souls, when dealing with men of good faith."[89]

---

[87]Markoe, "An Interracial Role," pp. 142-43.

[88]It seems that Curley had sent the manuscript to LaFarge, whom he had known from the Jesuit's Southern Maryland ministry and current involvement in the Cardinal Gibbons Institute, because the bishop did not have time to read it himself. He apparently had also been asked to write the foreword.

[89]LaFarge to Gillard, 11 May 1930; see also LaFarge to Gillard, 14 February 1930; LaFarge to Curley, 11 March 1930; Curley to Gillard, 12 March 1930; Gillard to Curley, 16 March 1930, all in Gillard Papers.

Although LaFarge had promised to promote the book, his review for the Chronicle included some of his initial objections, particularly his regret that Gillard had chosen to express personal views in an otherwise factual work. The nature of those opinions also bothered LaFarge. ". . . Fr. Gillard's remarks . . . give an impression of distrust, almost of pessimism, concerning the race."[90] Obviously Gillard was not pleased with LaFarge's remarks, and said so. He complained that LaFarge had "consigned my book to the limbo of apocryphal literature."[91] The Jesuit responded that he had felt it only fair to speak so forthrightly in the Chronicle, a journal of black opinion. He had avoided negative remarks in his America article. Gillard was apparently reconciled by this letter, for he wrote LaFarge about the need for various orders engaged in work among blacks to share ideas. He reiterated his conviction, however, that criticism might only encourage those intelligent blacks who were already only too willing to humiliate the Josephites.[92]

Two months after this exchange the two men had the opportunity to share ideas in person, for which LaFarge was grateful. He wrote that he could not understand, however, why Gillard felt the Josephites could not speak frankly to their bishops on the race issue.

---

[90]LaFarge, "Fr. Gillard's Study," p. 151.

[91]Gillard to LaFarge, 30 June 1930, Gillard Papers.

[92]LaFarge to Gillard, 1 July 1930; Gillard to LaFarge, 3 July 1930, both in Gillard Papers. The phrase Gillard used about humiliating the Josephites was more picturesque: to "take down the pants" of the Josephites!

> I believe that it is no longer prudence, but a grave imprudence, to be too timid in stating boldly and clearly the essential rights of the Negro as a human being; both in the natural order, and in the economy of the Church. I say advisedly as <u>a human being</u>, not as a member of this or that race. Passionate—in the case of Catholics, practically heretical—race prejudice has been met by passionate race defense. Fundamentally, it is not a question of race, but of humanity. The Church in this country is in serious danger of being neglectful on the preaching of fundamental human rights. Whether it applies to the Negro, or to the laborer, or to the unborn child, makes little difference. In each case human passion, the astuteness and malice of the evil spirit are arrayed against Christ's own teaching; and worldly reasons are alleged which can often deceive even the elect.[93]

LaFarge also disagreed with what he felt was Gillard's preference for priests speaking frankly among themselves, rather than before "unlettered Negroes," as in the <u>Chronicle</u>. The number of educated blacks was on the rise, LaFarge maintained, and even less educated blacks discussed racial issues more than whites realized. The Church must allow blacks a voice, even when it was crude and "un-Catholic." The important task was to get <u>beyond</u> a racial viewpoint.

> Our task is slowly, steadily, to guide them into the true Catholic manner of expression: to move from the primarily racial to the primarily human viewpoint. That we priests and white Catholics can only do, when we <u>ourselves</u> have laid aside the racial viewpoint—as anything <u>essential</u> in human life. And this is a matter of no small patience.[94]

At the executive committee meeting of January 1930, LaFarge had the opportunity to embody some of his hopes for a broad Catholic effort to secure basic human rights. It is not clear who actually

---

[93]LaFarge to Gillard, 30 September 1930, Gillard Papers.

[94]Ibid.

wrote the series of proposals to adopt Catholic Action as the objective of the Federation, but LaFarge was thanked for his great help at the meeting, and Markoe and Turner were not present. The ideas seem couched in a language peculiar to LaFarge. The goal of the Federation was transformed into a broadly Catholic one.

> The general objective of the Federation is the promotion of Catholic Action amongst the Negro Catholics of the United States. By Catholic Action is understood the participation of the layman in the apostolic work of the hierarchy of the Catholic Church.[95]

This meant that all activity would be seen in relation to the apostolate as an active force in the Church. This was to be no group established merely for annual conventions. Although its major concern would be with black Catholics, it would promote all phases of Catholic Action: liturgy, education, rural life, retreats. Even interracial efforts would be conducted with a new outlook.

> It means . . . that the Federation takes up interracial questions from the higher standpoint of Catholic Action, looking at them always from an apostolic and truly Catholic point of view. Where in the other lines of activities just mentioned the interracial problem occurs,

---

[95]"Catholic Action as the Objective of the Federation," Chronicle, March 1930, p. 51. This objective should be compared with that given for the Federation at its founding: "The purpose of the organization . . . is to bring about a closer relation and a better feeling among all Catholic negroes, to advance the cause of Catholic education throughout the negro population, to seek to raise the general church status of the negro and to stimulate colored Catholics to a larger participation in racial and civic affairs." (News article, "Colored Catholics Organize Society," 29 December 1924, Turner Papers). The original purpose of the organization was also embodied in article III of its constitution:--"The object of this Federation shall be to bring about a closer union and better feeling among all Catholic Negroes. . . ."The rest of the article is as the new article above. See "The Constitution of the Federated Colored Catholics of the United States," Chronicle, November 1929, pp. 27-29.

as it not infrequently does, it will also be considered from that standpoint. Hence there should be amongst the members of the Federation men and women who, spiritually formed and trained, will give particular thought to the truly Catholic view of these practical problems.[96]

Finally, the proposals suggested that at least one speaker address each phase of Catholic Action at the next convention; that committees be formed for each, with the chairman serving on a National Catholic Action Council; and that a Speaker's Bureau be established to provide Federation representatives to address other Catholic organization meetings. The last two suggestions, though favorably received, were never fully implemented. That they were LaFarge's ideas, however, seems evident both from correspondence with Turner, and from the fact that the Catholic Laymen's Union later incorporated them into its activities.[97]

LaFarge reported the events of the Detroit convention in an article for America entitled "What Do the Colored Catholics Want?" The question had been posed in Detroit. Hinting that a fuller statement would be forthcoming from black Catholics themselves, LaFarge listed the items he felt sure would be included. Black Catholics wanted economic opportunity, a Catholic education and freedom to pursue religious vocations for their children, the right to worship without humiliation and aid from other Catholics in building necessary institutions. They did _not_ seek social equality, "in the obnoxious sense attached to this word," he assured his white readers.

---

[96] Ibid., p. 524.

[97] Ibid., p. 66. See also LaFarge to Turner, 11 February 1930, Turner Papers. LaFarge, "The Laymen's Union," _Interracial Review_, April 1934, p. 42.

They do not want to interfere with the comfort or peace of mind of their white brethren, any more than can be helped. They do not wish to push themselves where they are not desired, but only to obtain the goods that God Himself wishes them to desire.[98]

---

[98]LaFarge, "What Do Colored Catholics Want?" p. 567.-"They want to earn a decent livelihood; free from interference based merely on racial attitudes.--They want such opportunity to extend to all legitimate forms of gainful employment, and to include adequate means of self-improvement through credit, housing facilities, recreation, and other public utilities.--They want their boys to be priests and their girls to be nuns.--They want such educational facilities as will fit their boys to be priests and their girls to be nuns.--They want to educate all their boys and girls in Catholic schools, from the primary school to the university, according to each one's native ability.--They want admission to Catholic institutions already frequented by the general body of white pupils (1) where the denial of such admission is not prescribed by law, as it is in the Southern States; (2) where such denial involves the loss of a tangible good, to which as Catholics and human beings they may legitimately lay claim; (3) where such exclusion is based on purely racial considerations, and not on objective standards of conduct, capacity, or decorum.--They want to attend Holy Mass and the services of the Church, to receive the Sacraments, and hear the Word of God, without suffering humiliating inconveniences based neither on the law of the land, nor on the practices of the Universal Church, nor on any objective, remediable conditions of the group, but merely racial considerations. --They want the practical charity of Catholics to aid them in obtaining such churches, schools, or welfare institutions, as will specially benefit their group, when, as a group, they experience special needs, due to depressed and disadvantageous conditions, location, poverty, vocational handicaps, etc.; when such establishments will be understood as fitting them for taking their full part in the life of the Church and the nation, and shall in no wise be looked upon as a means of excluding them from advantages legitimately theirs." (p. 566)--This list of needs was later used by the Federation for an official statement. LaFarge admitted to Turner that the list was "an expression of what is in justice due; not a statement of everything that one might possibly want as the ultimate ideal." He also insisted that if they were published elsewhere than in the Chronicle, they should come from the Federation "members" and not himself. See LaFarge to Turner, 5 October 1930, Turner Papers.--Apparently all white Catholics did not believe that blacks were not seeking "social equality." A November 29, 1930 comment in Ave Maria magazine took exception to the convention resolution calling for equality in education. The editor declared that many white Catholics were not ready for mixed schools. See Ave Maria, 29 November 1930, pp. 695-96. Markoe met this objection in an editorial for the Chronicle in January 1931. LaFarge also

Above all black Catholics wished to be treated not as a problem, but as human beings sharing in the Redemption of Christ. If white Catholics in their many organizations, priests and nuns would cooperate with the Federation's Catholic Action program, this could be accomplished.

LaFarge pursued this theme of viewing blacks as human beings in a radio address for the Interracial Hour in October 1931. He admitted a certain reluctance to talk about blacks, when members of the race could do so more effectively. His intention, however, was to overcome some of the "indifference and confusion" among white people.[99] The black man was most evident to white people in the city, where he was often seen merely as a problem. To solve this "problem," white people must come to view blacks not as a race but as a people. LaFarge recalled the portrait of blacks in "Green Pastures" as an example. A people was united by common experiences. Black Americans shared a common ancestry, a common plight of slavery and poverty and above all "the white man's attitude on race." If blacks were united racially it was in defense against a situation not of their own creation. Most blacks considered prejudice as an outgrowth of ignorance, LaFarge said. Once again he enumerated the black man's basic desires, this time more generally. Such goals would be met only by "painstaking study" by intelligent people working together. He left discussion of the Catholic contribution for a future talk.

---

made a passing criticism of the article in _America_. See LaFarge, "Poisoning Negro Youth,' _America_, 24 January 1931, p. 377.

[99]WLWL, "The Negro in the City," 15 October 1930. Copy in LaFarge Papers.

In January 1931, LaFarge addressed another audience, this time the American Interracial Seminar meeting in New York City. There he struck the theme of "The Negro and Security." Many white people had difficulty understanding why the black man objected so to "Little arrangments" which reminded him of the past. Why couldn't he forget the past? Because it extended into the present, LaFarge argued.

> We shall never get the public to understand the Negro's point of view until we can get before them a clear idea of the extent and significance of the American Negro's condition of insecurity.[100]

Even blacks themselves often failed to realize how little they resembled the portrait of a happy, carefree race. They lived instead in constant fear of lynching, unemployment, mistreatment of black women and ever present public discrimination. Oddly, however, these facts were not apparent to most whites.

> . . . they are not old stuff to the general public. They simply do not know these things; and they must be told, and their connection explained with what seems matters of pure sentiment.[101]

The solution to the race problem lay first not in psychological adjustments, but in ordinary justice. ". . . if men are provided with the security of the goods of life and of person which their nature demands," LaFarge insisted, "the psychological will take care of itself." Often it was true, justice was difficult to determine. When, for example, was it just to accept the provision of all-black

---

[100] LaFarge, "The Negro and Security," address delivered before the American Interracial Seminar, New York City, 2 January 1931, LaFarge Papers.

[101] Ibid.

facilities? LaFarge based his judgment on rules established at the recent Detroit convention.

> . . . in all such doubtful cases the thing to consider was precisely, does such a gift or provision contain, or not contain, an implicit threat of greater insecurity or injustice than now exists? While offering certain evident goods, <u>does it tend</u> to deprive the Negro of other goods, say civic or economic, to which, as a human being, or a citizen, he has an inalienable right?[102]

How could white men be motivated to grant the black man his just claims? Enlightened self-interest could be one motivating factor, since any institution based on less than sound principles would ultimately suffer from "the quaking sands of popular taste and distaste." This reasoning would never prove sufficient, however; disinterested charity would be needed for complete success.

> . . . in the last analysis, our contributions to the security of the Negro will depend on our willingness to recognize the principles of our absolutely common interests. . . . The higher our concept of the community of spiritual destiny, the more it contains of the eternal and not merely the temporal, the surer will be the foundation on which to build our security.[103]

The Detroit convention seemed to have given the Federation a renewed sense of purpose. In January 1931, LaFarge published an article entitled "Poisoning Negro Youth." In it he criticized an address by Clarence Darrow to the Howard University student body,

---

[102] Ibid. As an example of an all-black institution that blacks could consider justifiable, LaFarge later pointed to the new black Catholic hospital in St. Louis, in his <u>America</u> column. See "With Scrip and Staff," <u>America</u>, 6 December 1930, p. 216.-"It is felt that [the] cause of interracial understanding would be effectively promoted if a hospital for the colored were organized under the auspices of white Sisters."

[103] Ibid.

urging the latter to depend on their own resources rather than religion to solve the racial problem. This was what the future leaders of the race were exposed to daily, LaFarge declared. What about the black Catholics who were surely sitting in the audience? Why were they deprived of a decent Catholic education? Who was to blame? he asked.[104]

Turner and LaFarge apparently decided to find out, for Turner made initial contact with Dr. John Cooper at the Catholic University of America, to try to open the doors there.[105] For his part LaFarge began to write again of the Cardinal Gibbons Institute, now interpreting it as a form of Catholic Action. When the Institute appeared under attack as one more "back-to-the-farm" effort, LaFarge replied that it meant only to prevent the _total_ disruption of rural life. Its lessons were a solid preparation as well for those black youths who later migrated to cities.

> It's [Institute's] peculiar pertinence to Catholic Action resides therein that the principle underlying it is that of bettering the actual living conditions of the Negro group, by direct, concrete action, which is _one of_ the principal tasks the Church must undertake today.[106]

LaFarge reiterated this same view when he asked Turner to answer the criticisms of the Institute. Although the black man _was_ not a problem, LaFarge wrote, he surely _had_ problems. Therefore, Catholic Action

---

[104]LaFarge, "Poisoning," pp. 376-77.

[105]Turner to LaFarge, 7 February 1931; LaFarge to Turner, 13 February 1931, both in Turner Papers.

[106]LaFarge to Augustine Walsh, 16 April 1931, Turner Papers.

toward the race must mean not mere charity, but helping to <u>change</u> the economic conditions in which blacks found themselves.

> The Negro problem in the vulgar racial sense is, of course, fictitious. But the Negro has a very bitter economic and social-welfare problem, and it is not justice or kindness to him to ignore it. As I see it, the heart of the Institute work consists in the attempt not merely to minister to the Negro in the conditions in which he finds himself, but to actually remedy these conditions by whatever humble and persistent means are at our disposal and thereby fit him to take his part not <u>merely</u> in rural life but in whatever career, whether in city jobs, or in further educational work, or professional training, he may find himself.
>
> . . . The more I study the matter, the more conversations I have with experienced men both of the colored group and of the white the more convinced I am of the tremendous soundness of our program and its potentialities for good, provided it is linked up with Catholic principles.[107]

The remarks above indicate that the Detroit convention's emphasis on Catholic Action had produced the kind of interracial program which LaFarge heartily approved.

As the St. Louis convention approached, LaFarge began to prepare his <u>Chronicle</u> readers. If anyone doubted the Church's concern for economic questions, he wrote, he would learn differently in St. Louis. Indeed, every Federation delegate should bring a copy of the new papal encyclical, <u>Quadrigasimo Anno</u>, for it would be much discussed there. Pope Pius XI had merely summarized in the document a long history of Christian teaching on the subject.

> Catholic theologians and philosophers have always discussed matters relating to man's temporal welfare as well as his spiritual, once the question of right and wrong entered in.[108]

---

[107]LaFarge to Turner, 7 April 1931, Turner Papers.

[108]LaFarge, "Doing the Truth," <u>Chronicle</u>, July 1931, p. 489.

(So great would the emphasis be on the new encyclical that R. A. McGowan, in charge of the first day's discussion on blacks in industry, had talked with H. M. Smith about curtailing the time devoted to racial discrimination in industry.)[109]

Since Markoe could not attend the executive committee meeting in June, he wrote LaFarge about the arrangements for the convention which should be settled there, requesting that LaFarge "make them" settle a great deal at the meeting. The two priests did collaborate diligently to produce a successful convention, a fact greatly appreciated by Federation members.[110]

These well laid plans appeared in jeopardy the next month, however, when troubles began in Chicago and Philadelphia. As mentioned in Chapter II, LaFarge was directly involved in the Philadelphia controversy. When William Bruce threatened Father Dever's efforts to organize the Federation, LaFarge reacted swiftly. Father Dever was the Cardinal's duly appointed representative for the black apostolate, and thus the only key for the Federation's success in the archdiocese. What was more, to endanger relations with the hierarchy there was to do so everywhere, LaFarge felt.

> I see no other reasonable or practical course but the complete carte blanche to Fr. Dever to organize or have organized in Philadelphia the Federated Colored Catholics as, and by whom, he sees fit. It is a question not of this or

---

[109] McGowan to LaFarge, 9 June 1931, LaFarge Papers.

[110] Markoe to LaFarge, 27 May 1931, LaFarge Papers. See also "Plan Organization of Negro Catholics," New York Amsterdam News, 29 July 1931, p. 14; "Negro Catholics to Meet at St. Louis, September 5-7," New York Age, 1 August 1931, p. 5.

that individual priest; but of <u>the whole question of ecclesiastical authority</u>.[111]

LaFarge wrote that Bruce had been rude and was ill-qualified as a leader, and that Prater, the field agent, had acted with poor judgment. Both would have to be sacrificed. If they were not, LaFarge warned, he himself would resign.

> Unless once and for all we can wholeheartedly cooperate with the authorities of the Church, without evasion or danger of compromise, I shall have to resign from the Federation.
> . . . I am writing to you intimately and as a friend. I want to save the F.C.C. It can be saved, but there is only one way to save it.[112]

As mentioned in Chapter II, Turner acquiesced. It is not clear how much he was influenced by the threats of resignation.

When Markoe had written LaFarge about the convention earlier, in June, he suggested that LaFarge convince Gillard to appear on the St. Louis program. Obviously LaFarge had cultivated this association. The Josephite was reluctant to go to St. Louis, however, until LaFarge assured him that numbers would be needed quietly to oust Turner. Later Gillard felt that he had been betrayed in this promise, and wrote thus to his friends. How much LaFarge actually intended Turner's removal is unclear, since accounts must be taken from Gillard's impressions alone.[113]

---

[111]LaFarge to Turner, 13 July 1931, Turner Papers.

[112]Ibid.

[113]Gillard to Welbers, 5 May 1932, Gillard Papers.

Despite the growing problems, LaFarge continued to see the Federation as a necessary Catholic solution to the race question. The Church was the proper agency because she alone could differentiate essential from non-essential elements in the question. She taught, for example, that man's absolutely essential need was to save his soul, and that basic material goods were necessary to achieve that goal. Racial distinctions, on the other hand, were non-essential in the conduct of life. The Church could also provide the assistance all men would require, because they were instinctively selfish, to live by such standards. Even her power, however, had its limits.

> This is as far as the Church can go. She gives us the means to solve the problem. But it is up to each individual to use those means, and to put charity into practice himself. That this may be done, is one great aim of our Federation.[114]

LaFarge's report on the St. Louis convention revealed the part he envisioned for the Federation in the Church's solution to the race problem. It provided the "bridge" over the old abyss between rich and poor, black and white. It provided an organization in which black Catholics could be introduced, through contact with "those enlightened members of the general Catholic body," to their role in the Catholic Church.[115] By discussing their rights, they could obtain the means to perform their duties. In the same way, sharing solutions to their economic and social needs could eliminate those obstacles

---

[114]LaFarge, "Doing the Truth," *Chronicle*, September 1931, p. 580.

[115]LaFarge, "The Bridge of St. Louis," *America*, 20 September 1931, p. 586.

to the pursuit of personal salvation. The hallmark of the Federation, however, was its union of minds and hearts in the pursuit of justice. The lesson of St. Louis was that "the Federation is open to all who have the welfare of the Negro at heart," LaFarge proclaimed.[116] The seventh annual convention had obviously transformed the Federation in LaFarge's mind from a black Catholic organization to an interracial one.

Interracialism and the Controversy

One important organizational change at the convention was the election of Elmo Anderson as national organizer. Although LaFarge entertained hopes that Anderson could develop a center of operations in New York (perhaps initiating LaFarge's idea on regional vice presidencies--see Chapter II), the key fact was Anderson's election. He was the business manager of Our Colored Missions, published by Fr. Edward Kramer's Catholic Mission Board. Secondly, he was the president of the Catholic Laymen's Retreat Union. This group, as mentioned earlier, was composed of New York black Catholic men in business and the professions who had first met for a weekend retreat in 1928.[117] There are indications that Turner attended at least one of these retreats, in 1930, and that Victor Daniel of Cardinal Gibbons did so in 1931. The fact that Turner was unable to get to Tenafly in 1931 may have been one reason why a revised constitution was not

---

[116]Ibid., p. 587.

[117]Most of the information on the Union is contained in an article which LaFarge wrote for the Interracial Review: "The Laymen's Union," April 1934, p. 42.

enacted at the St. Louis convention that year. Apparently LaFarge, who had conceived the idea of a permanent secretariat for the Federation similar to that of the Catholic Rural Life Conference, had wished to discuss this with Turner during the 1931 retreat.[118] In any event, the retreats were a time for sharing as well as personal reflection.

As a result of the retreats the Laymen's Union was organized as a distinct group, with rules approved by Cardinal Hayes of New York, on February 15, 1932. The membership was by invitation only, and limited to twenty-five black Catholic business and professional men, although others could be admitted with the consent of the group. LaFarge was the spiritual director, with a small group of officers. The Union adopted a spiritual program which included the annual retreat, a bi-monthly renewal of spirit (Mass, meditation and a breakfast meeting), and a daily schedule of personal meditation, spiritual reading, examination of conscience and a morning offering of the day to God. The January renewal of spirit was held jointly with white members of the Catholic Evidence Guild.[119]

---

[118]Smith to Turner, 12 July 1930; LaFarge to Turner, 19 June 1931; Victor Daniel to Turner, 1 July 1931, all in Turner Papers.

[119]The daily program of the Union was quite similar to that of the Jesuit lay sodalities of Our Lady. The first of these had been founded in 1563 by a Jesuit for students at the Roman College. The organization emphasizes a program of spiritual growth and apostolic work. See New Catholic Encyclopedia, s.v. "Sodalities of the Blessed Virgin Mary," by A. J. Conley. The Catholic Evidence Guild was founded in London at the end of World War I to spread Catholic doctrine. Its most famous American members were Frank Sheed and Maisie Ward, the publishers.

The Union members also desired some form of outreach, so they developed a program of activities which they felt would be productive while not unreasonably demanding. Because they wished some preparation in the apostolate, they met in monthly study sessions on various Church-related topics (one per year). Seeking to reach the untapped resource of non-Catholic leaders in Harlem, as well as the "better element" among the white Catholic laity, the group agreed on several activities: a monthly forum, devoted to issues of social ethics that would interest a broad section of New York people. Various speakers of the day, such as Dr. Alain Locke, Dr. Arthur Schomburg, Dorothy Day, were invited to these sessions. The Union also sponsored the Interracial Hour over station WLWL, sent members to speak to white parishes and organizations and held several special events during the year. The addresses to various white groups were considered by the Union their most valuable work. In an effort to promote collaboration with other organizations, the Union became a member of the National Evidence Conference and eventually of the National Catholic Interracial Federation.

The Catholic Laymen's Union played its most important role in interracial activities on Pentecost Sunday, 1934, when it sponsored New York's first Catholic Interracial Mass Meeting in the Town Hall. Out of that assembly was born the New York Catholic Interracial Council, whose first vice president and chairman of the Board of Directors was Elmo M. Anderson, president of the Laymen's Union.[120]

---

[120]"The Catholic Interracial Council," Interracial Review, October 1934, pp. 125-26.

The fruits of the Catholic Laymen's Union were as yet unseen in 1931, of course, but LaFarge's concern for a truly interracial effort was growing. In a sermon for the dedication of a new black parish in Jersey City in December, LaFarge spoke of the joy not only for the black parishioners, but for the white donors of the church as well. The building stood as a symbol of what the Catholic Church could and would do for the black race. Recalling the condemnation of discrimination by Archbishop Ireland years earlier, LaFarge promised its renewal.

> It is only the dead weight of the wreckage of the past that has delayed these words being fulfilled. But that wreckage must be, it will be cleared away. . . . Your Most Reverend Bishop is determined that this river of charity shall flow into the hearts of all Catholics; and if it continues as it has begun today, it will carry away on its tide that wreckage of the past, those sorrows and grievances, which have so burdened the Negro race these long years.[121]

The specter of social equality haunted all interracial efforts. (Ave Maria's criticism of Federation demands had been a stern reminder of that.) LaFarge tackled the problem directly in his "Doing the Truth" column in the Chronicle.

> The catch lies in the fact that the word "social" means two entirely different things; it may refer merely to the enjoyment of other people's company; or it may refer to the rights and duties which we have in common as human beings.[122]

LaFarge admitted that persons who raised the issue were generally concerned with the first meaning. Did blacks wish to enjoy

---

[121] LaFarge, sermon delivered for the dedication of the Church of Christ the King, Jersey City, 20 December 1931, LaFarge Papers.

[122] LaFarge, "Doing the Truth," Chronicle, April 1932, p. 72. The fact that LaFarge handled this issue in the Chronicle may indicate that it was attaining a larger white readership.

the company of races other than their own? "Frankly, I do not know," LaFarge responded. It would seem there was diverse opinion among blacks. What should be remembered, however, was that meetings between races (as another author had pointed out in a recent <u>Chronicle</u> article) were meetings between different cultures, where misunderstandings could arise. Secondly, any social gathering for the most serious purpose required the observance of at least some social amenities. The "friendly intercourse of serious workers," however, did not necessarily imply mere mutual enjoyment, "which leads, naturally, to intimacies and prolonged relationships that may be good or bad for many or any reasons."[123] (Few references to miscegenation have been more oblique!)

As for the second meaning of "social equality," blacks were bound to seek the same rights as all men in order to fulfill their duties as human beings. The connection between right and duty was the key to the argument.

> Take away our common DUTY, and we cease to have anything in common in the way of rights; we would cease to find anything in which we <u>could</u> be equal. Take away our common duty, and we should <u>be</u> nothing but a great herd of unrelated units, each struggling with the other to get ahead, and "devil take the hindmost."[124]

The only true equality was that brought by Jesus Christ, who made us by his redemption children of the same heavenly Father.

LaFarge was careful to emphasize that working <u>with</u> the black man did not mean doing for him what he could do himself. In an address

---

[123]Ibid., pp. 72-73.

[124]Ibid., p. 73.

to the eleventh annual convention of the National Council of Catholic Women in April 1932, he defined interracial justice.

> . . . a virtue which seeks to provide for any racial group—presumably those of a different race from ours—those goods of life, fortune, body and soul, of which they are unjustly deprived.[125]

What the black man truly needed was his own leaders, he told the women, that the race might attain its potential.

> Interracial justice, practically considered, may mean not so much stooping down and binding up the physical wounds of the man on the road to Jericho. It may mean going out before the public and courageously overcoming the apathy, timidity or downright hostility which will prevent the training of thousands of young men and women who would bind up the wounds not of this or that chance individual, but of an entire race. It may mean not only paying the inn-keeper, but having the courage to appear at the inn at all in the custody of so unwelcome a guest.
> . . . The problem of the American Negro is the white man, not the Negro. A great part of the apostolate for those of other races finds its object in our own race.[126]

LaFarge ended with a quotation from the Catholic industrialist, Leon Harmel, "Work for the workingman by working *with* the workingman, never without him."[127]

Meanwhile, of course, the details of Federation endeavors, as well as the Institute and other works, continued. The St. Louis convention had produced a check from Father Kramer, through LaFarge,

---

[125]LaFarge, "Interracial Justice," Catholic Action 14 (April 1932): 13.

[126]Ibid., p. 30.

[127]Ibid.

which appeared a symbol of better relationships with official Church structures. It was true, on the other hand, that one Josephite had written an unfavorable report of the convention for Our Colored Harvest. LaFarge's reaction to this was typical of his bent for avoiding controversy. He wrote a response for the Chronicle and recommended that Turner not publish a second one immediately (see Chapter II).

> In controversy, I believe, it is better to make one move at a time; meet just one or the other point; then see what they do [128]

In November Turner and his small committee went to Catholic University to talk to the bishops. LaFarge provided whatever information he had to strengthen the argument for black Catholic education, and advised Turner to use diplomacy with the bishops.

> The pitfall into which many have fallen, in trying to get across ideal to them, is that of appearing to "tell them" what to do.[129]

Cardinal Gibbons Institute during this period was experiencing financial difficulties, for which LaFarge now held some responsibility. Victor Daniel became ill, to add to LaFarge's burdens. The Jesuit began to feel the weight of distances. Turner tried to meet with LaFarge and Anderson in New York when he could, and LaFarge handled Federation business when he traveled to Ridge.[130] Despite the problems, LaFarge pursued his ideas on revisions in the Federation structure. He felt the need to incorporate the regulations of the Detroit

---

[128] LaFarge to Turner, 16 October 1931, Turner Papers.

[129] LaFarge to Turner, 4 November 1931, Turner Papers.

[130] LaFarge to Turner, 23 November 1931; Turner to LaFarge, 7 December 1931; LaFarge to Turner, 27 December 1931, all in Turner Papers.

convention in the constitution, to avoid any repetition of the misunderstandings in Philadelphia. He still favored his plan of vice presidents elected from various regions of the country, and a generally more efficient operation of Federation affairs.[131]

By now the decision had been made to hold the 1932 convention in New York City. LaFarge asked Markoe to come in advance of the meetings to aid in their preparation (see Chapter III). In May his "Doing the Truth" column proposed an important subject for consideration at the convention. LaFarge reported on a paper delivered by Dr. Maurice Sheehy of Catholic University to the Catholic Association for International Peace meeting in Cleveland. His study of Catholic school children had indicated that racial prejudice was learned, not innate, in youngsters. LaFarge urged the Federation to consider what specific programs should be included in schools, examination of textbooks, individual counselling and religious instruction, to avoid harmful prejudicial influences.[132]

LaFarge had tried to explain the truer, deeper motivations for prejudice in a talk over WLWL in January 1932. The first truth to be understood was that prejudice was *not* inevitable.

> There is nothing profound, mysterious, or recondite in the matter of relations of races. Race is a mere accident. Vast civilizations have extended themselves over the world and have been practically untroubled by the problem of races. . . . The difficulty in race relationships, in other words, is not in the question of race itself; the difficulty arises from other entirely different issues which are attached to the question of race. In this way racial conflicts become

---

[131] LaFarge to Turner, 27 December 1931, Turner Papers.

[132] LaFarge, "Doing the Truth," *Chronicle*, May 1932, pp. 90-91.

> a symptom, not of any inherent antagonism of race which is nonexistent, for there are no groups of the human family inherently antagonistic to one another, but they are symptoms of other conflicts which are disguised or symbolized under the appearance of race.[133]

The case of the black American was no exception. The roots of prejudice lay in economic and social conditions. Their solution was to be found in the same place.

> The greatest obstacle to the healing of the interracial relationships in the United States is not the racial situation of the Negro himself, but the lack of confidence as yet placed in him by so many of his fellow citizens.[134]

The best way to display confidence in blacks was to aid black leaders in the solution of their own problems.

In May 1932 Turner sent LaFarge a letter concerning the reestablishment of a Federation chapter in Baltimore. The archbishop had suggested Gillard as the spiritual director, a post he subsequently declined (see Chapter II). The relationship with the Josephites was declining rapidly at this point. The Josephite Fr. L. J. Welbers had expressed his concerns about black Catholic apathy to Markoe, who had forwarded the letter to Turner. When Welbers expressed dissatisfaction with Turner's response, Markoe sent that letter to LaFarge! Meanwhile, Welbers was requesting advice from Gillard on the situation.[135] The entire mosaic is an interesting insight into

---

[133]WLWL, "Race Relations," 20 January 1932. Copy in LaFarge Papers.

[134]Ibid.

[135]Welbers to Markoe, 5 April 1932; Teabeau to LaFarge, 8 April 1932, both in LaFarge Papers. Also Gillard to Welbers, 5 May 1932, Gillard Papers.

communication within the Federation. Unfortunately, it revealed only growing difficulties for the organization.

Fr. Vincent Dever had been assigned the task of writing a constitutional revision. The objections of LaFarge and other Federation members to the results have already been discussed. LaFarge reiterated his view throughout that the Federation must embody a program of <u>action</u> if it were to be successful in solving the racial problem. For the Jesuit that action must be primarily educational, specifically enlightening the white Catholic public on the correlation between Catholic principles and specific instances of racial injustice. He also repeated his belief that black Catholic laymen were the proper personnel for this task, since time would not permit waiting for black priests to begin the work.[136] Although Turner seemed to agree, as mentioned before, he emphasized the need to protect the Federation from hierarchical censorship, while LaFarge stressed organizational efficiency and cooperation with the clergy. Beyond that, LaFarge insisted that the primary objective of the Federation must be broader than the acquisition of black rights within the Church. Such rights were dependent upon the application of Christian principles to specific issues, which in turn was dependent upon "the establishment (in general) of race relationships based upon Christian principles." These relationships were so vital because justice was impossible without love. "Justice, though theoretically self-sufficing,

---

[136]LaFarge to Turner, 6 August 1932, Turner Papers.

is actually not capable of being actuated save through supernatural love," LaFarge insisted.[137]

In his column for the Chronicle in July 1932, LaFarge went one step further. Noting requests at the executive committee meeting in June for a change in the Federation's name, he admitted that revisions in the constitution made the proposed name, National Catholic Interracial Federation, a reasonable one.

> This writer believes that the name "National Catholic Interracial Federation," whether desirable or not, does express what has developed to be the primary purpose of the organization. This purpose may be summed up in eleven words as "the promotion of relations between the races based on Christian principles."[138]

Interestingly, LaFarge was admitting that this view of the Federation as an interracial organization had developed through its history. He repeated his conviction on the fundamental importance of proper race relationships, which in turn presupposed a proper understanding of good race relations. The problem, in other words, was basically a conceptual one.

> . . . the stronghold of discrimination and injustice lies in the huge dead-weight of misconception as to the true character of the Negro and the Christian ideal of race relations which is spread over the Catholic and the non-Catholic population of this country. When this stronghold is invaded, when these misconceptions are destroyed, the Church, as well as the State, will function normally for all.[139]

---

[137] Ibid.

[138] LaFarge, "Doing-the Truth," Chronicle, July 1932, p. 130. Interestingly, Markoe later listed this article on his personal card index as "Beginning of the Federation Split." See Catholic Interracial Council files, New York City.

[139] Ibid., pp. 130-31.

The logical program to support these theories was an educational one.

> Without education, the right kind of direction cannot be given to race relationships; nor can the men be found whose knowledge and example will overcome passion and ignorance, and command the respect that will break down prejudice.[140]

To show an example to others of the ideals it sought, and, as a prerequisite, therefore, to the goals the Federation had always held, the organization's activities must be interracial. On this point LaFarge was quite clear. Even black Catholic unity depended upon an interracial approach.

> The promotion of union among all colored Catholics in the United States, as well as the promotion of education, which the Federation has always considered among its prime objectives, flows from a primarily interracial program.[141]

LaFarge advised Turner that he was not necessarily advocating a name change, but felt that it should be considered.[142]

Little material is available about LaFarge's actual participation in the 1932 convention. He and the New York chapter were hosts of the meeting, but it was apparently Markoe who was most active. His memoirs reveal, in fact, attempts to gain LaFarge's support for the name change in all its ramifications. It was Markoe who recalled that LaFarge did finally agree, and spoke so vehemently on behalf of an interracial approach that even his friends were shocked.[143]

---

[140]Ibid., p. 131.

[141]Ibid.

[142]LaFarge to Turner, 25 August 1932, Turner Papers.

[143]Markoe, "An Interracial Role," pp. 235-36.

That appears, however, the last major role (except for his suggestion to Markoe that the <u>Chronicle</u> be renamed the <u>Interracial Review</u>) which LaFarge played in the controversy, and perhaps in Federation affairs. He did report on the convention for <u>America</u>, but not until two months after the famous Chicago meeting which ousted Turner. His column for the new <u>Interracial Review</u> avoided the subject during approximately the same period. In <u>America</u> LaFarge repeated his belief that most thinking blacks were convinced that educating the white Catholic laity was the primary means of acquiring justice in the Church. Then he explained why.

> The pastor, the teacher, or the head of the institution is confronted with the question of lay sentiment at every turn. Not that <u>all</u> turns upon the laymen; not so facile a matter as that. But if the body of Catholic laymen <u>do</u> know the facts, if they realize the importance of the <u>facts</u>, the task of those who are devoting their lives to the Negro's welfare will be comparatively simple. For few of the Negro's problems are created, in the last analysis, by the Negro himself.[144]

Interracial cooperation gave the white man the chance to ask honestly, "What does the Negro want," and the black man the opportunity to ask, "What are the white man's intentions?" This required enlightened men on both sides and a great deal of patience. LaFarge summarized in the words Archbishop McNicholas had written George Conrad when he succeeded Turner: all sides should take their example from the Church,

---

[144]LaFarge, "Catholic Negroes Take Stock," p. 431.

. . . that they learn from her how to be patient and forbearing, yet steadfast in their purpose to do away ultimately with injustice.[145]

Apparently LaFarge's only connection with the Chicago meeting which ousted Turner was to send a telegram to Markoe at that time. Most articles publicizing the controversy spoke of LaFarge only in association with Markoe. Only Cora Grace Inman's attack (which was directed against the America article described above) singled out LaFarge for comment. Many accounts ignored him altogether, which it seems was his preference. He was not present for the attempted reconciliation in Washington, D.C., between Turner and Markoe, although the latter reported to LaFarge immediately afterward.[146]

LaFarge chose the indirect approach to the entire question. He wrote an article for the Interracial Review in apparent response to a friend's query: "What Is Interracial?" In it he pointed out that interracial activity in itself was not a good; after all, one could have an interracial fight.

---

[145]Ibid. Markoe had lamented this same letter from McNicholas, as advising an already timid Conrad to become even more cautious. See Chapter III.

[146]Much of LaFarge's absence from publicity surrounding the controversy is probably due to his non-involvement in the Chicago meeting. That the Jesuit was interested in developments of the controversy as reported in the press is evident from the collection of articles on the subject among his private papers. For reference to the LaFarge telegram to Markoe, see Markoe to LaFarge, 27 December 1932, LaFarge Papers. Apparently LaFarge had no further contact with Turner once the controversy began. There is one brief letter from LaFarge to Turner requesting information on an unrelated subject in 1940. Not a single piece of correspondence with Turner could be found in the LaFarge Papers.

> ... the interracial action which the Federation undertakes to promote, is not merely interracial action, as such and no more. It is a specific type of interracial action; namely, action directed towards the betterment of the Negro race, and of the country in general, by members of either group who are qualified to engage in it. It is the collaboration of the most unselfish, the most capable members of either race for the highest of ideals, for the improvement of the situation of the Negro in this country, for his education and advancement, and for the spread of Christ's Kingdom upon earth.[147]

The value of interracial collaboration should not rule out other approaches. Rather, each activity would call for its own response, which the black man was best able to judge.

> Many an arrangement which to the white man will seem eminently fair, will present, in their [Negroes'] judgment, elements of danger; while, on the other hand, they will at times advise a course to be followed which might seem to favor the very things against which they are contending.[148]

What the Federation offered was the opportunity for men of widely different backgrounds to work constructively in the solution of problems.

When white students at Manhattanville College attempted awkwardly to do their part in the interracial movement, LaFarge interpreted them to others. He wrote to readers of the Interracial Review that while the young women's statement might appear patronizing, the important fact was that it had been issued at all.[149]

---

[147]LaFarge, "What Is Interracial?" Interracial Review, March 1933, p. 54.

[148]Ibid., p. 55.

[149]LaFarge, "Doing the Truth," Interracial Review, August 1933, p. 152.

The Aftermath

LaFarge did attend the convention of the National Catholic Interracial Federation in Cleveland in September 1933, but seemed to become little involved in its executive committee meetings and general affairs (except for his contributions to the Interracial Review). The Cardinal Gibbons Institute had become a growing concern for him, as it was forced to close in December 1933. He spent endless hours in the following months trying to reopen it. Other more positive developments also occupied him. The Catholic Laymen's Union had a solid program of activities for which LaFarge was always the guiding force. Unlike the Institute or the Federation, the Union conducted its affairs almost exclusively in New York. In May 1934 the Catholic Interracial Council was born. Elmo M. Anderson's comment at the Council's appearance could have been made by LaFarge himself.

> For many years it has seemed to me that the fundamental difficulty in the problems confronting the Negro in America is interracial and will require a solution based on interracial understanding and cooperation.[150]

The issue of the Interracial Review which reported the establishment of the first Catholic Interracial Council also announced that the Review had become the official organ of the Council. As described in Chapter III, Markoe had transferred the magazine to New York when he could no longer publish it himself. George K. Hunton, whom LaFarge had introduced to Markoe in 1932, and who had promoted

---

[150]"The Catholic Interracial Council," p. 126.

the Institute, became the new editor. His years with the Catholic Interracial Council are a legend all their own.[151]

In this same issue of the Review, LaFarge wrote once again on the subject of interracial justice, basing his discussion largely on recent sessions of the Summer School of Catholic Action, sponsored by the Jesuits in New York. The article was a brief summary of his basic position. He began by defining a racial group as "a social group identified by physical traits due to a common inheritance." Interracial justice was the

> . . . organization of society so that each racial (or minority) group obtains an equal share in those common benefits to which it has an equal claim.[152]

What was the rationale for the practice of such justice? The unity of mankind through creation and redemption. How did one determine what was just? Here LaFarge used the rule of thumb devised by Parsons (but similar to his own): MUSTS (obligations) equals MAYS (claims). The duties which all men shared were differentiated by their roles. Men had obligations as individuals (health, education), as members of a family (employment, education of offspring), as citizens (vote, education to citizenship) and as members of the Church (not to scandalize others or prevent their practice of the

---

[151] See Hunton's own memories in George K. Hunton, All of Which I Saw, Part of Which I Was; the Autobiography of George K. Hunton as Told to Gary MacEoin (New York: Doubleday, 1967. Interestingly, some of the same men who were original members of the Federation later became charter members of the Washington Catholic Interracial Council, such as Dr. Eugene Clarke. Interview with William and Mary Buckner, Washington, D.C., November 1974.

[152] LaFarge, "Interracial Justice," Interracial Review, October 1934, p. 121.

Faith). LaFarge once again placed the source of interracial injustice in the realm of concept; men had false, unchristian ideas of society and unreasoning prejudice. The latter could be overcome only by dissection of it. Interracial justice depended in general on an increase of supernatural charity, and in particular on the application of this charity to racial problems, collaborating with others in their solution. LaFarge saw Catholic Action groups, of course, as the best agencies for achieving this goal.

The Catholic Interracial Council was only one of several interracial movements for LaFarge. In November 1933 he had met with several priests in the East to form the Northeastern Clergy Conference on Negro Welfare. Until 1942 this group of priests engaged in work in the black community shared experiences and developed a program of race relations. Other groups were formed later modeled on this one.[153]

Obviously John LaFarge had found his path in the interracial movement, one he felt was a natural outgrowth, indeed the blossoming of those ideas first conceived but never fulfilled in the Cardinal Gibbons Institute. In April 1938 LaFarge traveled to the International Eucharistic Congress in Budapest, viewing "the gathering storm" in Europe and the world. While abroad, LaFarge met with Pius XI in special audience. The pope had just finished reading LaFarge's latest

---

[153]LaFarge, The Manner, pp. 339-40. There is some correspondence in the Gillard Papers which indicates that LaFarge tried to interest Gillard in joining the Clergy Conference on Negro Welfare, but the latter refused attendance after his remarks at one meeting had been repeated outside it. See LaFarge to Gillard, 19 January 1934; Gillard to LaFarge, 22 January 1934; LaFarge to Gillard, 26 January 1934; Gillard to LaFarge, 31 January 1934.

book, Interracial Justice, published in 1937. It has been revealed recently that the pope, greatly pleased with LaFarge's book, commissioned the Jesuit to draft an encyclical on racism based upon the ideas presented in Interracial Justice. LaFarge was given the charge under the greatest secrecy, and kept that seal until nearly the end of his life. The draft form was written in collaboration with Fr. Gustave Gundlach of the Gregorian University, Rome, and Fr. Gustave Desbuquois of Action Populaire in Paris. Even today it is difficult to judge the authorship of each section. The actual work was never used by Pius XI and may or may not have affected the work of his successor, Pius XII. For a full discussion of this episode in LaFarge's life, see the work of Edward Stanton, "John LaFarge's Understanding of the Unifying Mission of the Church, especially in the Area of Race Relations." Stanton discusses not only the draft encyclical, but also the thought of John LaFarge developed in his later, more fruitful years. It should be kept in mind that what has been presented here is based upon the early period of a man who spent many more years in the field of race relations.[154]

On July 12, 1942, LaFarge was appointed executive editor at America, and in October 1944, editor-in-chief. But he fell ill in 1945, and did not fully recover until 1947. When he did, he made a tour of Europe. Robert C. Hartnett was appointed to LaFarge's post in 1948, and LaFarge became once again an associate editor. His career was far from over, however. In 1951 the State Department

---

[154]Edward S. Stanton, "John LaFarge's Understanding of the Church, especially in the Area of Race Relations" (Ph.D. dissertation, St. Paul University, 1972), pp. 168-95.

asked LaFarge to visit theology schools in occupied Germany and report on their social studies programs. Finally, John LaFarge reached the culminating point in his long struggle for racial justice in 1963, when at the age of eighty-three he participated in the famous March on Washington. He died the same year, just three days after President John F. Kennedy, on November 24, 1963. The story of LaFarge's lifelong effort to comprehend the roots of true racial justice is best summarized in his own words.

> We need light from above in order consistently and universally to see all men as Christ our Lord saw them, transcending outward appearances. I myself had to learn my lessons through long observation and experience, not from anybody's say-so. It needs more than unaided human strength to translate such an understanding into practical deeds, such as the defense of basic human rights, when you are personally not inconvenienced . . . it is not easy to steer a straight course between a doctrinaire spirit and a spirit of compromise.[155]

---

[155]LaFarge, The Manner, p. 337.

CHAPTER V

CONCLUSION

Fr. Thomas J. Harte, in a 1947 study of Catholic interracial organizations, concluded that the basic issue of the Federation controversy was methodology. Father LaFarge and Father Markoe favored a "gradualist" approach, while Dr. Turner sought "direct" methods.[1] This analysis, while basically accurate, does not go deep enough. Fundamental disagreements existed about the nature of the race problem, the Church's role in solving it, and the purpose of the Federation. Each of these will be examined in the light of the three men's views.

I. The Problem

All three men agreed that the "Negro problem" was really the white man's problem of racial prejudice. They disagreed, however, about the white man's role in resolving the issue.

A. Turner

For Turner, the race problem was an existential one. It was not something he chose to be concerned about; he lived with it daily. He had experienced the invalidity of the proposition that once a man lifted himself out of poverty and ignorance, he would be treated as an equal by his fellow white Americans. While en route to a science convention to

---

[1]Harte, Catholic Organizations Promoting Negro-White Race Relations in the United States, p. 7.

deliver a paper before his professional peers, he could still be told to sit in the back of a Catholic church, or to take the freight elevator in the hotel where he was to give his address.[2] He had been deprived of a Catholic education, and then taught another generation of black Catholic students who suffered the same loss. As a scientist, he knew that racial theories of superior and inferior races were inaccurate, but nonetheless imbedded in the popular mind.

Mention has already been made of the profound effect of an interview with General John Eaton as Turner was leaving Howard University. The event set him on a course of active involvement in civil and religious rights which continued throughout his life.[3] His interest in teaching science to the rural black child was not to keep him "down" on the farm, but to bring him the latest scientific technology.[4] As a scientist he insisted on adequate laboratory facilities, and the opportunity for his own professional development. He attended conventions, at times reading papers before them. Turner's students profited from his concern for excellence. Two members of his first class of students at Hampton later earned their Ph.D. degrees. Turner educated blacks not to fit in to white society, but to make their own place according to their talents.

Coming from Maryland, Dr. Turner admitted that he did not experience white racist attitudes in the deep South, except on occasion. Although he worked for many years in Virginia, his life was circumscribed

---

[2]NPR, "Options," April 1974.

[3]See Chapter II.

[4]Turner, "Nature Study," pp. 496-503; "Biology Teaching," pp. 349-52.

a good deal by the work at Hampton Institute and the particular environment of that black educational institution. When he encountered white society, he expected to do so on his own terms. When he was "Jim Crowed," he protested, often successfully.[5] While he did not speak at great length about white men, he placed the blame for racial injustice upon their shoulders, for he considered racial prejudice an immoral attitude, not to be tolerated.[6] Turner felt that the only sure means for obtaining racial justice was for the black man to fight for it wherever and whenever possible. He put little faith in changing white men's minds, but wanted curtailment of their unjust activities. This was to become, of course, the basic methodology of the N.A.A.C.P.

Turner's membership in the N.A.A.C.P. is significant. He helped to organize its first chapter in Baltimore. Even more importantly, however, he was among the first members of the Washington chapter while a professor at Howard University. Turner had come to Washington in the year Woodrow Wilson took office, 1913. The Wilson administration was marked by increased segregation in federal agencies in the District, and a reduction in black appointments. The deteriorating status of blacks under the Roosevelt, Taft and Wilson administrations helped to develop a new sense of militance among black Washingtonians. It united

---

[5]Turner admitted the limitations of protest when traveling in the deep South. He recalled several incidents when he did speak out, repeating the stories for me, but was generally reluctant to dwell on such unpleasant memories at great length. Interview, March 1973.

[6]Turner, "After the Parish School," p. 653. For full quotation, see Chapter II, p. 26. See also Turner to Fr. Ignatius Smith, 8 February 1916, Turner Papers. For full quotation, see Chapter II, p. 30.

a group of black men whom Booker T. Washington described as "so discouraged and so bitter."[7]

In 1912 the Washington branch of the N.A.A.C.P. was organized. Some of the men most prominent in this new wave of black militancy, Kelly Miller and the Grimke brothers, for example, were Turner's friends and coworkers. He joined them in that movement at a time when his own thoughts about racism in the Church were developing.

The race problem was for Turner, then, a fact of life he dealt with directly. Its cause, prejudice, was a white man's problem. Turner as an educator used his talents to develop black minds to the best of their ability. He was willing to combat discrimination where he met it, support its demise, and accept but not depend upon white assistance in that cause. This was in keeping with his conviction that only the black man truly perceived the problem, had the courage to meet it directly, and thus should provide the leadership in racial activity. Interracial for him meant a willingness to cooperate with white men, but not to be dominated by them. The early N.A.A.C.P. as an interracial organization was consonant with his concept.

B. Markoe

William Morgan Markoe admitted that blacks were practically unknown to him before his college days in St. Louis. His involvement

---

[7]For a description of this era among blacks in Washington, see Constance McLaughlin Green, The Secret City (Princeton, New Jersey: Princeton University Press, 1967), pp. 155-83. Dr. Turner recalls his involvement in the early days of the Washington N.A.A.C.P. He mentioned collaborating with Carter Woodson, the founder of the Association for the Study of Afro-American Life and History, in the development of a plan subsequently adopted by the N.A.A.C.P. in its first city-wide recruitment drive. Interview, 24 December 1974.

in the race problem was circumstantial, but he quickly made it a personal cause. He vowed to serve the black community. The first blacks Markoe met were almost destitute. His was a beneficent role, both at Florissant and later in St. Louis. Even though the parish of St. Elizabeth's was located in the "better" black neighborhood, Markoe's first catechetical work had been among the newly arrived Southern blacks east of Grand Avenue. Their condition was pitiful, and his work was as much material as spiritual.

Catechetical instruction and conversion of non-Catholic blacks in St. Louis convinced Markoe that the Church had before her a tremendous challenge, especially in the North. If she met it sucessfully, she could bring the black race into the Faith. Markoe also realized, however, that the greatest obstacle to that conversion was the prejudice of white Catholics.[8] Thus he set about the task of a missionary to non-Catholic blacks on the one hand (through home visits, schools), and to white Catholics on the other (through *America*, the Claver Clubs). Through this dual participation he established his own interracial role. This methodology was solidified when Markoe became a pastor. The great tornado which hit St. Louis in 1927 forced him to seek financial assistance from local white parishes. This cooperation continued through the city-wide fund drive for a new St. Elizabeth's, which brought together representatives of black, white, Catholic and nonCatholic organizations in St. Louis. The interracial musicals which some of these groups produced were an example of this new joint effort.

---

[8]Markoe, "An Interracial Role," p. 17.

Finally, Markoe himself joined the Urban League, a body devoted to interracial cooperation in solving the problems of black people in cities.

In all this Markoe maintained a conviction that the white man, while responsible for discrimination, could be changed in his attitudes and, above all, was necessary to the advancement of blacks.[9] Markoe admitted that the race problem was rooted in a horror of miscegenation (resistance to interracial schooling seemed to evidence this) and a general ignorance of the viewpoint of blacks. Markoe met the first problem by stressing the black man's rights in the Church, including his right to a formal Catholic education.[10] Since the purpose of the Catholic school was a religious one, social relationships should be given secondary consideration. These were Markoe's words, however, rather than his practice.

In the beginning, he did not press even the issue of integrated schools, although he realized the folly of a separate system in the North. Rather, he continued stressing an ongoing education to change white attitudes, until discrimination in schools was eliminated.[11]

As for the second obstacle, ignorance of the black man's viewpoint, Markoe advocated increased black-white contact. As preparation for that, he presented himself as a spokesman for blacks, speaking and writing about the "Negro viewpoint." That he attempted to learn

---

[9]Markoe, "Social Equality," p. 352. Catholics especially could be taught to grant Negroes justice. See "Prejudice Outlawed," p. 245.

[10]Markoe, "Solution," p. 125.

[11]Markoe, "Social Equality," p. 352.

that mind by frequent contact with blacks is amply evident.[12]

While serving as a spokesman for blacks, he also administered separate parochial institutions, stressing they were interim measures. He believed that the segregated parish of St. Elizabeth's, as well as the separate schools he had begun, were institutions whose aim should be their own abolition. In this sense, Markoe, unlike many in the Church, saw the need for an end to his mission role. Converted blacks were to be assimilated into the rest of the Church.

His single aim was to achieve results, in this instance the advancement of blacks through membership in the Catholic Church. The black parish, the black school, the black newsletter or journal, Claver Clubs, White Friends of Colored Catholics, America magazine and the Federation itself could all be used as instruments to assist the abolition of racial prejudice and to establish racial justice. One critical issue, however, was that he was convinced that white cooperation was essential to this goal. Those organizations such as Claver Clubs and an interracial Federation, which promoted such cooperation, were examples of the only methodology he believed would work. To emphasize race in any way was, for Markoe, heretical, immoral and self-defeating.

Markoe did not stand alone in this conviction. Many members of the Federation, particularly in the North, shared his belief that black separatism was merely Jim Crow by choice. In Markoe's methodology the interracial day at the Federation conventions, devoted to the dis-

---

[12]Markoe, "The Negro's Viewpoint," p. 3. An interview with Father Heithaus, of St. Louis, as mentioned in chapter three, revealed Markoe's preference for the company of his black parishioners and friends.

cussion of common industrial problems, reflected the kind of cooperation which was at the heart of all black progress.

C. LaFarge

John LaFarge regarded race relations as only one among many concerns. His interest in social justice had been aroused first by study of the Church's social doctrine in Europe. He became convinced that the social disorder which the Old World was experiencing in the early twentieth century could spread to the New. Those elements of American society which suffered most from injustice could easily join the new revolutionary movements of Europe, particularly Communism, then gaining strength. The only way to prevent this possibility was for the Church to reconstruct the social order on a religious basis, giving hope and justice to these disaffected peoples, blacks among them.

LaFarge's first real contact with blacks was in a rural setting. He became a strong admirer of Booker T. Washington's effort at Tuskegee. Cardinal Gibbons Institute was LaFarge's version of that institution.

Although he had greater faith in rural solutions to social problems, LaFarge knew that many blacks would continue to migrate to the cities of the North. He agreed with Markoe that this movement presented both an opportunity and a challenge to the Catholic Church. He also agreed that the discrimination of white Catholics was the greatest obstacle to black conversion. He saw racial prejudice as immoral, and devastating to the black man's self-image. It was particularly harmful to the black Catholic because it deprived him of an all-essential religious education. At the same time, he believed strongly that prejudice was caused by ignorance and perpetuated by economic and political factors. Since it was itself an unreasonable position, LaFarge believed it could be eradicated by education.[13]

The social doctrine of the Church could provide the image of justice in race relationships, distinguishing between essential issues of basic rights, and non-essential issues, such as intimate "social equality."[14] Blacks themselves could best describe the concrete effects of discrimination. Those who had become educated, with a particular emphasis on character formation, could demonstrate that they were just as intelligent and moral as other men.[15] Such meetings of the mind would best begin, in LaFarge's view, among the highly educated, and deal with common problems felt by both races. These leaders would in turn instruct the masses. LaFarge believed the cooperation of white men was essential to success, although he often saw them as supporters of black leadership, and educators of other white men.[16]

He seemed to rely most heavily upon an intellectual confrontation, which would result in changed white attitudes. That, he believed, would initiate social change. For LaFarge, as for Markoe, the attitude of the average white man was essential to all black progress.

II. The Catholic Church

Before the Second Vatican Council the vast majority of Catholics viewed the Church as an hierarchical institution which administered the

---

[13]LaFarge, "The Negro and Security." WLWL, "Race Relations," 20 January 1932. "Doing the Truth," Chronicle, July 1932, pp. 130-31.

[14]See Chapter IV, pp. 256-57, 267, 269.

[15]LaFarge, "The Catholic's Voice, "p. 33.

[16]LaFarge, "Interracial Justice," Catholic Action, p. 30.

faith and sacraments to its members. Few who spoke of the "Church" meant the people who composed it. Turner, LaFarge and Markoe all made this distinction on the question of racial justice. The "Church" was separated from those prejudiced white members within it. The "Church" did not teach discrimination, although some Catholics (even clergy) might practice it. The three placed their faith in the papacy and its documents. There was even a suggestion at one point about sending Turner to Rome as a representative of black Catholics.

The three men differed, however, in their estimate of the Church's role in solving the race question. First, the two priests were principally concerned about the conversion of non-Catholic blacks and the discrimination of white Catholics as an obstacle to that conversion. Turner, while willing to discuss conversion, was more concerned with the treatment of blacks in the Church as a problem in its own right. Conversion of the race was consequent upon justice granted to these members, and the development of a black clergy. Second, while the two priests saw the Church as the ultimate instrument for solving the entire race question, Turner centered his efforts on those services of the Church in the development of the black Catholic community. Finally, while all three understood the hierarchical nature of the Church, Markoe and LaFarge were convinced that white lay Catholics held the Church's key to racial justice. Until their resistance could be overcome, little would be accomplished. Turner, on the other hand, appealed directly to the hierarchy. Prejudice was sinful and should receive only condemnation. The bishops should grant the black man forthwith his just due.

A. Turner

Non-Catholics of both races are apt to ask black Catholics, even today, "Why have you remained in a Church that has been so discriminatory?" To the black Catholic, particularly one whose history in the Church goes back several generations, the question often makes little sense. The Church is the one true Faith. To leave it is to leave all religion, for there is no other. Turner once answered such a question with another: "Where would I go?"[17]

While loyal to the Church, Turner developed an attitude toward non-Catholics which reflected his need to seek advantages outside the Catholic community. He realized his only education in Latin and liturgy had come from an Episcopal priest.[18] Dr. Turner taught all his life in secular institutions, often as the only black Catholic. He collaborated with black churchmen of other faiths and made necessary use of such facilities as the Y.M.C.A. That may seem commonplace today, but was not so among white Catholics, prohibited from joining non-Catholic religious organizations, forty or fifty years ago. Since he was neither a cleric nor a missionary, conversion was not preeminent in his thinking. Rather, his experience in the Catholic faith gave him an awareness of its limitations, and an appreciation of non-Catholic efforts in the cause of civil rights.

Turner's black associates, however, viewed him as a representative of Catholicism among his own race. Since he was a natural leader

---

[17] Interview with Turner, March 1973.

[18] Ibid.

in the black community by reason of his advanced education, he gradually envisioned his contribution to race relations in a unique position as a black Catholic. As a layman, however, his Church involvement was not all-consuming. For Turner other agencies outside the Church offered valid services to the black community. The Church could begin by justly aiding her own black members. Turner emphasized that the Church must do her part, rather than do everything.

Turner stressed access to a Catholic education and the need for a black clergy in the development of black Catholic leadership. He was painfully aware of his own lack of a Catholic education and the effect of the same on his Catholic students. In many respects he was aware as much of the psychological damage of Church prejudice as of the actual loss of educational opportunities.[19]

Turner admitted that he lacked the background to speak in "Catholic" terms. It may have affected him in other ways. His direct appeals to the bishops were honest, but he did not perceive the power of white lay Catholic opinion. His contact within the Church—religious orders, pastors, organizations—was not sustained in such a manner as to serve his cause. His was a strong voice, but one speaking to a largely indifferent audience. While he had grasped the truth that authority in the Church rests at the top, he could not have realized all the dynamics affecting the use of episcopal power. His demand that the Church rid herself of racism despite white resistance, was a call to justice which

---

[19]Turner, "After the Parish School," p. 653.

remained largely unheeded. Even the white priests who assisted him were unwilling to challenge the system fully. He was left "clinging to the banner of the Lord Jesus Christ" as his Church.

B. Markoe

Markoe vowed early to spend his life in service to the Negro. He believed firmly that the Church alone possessed the ultimate answer to the race question, despite the fact that often his own work received little official support. He was convinced that only the Church could enable the white man to view the black man "supernaturally"; that is, see him in the light of his spiritual destiny as a child of God.[20] If white Catholics could be persuaded to grant blacks their religious rights, the other rights would soon follow.

Markoe's own location in St. Louis at a time when the city was experiencing a great influx of Southern blacks impressed him, as has been mentioned, that the time was crucial for black conversion.[21] The reception which his own kindness gained for him, and the generous assistance of numerous white seminarians, religious and lay people enabled Markoe to believe that racial prejudice could be eliminated.

In many respects, Markoe's "maverick" activities brought the Church to the black man in spite of itself. He was not reluctant to criticize official structures on that account. He warned black converts that they would experience prejudice in the Church. At the same time, he preached a defense of the Church's stand on slavery, believing

---

[20] Markoe, "Viewing the Negro," p. 202.

[21] See Chapter III, pp. 142-44.

that the general public had misunderstood the true teaching of the Church on such issues.[22] This was consonant with his need as a cleric to retain the Church, despite her racism, as the "answer" to the race problem.

On the other hand, Markoe generally dismissed philosophic approaches to race. He was preeminently an active missionary. Reaching out to welcome blacks, he urged white Catholics not to feel threatened by this new presence. Markoe envisoned the Church as that structure which, in its catholicity, could reflect the model of true interracial justice.[23] He spiritualized this approach, however, thus effectively maintaining white control over the pace of this integrative process.

As a journalist he spread his message through his writings. He envisioned St. Louis as a focal point for Catholic interracial work. The nation seeing an example of true cooperation between black and white people could take heart in a possible end to racial conflict.

There is ample evidence that Markoe was surprisingly successful in several efforts. His early catechetical centers produced many converts. His fund drive for St. Elizabeth's, despite its eventual demise, created a city-wide response which was truly impressive. The musicals which accompanied the drive gave St. Louis some of its first interracial entertainment. Unfortunately, these efforts were often maverick. They were conducted within the framework of an episcopal administration which often contradicted Markoe's thrust by evident neglect of black Catholics, and under Jesuit superiors who felt compelled at times to curtail their

---

[22]Markoe, "The Catholic Church," pp. 415-17. "An Interracial Role," pp. 261-71.

[23]Markoe to Brunner, 20 September 1930.

subject's activities. The result was that Markoe's departure from a situation often meant the cessation of his projects. He took his role as "shepherd" over a docile "flock" so seriously that his departure left no one else to assume command.

C. LaFarge

Unlike Markoe, John LaFarge did not shun an intellectual approach to race relations. For him the role of the Church in western civilization was preeminently that of teacher, imparting to each generation the deposit of faith entrusted to her. That civilization had as its hallmark the development of not merely a few individuals, but many strong well-rounded characters.[24]

As he traveled on horseback through the Maryland countryside LaFarge could see that black Americans were not receiving the benefit of the Church's teaching. His response was to establish schools. The social doctrine of the Church which he had been exposed to in Innsbruck had a particular message for this situation. That doctrine, however, called for a reconstruction of the entire social order. In LaFarge's view the Church should provide the foundation for that social change by renewing the religious life of its members. Learning the principles of true justice and charity, worshipping in genuine communities, men could build the kind of society in which human problems could be adequately solved.[25]

LaFarge emphasized the Church's role in educating strong black leaders grounded in Christian principles. He believed that the black man

---

[24]LaFarge, "Full Measure," p. 197.

[25]LaFarge, The Manner, pp. 246, 248.

alone fully grasped his own situation, and the race would listen best to its own representatives. This approach also reflected his conviction that education as well as social reform must proceed from the top down.[26] Concretely, Cardinal Gibbons Institute and the Catholic Laymen's Union were expressions of these principles.

LaFarge saw, however, that racism was a matter of relationship. Although he considered prejudice a white man's problem, he felt the black man must share in its solution. Human misunderstandings were handled best through a meeting of minds. Once the white man and the black man truly communicated, prejudices could be diminished. Eventually, LaFarge devised a plan for this communication. Men must learn true Christian principles of race relations, then the actual situation in society (through the eyes of the black man himself) and finally, make the application of principle to event. In keeping with his elitist approach, LaFarge stressed meetings of educated minds first, then a gradual dissemination of the process to the masses.[27]

LaFarge predicted that eventually circumstances would cause the two races to cooperate by virtue of common needs. Like Markoe, however, he saw the imminent need of white cooperation if blacks were to be won to the Faith. LaFarge was basically optimistic about such cooperation, largely because he believed that many white Catholics were merely ignorant of the effects of prejudice on blacks.[28] He had also received

---

[26]LaFarge, "The Immediate Negro Problem," p. 221. "Opportunity for the Negro," p. 407.

[27]LaFarge, "The Catholic's Voice," pp. 33-34. LaFarge to Turner, 8 August 1932.

[28]LaFarge, "The Negro and Security."

favorable white response in the beginning to the common effort of Cardinal Gibbons Institute.

The educational approach evoked less controversy than more direct demands. The framework was familiar to church authorities and personnel. While the question of interracial education in the North was inevitable, LaFarge advised blacks to see this as a long-term goal.[29] He proposed starting with leaders in both races, the ground of least resistance. He was not disappointed. The proliferation of Catholic Interracial Councils was evidence of that. At the same time, the ultimate goals to reconstruct the social order on Catholic principles, and to convert blacks to the Catholic Faith were not achieved. Although the institutional Church was willing to educate, she remained eminently color conscious in her choice of pupils.

III. The Federation

Turner, LaFarge and Markoe all agreed on the necessity of the Federation. In the beginning they appeared to hold a common view of its purpose (with the possible exception of Markoe, who later claimed a different opinion). There seems little doubt that the Federation's purpose changed through the years. The crux of the problem was each man's perception of those changes.

The transition of the Federation from an all-black organization to an interracial one occurred in three stages. The initial Federation, an outgrowth of Turner's Committee for the Advancement of Colored Catholics, stated the following purpose in its 1925 constitution:

---

[29]LaFarge, "The Crux," p. 81.

> The object of this Federation shall be to bring about a closer union and better feeling among all Catholic negroes, to advance the cause of Catholic education throughout the Negro population, to seek to raise the general Church status of the Negro and to stimulate colored Catholics to a larger participation in racial and civic affairs.[30]

A series of directive regulations drafted at the 1930 convention in Detroit and afterwards adopted by the executive committee, listed the following objective of the Federation, which emphasized Catholic Action.

> The Federation's prime objective is to unite all colored Catholic parishes and already existing colored Catholic societies for the purpose of national Catholic action in all its phases.[31]

The shift in emphasis was from black Catholics generally to those officially organized in Church structures, and from specific black interests to the Church work of "Catholic Action." Since these directive regulations were not incorporated into the constitution at that time, their legal force became a cause of misunderstanding, as has been explained.[32] To deal with this difficulty, the executive committee planned a constitutional revision to be presented at the 1932 convention. In the new constitution the purpose stressed black concerns once again, but this time within the framework of an interracial organization.

> The object of this Federation shall be to bring about a clearer union and better feeling among all Catholics; to promote relations between the races based on Christian principles; to advance the cause of Catholic education throughout the Negro population; to seek to raise the

---

[30]"The Constitution of the F.C.C.," pp. 27-29.

[31]"Catholic Action as the Objective," p. 51.

[32]See Chapter II, pp. 73-75.

general status of the Negro in the Church; and to stimulate Catholic Negroes to a larger participation in racial and civic affairs of the various communities and of the whole country.[33]

In some respects, the original purpose was Turner's, the thrust toward Catholic Action, LaFarge's, and the revised constitution, Markoe's. The last revision reflected both Markoe's and LaFarge's thought, but its adoption was due largely to Markoe's campaigning.

A. Turner

To understand Dr. Turner's concept of the Federation, it is important to recall the group's beginnings. It was an outgrowth of an ad hoc committee founded by Turner. This movement was in response to the discrimination experienced by a small number of black Catholics in Washington, D.C. The project gained impetus through the need to find job placements for black Catholics in World War I cantonments. The success of that endeavor encouraged the committee to continue. Since racial discrimination was not about to disappear, there were many opportunities for new forms of protest. A general pattern emerged, wherein the committee directed its attention largely toward authority figures who, it felt, had the power to change conditions. The very name, "Committee against the Extension of Race Prejudice in the Church," made clear its purpose. With time and numbers a permanent organization seemed advisable. What is important to keep in mind, however, is that the thrust remained the same. The committee had changed its name in between to the more positive "Committee for the Advancement of Colored

---

[33]"Constitution of the National Catholic Federation," p. 201.

Catholics," but the concentration was still on race discrimination. The original constitution of the Federation mentioned the goals, as listed above, of black Catholic unity and educational opportunity, but early activities centered on the question of Church equality.

Turner was advised, as often happens in the case of protest groups, that the organization would need a thrust perceived by critics as positive, to stay alive.[34] He listened, and apparently agreed. At his own suggestion, an interracial committee was formed to work with the N.C.W.C. The "interracial days" were begun. In Detroit, Turner agreed to stress Catholic Action. He admitted a need for white support and hierarchical blessing if the Federation were to prove successful. The Chronicle seemed to him a real boon, and he welcomed the counsel of LaFarge and Markoe.

On the other hand, there were some initiatives he did not take. He made only one attempt to penetrate the deep South, seeking the support of the Knights of Peter Claver while in New Orleans. But the subject was not pursued at great length. General Josephite opposition to the Federation then guaranteed the project would die a natural death. The result was that few local units of the Knights of Peter Claver, the largest single black Catholic fraternal organization in the country, ever joined the Federation. As a consequence, the Federation never reached that area where the majority of black Catholics lived. Turner promoted the Federation on his annual trips to science conventions, but his time was severely limited.

---

[34] Kramer to Turner, 28 December 1932.

Indeed, this fact is vital. In this Catholic organization administered by unpaid laymen, the clerics in advisory positions had more time to devote to the work than the officers.[35] It is interesting to note in this connection that the last two men chosen for the post of national organizer were Father Markoe and Elmo Anderson, who worked for Father Kramer's Board of Colored Missions. As the Federation approached the depression years, time and money became even more important commodities for all members.

Turner did not accept nor perceive the emphasis on Catholic Action. The Federation remained for him a reception house for complaints of discrimination, a vehicle for organizing an annual convention and a voice to speak to the hierarchy on behalf of black Catholics. That some of his followers felt the same way is evident in correspondence preceding the New York convention. Eugene Clarke and H. M. Smith urged Turner to see that the original purpose of the Federation, to combat discrimination, was not lost in the new constitutional revision.

This analysis of Turner's view seems borne out by the fact that the branch over which he presided after the split dissolved, according to its members, at that point when most felt that the conditions against which they had protested were largely resolved.[36] Actually, the membership itself had grown older with time. Few new members had been added.[37]

---

[35] Perhaps Vincent Dever's resignation from the executive committee in 1932 was prompted by the realization that clerics with more time to devote to the Federation might eventually control the lay organization more than they should.

[36] Program for testimonial dinner, 1952.

[37] New Catholic Encyclopedia, s.v. "Federated Colored Catholics," by Thomas J. Harte.

Finally, Turner's approach was subject to an age-old dilemma in all protest movements: how to remain within a structure while attempting to transform it. Turner tried to situate his group on the fringes of the institution.[38] While acknowledging the existence of a spiritual director (Archbishop Curley) and loyalty to the Church, he determined not to allow any cleric to bury the truth. He did so by maintaining a cautious stance toward white clerical involvement in the Federation.[39]

It is difficult, however, to operate in such a cautious position in a hierarchical Church. The layman possesses little independent authority. It was for this reason that LaFarge and Markoe seemed to thrust the Federation toward the center of the Church by giving it a Catholic Action program. Catholic Action as it was defined then by Pius XI was the laymen's participation in the pastoral work of the bishop.[40] Consequently, protest against the Church would become not only impossible but ridiculous. The bishop (as LaFarge finally wrote Turner)

---

[38] One of the first remarks which Turner made to me about the Federation is that he had tried to make it not a Catholic organization, but an organization of Catholic men. This was his understanding of the distinction which had enabled the Knights of Columbus to operate as a lay organization without clerical interference in the Church. Interview with Turner, March 1973.

[39] Turner's caution toward clerical involvement was so great that Curley later proclaimed himself virtually ignorant of the Federation's activities, as the reader may recall. See Curley to Turner, 8 October 1932. It should also be remembered, of course, that Curley never appeared anxious to know more than he did about the Federation's work.

[40] The Detroit resolutions indicated an acceptance of this interpretation of Catholic Action for the Federation: "By Catholic Action is understood the participation of the layman in the apostolic work of the hierarchy of the Catholic Church." "Catholic Action as the Objective," p. 51.

had the power not only to advise but to "prescribe the norms" according to which a lay organization could operate.[41] Furthermore, the purpose of Catholic Action was to further the ends of the Church, not of any one group within it. Turner did not accept the fact that Catholic Action meant the cessation of protest. In a later day, it is perhaps possible to interpret Catholic Action broadly enough to incorporate the original orientation of the Federation. In 1930, however, the task would have been difficult. In any event, LaFarge and Markoe by proposing Catholic Action did not intend to preserve the original Federation. Each later admitted he wished to transform the group. Unfortunately, Turner did not realize that until the facts were irreversible. He had been deceived by two individuals who no longer respected him.

B. Markoe

William Markoe was a latecomer to the Federation. Although his original impression of the existing group was that it was a Jim Crow organization, he apparently saw enough of worth to give his time as the official editor. It was less than a year later that Markoe wrote his first critical article on "Our Jim Crow Federation." Every effort was made from that time forward to introduce an interracial orientation into Federation activities. Not that the group was entirely separatist. There had always been white involvement. The question was the centrality of that involvement. Beginning with the format of the Chronicle and trips to promote the magazine, Markoe began to preach his message. The St. Louis convention provided the greatest opportunity to present a concrete

---

[41]LaFarge to Turner, 20 August 1932.

portrait of interracial cooperation. The hosts were members of St. Elizabeth's parish, but to a lesser extent, St. Louis University (white and segregated) and the White Friends of Colored Catholics.

These activities were in keeping with Markoe's efforts prior to Federation membership. He had never worked among the black race except on an interracial basis. His catechetical centers, parish activities and newsletters, as well as civic endeavors, had all been interracial. To Markoe any other approach was, as mentioned before, heretical, for the unique gift the Church had to offer was a portrait of the truly catholic society.[42]

It is evident in retrospect that Markoe considered the Federation a convenient vehicle for spreading his own St. Louis efforts. He had lost his national forum when *America* no longer published his articles. The *St. Elizabeth Chronicle* had some outside circulation, but could reach far greater numbers as the organ of a national organization. In addition, an already existing group provided an initial audience. There seems little doubt that Markoe felt that he and Northern black Catholics had developed a philosophy which should supersede that of the Southern founders of the Federation. He had hoped that it would become the basis of activity among black Catholics throughout the country. However, he too failed to win the support of the deep South. Even though his forthright speeches were applauded by the Knights of Peter Claver, many of their white pastors felt the Jesuit far too radical, and impractical.

Markoe once wrote the he regretted not having developed the

---

[42]Markoe, "An Interracial Role," pp. 238-39.

Claver Clubs more fully, because they could have predated the Catholic Interracial Councils by many years. His desire to be "first" is indicative of his nature. While his understanding of blacks evolved over time, he never lost that single-minded thrust which was driven by his own self-proclaimed grasp of the "Negro viewpoint." This led him to seek control, even in the black community, never fully grasping the contradiction of a white man "taking over" a black organization. Despite his successes and obvious popularity at times, he never really understood that his personal struggles with racial identity gave him a crusading edge that frequently became a two-edged sword.

C. LaFarge

John LaFarge's interest in the Federation closely paralleled his concern for the Cardinal Gibbons Institute. Many of the original members of the Federation supported the Institute, located geographically near Washington, D.C. As mentioned earlier, LaFarge later referred to the Federation as an outgrowth of the Institute, although that is disputable.

As early as 1927, LaFarge urged Turner to consider positive programs for the Federation. The Jesuit's own involvement in other movements, rural life, liturgy, peace, gave him a number of models to work with. He apparently studied the causes of success in various Catholic organizations. From time to time he proposed plans for reorganizing the Federation. His particular concern was to develop an active program that could be applied at the local level, so that the organization would not deteriorate into a mere vehicle for an annual convention.[43]

---

[43]LaFarge to Turner, 8 August 1932.

LaFarge's first emphasis was upon Catholic Action, both because it drew the Federation into more positive relation to the rest of the Church's organizations, and because it gave each chapter of the Federation a specific goal (renewal of rural life, liturgy) other than Federation membership. With time LaFarge saw more clearly the possibility that the Federation on a national level would develop specific programs of action to promote better race relations. These were always educational endeavors, in keeping with his conviction that the race problem was rooted in misconceptions, of Christian principles governing race relations and the proper application of those principles.

Although LaFarge too stressed the need for white cooperation, and an interracial approach, he also saw the value of all-black efforts. He did not view them as inherently uncatholic.[44]

The Jesuit was more the planner than the administrator in Federation affairs. He asked Markoe, for example, to organize the convention in New York City, which LaFarge was sponsoring. One reason for this was his own nature. He preferred conception to administration. Another was the breadth of his interests. His activities encompassed too many fields for him to be involved in Federation details. Perhaps for these reasons LaFarge preferred the elitist to the mass approach in race relations. It worked well for him. His Catholic Laymen's Union developed a strong core of leaders who were quite capable of launching the Catholic Interracial Councils. The _Interracial Review_ enjoyed success under the able hand of George K. Hunton and LaFarge. In many respects he had read the times well.

---

[44]LaFarge, "What is Interracial?", p. 55.

On the other hand, the Federation was not an elitist group. At one point, in fact, its every effort had been directed toward gathering as many members as possible. LaFarge envisioned programs which a central administration, possibly a secretariat, could carry out for the entire organization. He had in mind an operation similar to that of the National Catholic Rural Life Conference.[45] Civil rights could not wait, however, even in the Church, for such long-range plans. In addition, LaFarge ultimately betrayed a trust in the one man who had been his ally in the earliest days of the Federation; that is, Dr. Turner. The irony was that LaFarge had preached black leadership, but abandoned it whenever his own hierarchical structure seemed threatened.

IV. Summary

It is too easy merely to characterize the founders of the Federation as men either behind or ahead of their times. Basically they attempted to read their times honestly, asking more of the church institution than it was ready to give, but depending upon the ideals of the institution to carry it truly above the realities of every day. Ultimately they were betrayed by two priests who felt a primary loyalty to their institution, good or evil, and then to the black community. The legitimate question which Turner asked bears repetition in every generation:

> The eternal question is, "Are we capable of managing our own affairs or are we to surrender all initiative to the dominant group?" This organization believes in capable

---

[45]LaFarge to Turner, 19 June 1931.

Negro leadership. We don't want to wait for our so-called friends to "sell us." We want a fair chance to prove our own worth.[46]

Between the demise of the Federation and the late 1960s the interracial approach of the Catholic Interracial Councils and, eventually, the National Catholic Conference on Interracial Justice, generally held sway. The Knights of Peter Claver, in existence since 1909, continued to serve as a strong black Catholic fraternal organization, especially in the South.[47] In the light of the Federation's constant plea for more black priests, it is significant that the first black initiative to follow the Federation was the formation of a Black Catholic Clergy Caucus. They met in April 1968, soon after the assassination of Dr. Martin Luther King, Jr. Assessing their own position within the Church and within the black community, these clergy concluded that "the Catholic Church in the United States [is] primarily a white racist institution."[48] They directed their subsequent demands for reform to the National Catholic Conference of Bishops and the Conference of Major Superiors of Religious Orders of Men. Among these demands were provisions for the inclusion of black clergy in decision making on the diocesan level, recruitment of more black priests and the

---

[46] Resolutions of the executive committee, 8 January 1933. Reported in <u>Baltimore Afro-American</u>, 14 January 1933, pp. 1-2.

[47] As mentioned earlier, this organization was founded in 1909 in Mobile, Alabama. See "Disparate Unanimity/the Common Goal," <u>Freeing the Spirit</u>, Summer 1972, p. 52.

[48] Ibid., p. 27. The information for this history of the current movement was taken from this volume, plus a private interview with Brother Joseph M. Davis, S.M., Executive Director of the National Office for Black Catholics, Washington, D.C., 17 December 1974.

training of white priests in the black community. Eventually a demand was added for the establishment of a National Office for Black Catholics, now in existence.[49]

A National Black Sisters' Conference was also organized in 1968, whose major concern has been black Catholic education. The first national convention of Black Lay Catholics met in August 1970, in Washington, D.C. The city had been the scene of the first meeting of the Afro-American Catholic Congress in 1889, and the Federated Colored Catholics in 1925. Black lay Catholics also called for the establishment of a national office. Their other demands reflected the passage of time since the Federation years. They called for the consecration of four regional black bishops, elected by their own black people, black pastorates, decision-making power for laymen in their parishes, an adequate liturgy, and the voice of black youth in Catholic youth organizations. They emphasized as well their right to direct the Catholic education of their children. Most interesting, however, was their proposal to send a delegation to Pope Paul VI to put before him their urgent needs.[50]

Conscious of the history of the Afro-American Catholic Congresses and the Federated Colored Catholics, black Catholics today realize that they stand in a long tradition of protest which has called the Church to accept fully the Gospel which she proclaims.

---

[49]Ibid., p. 33.

[50]Ibid., p. 42.

BIBLIOGRAPHY

Books

The American Catholic Who's Who, 1948-49. Gross Pointe, Michigan: Walter Romig, Publisher.

Faherty, William Barnaby. Dream by the River. St. Louis: Piraeus Publishers, 1973.

Foley, Albert S. God's Men of Color. New York: Farrar, Straus, 1955.

Gillard, John T. The Catholic Church and the American Negro. Baltimore: St. Joseph's Society Press, 1929.

_____. Colored Catholics in the United States. Baltimore: St. Joseph's Society Press, 1941.

Green, Constance McLaughlin. The Secret City. Princeton: Princeton University Press, 1967.

Harte, Thomas. Catholic Organizations Promoting Negro-White Race Relations in the United States. New York: Paulist Press, 1947.

Hunton, George K. All of Which I Saw, Part of Which I Was: The Autobiography of George K. Hunton as Told to Gary MacEoin. New York: Doubleday, 1967.

LaFarge, John. Interracial Justice. New York: J. J. Little and Ives Company, 1937.

_____. The Jesuits in Modern Times. New York: America Press, 1928.

_____. The Manner Is Ordinary. New York: Harcourt, Brace and Company, 1954.

_____. The Race Question and the Negro. New York: Longmans, Green and Company, 1944.

Reynolds, Edward D. Jesuits for the Negro. New York: The America Press, 1949.

Tenth/Two Hundredth Anniversary of the Church of SS. Paul and Augustine. Washington, D.C. By the Church. 1971.

Encyclopedia Articles

New Catholic Encyclopedia (1967). S.v. "Federated Colored Catholics,"
by Thomas J. Harte; "National Catholic Educational
Association," by M. Irwin; "National Catholic Welfare
Conference," by F. T. Hurley; "Negroes in the United States,
IV (Apostolate to)," by P. E. Hogan and J. B. Tennelly;
"Newman Apostolate," by C. Albright; "Paulists," by V. F.
Holden; "St. Frances Xavier Cabrini," by A. M. Melville;,
"St. Peter Claver," by H. Vivas Solas; "Sodalities of the
Blessed Virgin Mary," by A. J. Conley; "Xavier University
of Louisiana," by M. N. Conroy.

Magazines and Journals

Banks, Antoinette. "Fr. Stephen L. Theobald." Chronicle, August 1932,
p. 155.

"Catholic Action as the Objective of the Federation." Chronicle,
March 1930, p. 51.

"The Catholic Interracial Council." Interracial Review, October 1934,
pp. 125-26.

"The Church Still Lives." Interracial Review, January 1933, p. 9.

"Constitution of the National Catholic Federation for the Promotion of
Better Race Relations." Interracial Review, October 1932,
p. 201.

"The Convention." Chronicle, October 1929, pp. 14-15.

Daniel, Constance E. H. Review of The Catholic Church and the American
Negro, by John T. Gillard. Opportunity, August 1930,
pp. 247-48.

Daniel, Victor H. "Seven Years of Cardinal Gibbons Institute."
Chronicle, November 1931, pp. 664-65.

"Disparate Unanimity/the Common Goal." Freeing the Spirit, Summer
1972, p. 52.

"Executive Committee Meets to Plan Convention." Chronicle, July 1932,
p. 140.

"Executive Committee of the Federated Colored Catholics." Chronicle,
February 1932, pp. 37-38.

"Fr. Theobald." *Chronicle*, August 1932, pp. 157-58.

Feagin, Joe R. "Black Catholics in the United States: an Exploratory Analysis." *Sociological Analysis* 29 (Winter 1968): 186-92.

"Federated Colored Catholics--Constitution, 1929." *Chronicle*, November 1929, pp. 27-29.

"Federation's New Name Spells Progress." *Interracial Review*, December 1932, pp. 245-46.

Hannigan, Charles. "Report of the Formation of the National Catholic Association for the Advancement of the Colored People." *Catholic Educational Association Bulletin* 16 (November 1919): 418-22.

"John LaFarge, S.J. (1880-1963)." *America*, December 7, 1963, p. 725.

"Just Watch Us Grow." *Chronicle*, June 1930, pp. 132-33.

LaFarge, John. "After Two Centuries." *America*, October 1, 1927, pp. 584-85.

_____. "American Catholic Life in 1928." *America*, January 5, 1929, pp. 304-306.

_____. "The Bridge of St. Louis." *America*, September 20, 1931, pp. 586-87.

_____. "The Cardinal Gibbons Institute." *Commonweal*, February 17, 1932, pp. 433-35.

_____. "A Catholic Folk School." *America*, June 8, 1927, pp. 233-34.

_____. "Catholic Negroes Take Stock." *America*, February 4, 1933, pp. 429-31.

_____. "The Catholic's Voice in Negro Guidance." *America*, October 23, 1926, pp. 32-33.

_____. "Colored Catholics Discuss Their Situation." *America*, September 14, 1929, pp. 544-46.

_____. "The Crux of the Mission Problem." *America*, November 6, 1926, pp. 80-81.

_____. "Doing the Truth." *Chronicle*, July 1931, pp. 489-90.

_____. "Doing the Truth." *Chronicle*, August 1931, pp. 512-13.

_____. "Doing the Truth." *Chronicle*, September 1931, pp. 579-80.

LaFarge, John. "Doing the Truth." Chronicle, April 1932, pp. 72-73.

_____. "Doing the Truth." Chronicle, May 1932, pp. 90-91.

_____. "Doing the Truth." Chronicle, July 1932, pp. 130-31

_____. "Doing the Truth." Interracial Review, August 1933, pp. 151-52.

_____. "Eucharistic Honor in Colonial Maryland." America, September 22, 1928, pp. 565-66.

_____. "Fr. Gillard's Study of the Catholic Negro." Review of The Catholic Church and the American Negro, by John T. Gillard. Chronicle, July 1930, pp. 151-52.

_____. "The Federation of Colored Catholics." America, January 1, 1927, p. 284.

_____. "Full Measure for the Negro." America, December 17, 1921, pp. 197-98.

_____. "Hard Corner." America, November 11, 1926, pp. 109-11.

_____. "The Immediate Negro Problem." America, December 24, 1921, pp. 221-22.

_____. "Interracial Justice." Catholic Action, April 1932, p. 13.

_____. "Interracial Justice." Interracial Review, October 1934, pp. 121-23.

_____. "The Laymen's Union." Interracial Review, April 1934, p. 42.

_____. "The Meaning of the Cardinal Gibbons Institute." Chronicle, November 1929, pp. 7-9.

_____. "Opportunity for the Negro." America, February 2, 1929, pp. 406-407.

_____. "Poisoning Negro Youth." America, January 24, 1931, pp. 376-77.

_____. "The Unknown Field of Negro History." America, July 21, 1928, pp. 349-50.

_____. "What Do Colored Catholics Want?" America, September 20, 1930, pp. 565-67.

_____. "What Is Interracial?" Interracial Review, August 1933, pp. 151-52.

_____. "Why Rural-Life Education?" Chronicle, December 1929, pp. 21-22.

LaFarge, John. "With Scrip and Staff." America, December 4, 1926, p.185.

_____. "With Scrip and Staff." America, August 18, 1928, p. 451.

_____. "With Scrip and Staff." America, April 27, 1929, pp. 66-67.

_____. "With Scrip and Staff." America, December 6, 1930, p. 216.

Letter to the editor. America, December 18, 1920, pp. 208-209.

_____. America, January 8, 1921, pp. 286-87.

_____. America, January 15, 1921, pp. 308-309.

_____. America, January 22, 1921, p. 333.

_____. America, January 29, 1921, p. 357.

_____. America, February 12, 1921, pp. 406-407.

_____. America, February 19, 1924, p. 429.

_____. Interracial Review, December 1932, p. 249.

_____. Interracial Review, March 1933, p. 59.

McKenna, Horace B. "Colored Catholics in St. Mary's County." Woodstock Letters, February 1950, pp. 55-78.

Markoe, William M. "The Annual Convention." Chronicle, June 1931, pp. 457-58.

_____. "Catholic Aid for the Negro." America, February 18, 1922, pp. 417-18.

_____. "The Catholic Church and Slavery." America, February 12, 1923, pp. 415-17.

_____. "Catholics, the Negro, a Native Clergy." America, September 24, 1921, pp. 535-36.

_____. "Claver Clubs for Colored People." America, August 4, 1923, pp. 368-69.

_____. "Claver Clubs in Operation." America, April 5, 1924, pp. 590-92.

_____. "A Great Migration." America, February 9, 1924, pp. 396-9

_____. "How Help the Negro?" America, January 3, 1925, pp. 271-72

Markoe William M. "The Importance of Negro Leadership." America, October 13, 1923, pp. 605-606.

_____. "The Importance of Negro Patriotism." America, January 27, 1923, pp. 344-45.

_____. "'Kingfish' Race Leaders." Interracial Review, February 1933, p. 29.

_____. Letter to the editor. America, August 9, 1919, p. 451.

_____. "The Mission Crusade and Negro Education." America, June 3, 1922, pp. 154-56.

_____. "The Need of Another Claver." America, September 9, 1922, pp. 486-88.

_____. "The Negro and Catholicism." America, February 23, 1924, pp. 449-50.

_____. "The Negro Helps His Own." America, May 2, 1925, pp. 56-57.

_____. "Negro Higher Education." America, April 1, 1922, pp. 558-60.

_____. "Negro Morality and a Colored Clergy." America, November 12, 1921, pp. 79-80.

_____. "The Negro's Progress." America, May 24, 1924, pp. 127-28.

_____. "The Negro's Viewpoint." St. Elizabeth's Chronicle, April 1928, p. 3.

_____. "Negro Virtue." America, April 15, 1922, pp. 606-608.

_____. "The New Race Problem." America, October 9, 1920, pp. 582-84.

_____. "Our Jim Crow Federation." Chronicle, July 1930, pp. 149-50.

_____. "Plans for the National Convention." Chronicle, July 1931, p. 488.

_____. "Race and Religious Prejudice." America, May 12, 1923, pp. 77-78.

_____. "Report on the Chronicle." Chronicle, November 1931, p. 664.

_____. "The St. Elizabeth's Chronicle." St. Elizabeth's Chronicle, March 1928, p. 7.

_____. "Special Equality and Catholic Schools." America, January 29, 1921, pp. 350-52.

Markoe, William M. "Solution to the Race Problem." America, November 27, 1920, pp. 125-26.

_____. "The Soul of the Colored Man." America, March 5, 1921, pp. 474-75.

_____. "Viewing the Negro Supernaturally." America, June 19, 1920, pp. 200-201.

Moeslein, Mark. "Colored Catholicism." Sign, September 29, 1928, pp. 135-38.

Murphy, D. I. "Lincoln, Foe of Bigotry." America, February 11, 1928, pp. 432-33.

"A National Catholic Inter-Racial Organization." Chronicle, September 1932, p. 177.

"The Negro and the Immigrant." Interracial Review, February 1933, pp. 30-31.

Prater, William A. "The Federated Colored Catholics of the United States." St. Elizabeth's Chronicle, June 1929, p. 17.

_____. F.C.C. to Convene in Baltimore." St. Elizabeth's Chronicle, September 1929, pp. 13-14.

_____. Report of the Field Agent." Chronicle, November 1931, pp. 665-66.

"Prejudice Outlawed." Interracial Review, December 1932, pp. 244-45.

Smith, H. M. "An Outline History of the F.C.C. of the U. S." Chronicle, December 1929, pp. 3-5.

_____. "Report of the Secretary." Chronicle, November 1931, p. 666.

_____. "Solving Our Own 'Problem.' " Interracial Review, January 1933, pp. 8-9.

Spalding, David. "The Negro Catholic Congresses, 1889-1894." Catholic Historical Review 55 (October 1969): 337-57.

Teabeau, Hazel McDaniel. "Federated Colored Catholics Make History in New York Convention." Interracial Review, October 1932, p. 195.

_____. "September 5, 6, 7—The Seventh Annual Convention, St. Louis, Missouri." Chronicle, August 1931, pp. 522-23

Turner, Thomas W: "Actual Conditions of Catholic Education Among the Colored Laymen." Catholic Educational Association Bulletin 16 (November 1919): 431-40

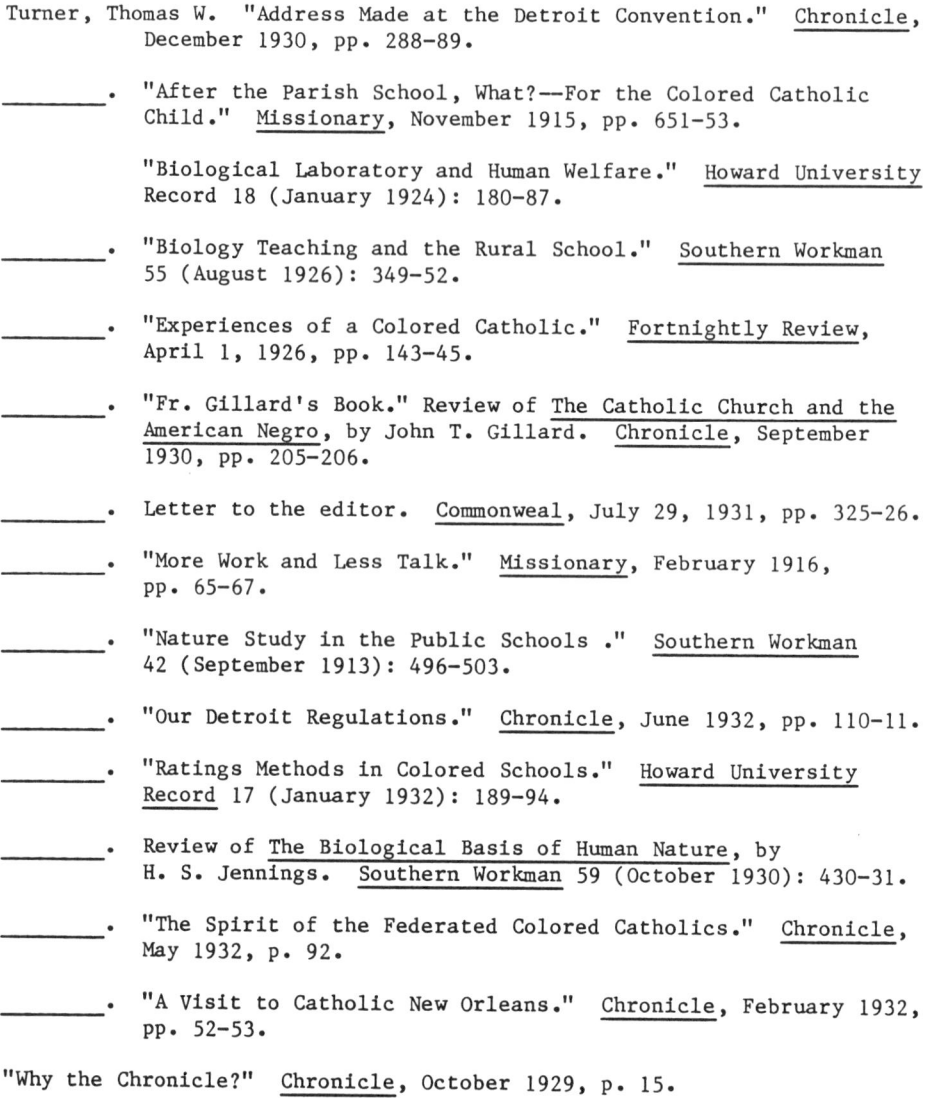

Turner, Thomas W. "Address Made at the Detroit Convention." Chronicle, December 1930, pp. 288-89.

_____. "After the Parish School, What?—For the Colored Catholic Child." Missionary, November 1915, pp. 651-53.

_____. "Biological Laboratory and Human Welfare." Howard University Record 18 (January 1924): 180-87.

_____. "Biology Teaching and the Rural School." Southern Workman 55 (August 1926): 349-52.

_____. "Experiences of a Colored Catholic." Fortnightly Review, April 1, 1926, pp. 143-45.

_____. "Fr. Gillard's Book." Review of The Catholic Church and the American Negro, by John T. Gillard. Chronicle, September 1930, pp. 205-206.

_____. Letter to the editor. Commonweal, July 29, 1931, pp. 325-26.

_____. "More Work and Less Talk." Missionary, February 1916, pp. 65-67.

_____. "Nature Study in the Public Schools." Southern Workman 42 (September 1913): 496-503.

_____. "Our Detroit Regulations." Chronicle, June 1932, pp. 110-11.

_____. "Ratings Methods in Colored Schools." Howard University Record 17 (January 1932): 189-94.

_____. Review of The Biological Basis of Human Nature, by H. S. Jennings. Southern Workman 59 (October 1930): 430-31.

_____. "The Spirit of the Federated Colored Catholics." Chronicle, May 1932, p. 92.

_____. "A Visit to Catholic New Orleans." Chronicle, February 1932, pp. 52-53.

"Why the Chronicle?" Chronicle, October 1929, p. 15.

Woodson, Carter G. Review of The Catholic Church and the American Negro, by John T. Gillard. Journal of Negro History 15 (July 1930): 373-76.

Newspapers

"Catholic Body Ousts Turner, Elects Conrad." Baltimore Afro-American, 17 December 1932.

"Catholic Church Praised by Dr. Turner's Successor." Philadelphia Tribune, 22 December 1932.

"Catholic Editor Talks." St. Louis Courier, 5 January 1933.

"Catholic Head to Disregard "Rump Ouster.' " Baltimore Afro-American, 24 December 1932.

"Catholics Oust Dr. Turner." Baltimore Afro-American, 17 December 1932.

"Chicago Officer Sustains Action." Californian, 30 December 1932.

"Conrad's Former Neighbor Will Support Dr. Turner." Baltimore Afro-American, 7 January 1933.

Cowans, Russell J. "Turner Re-elected to Lead Catholics." Chicago Defender, 6 September-1930.

Daniel, Victor. Letter to the editor. Baltimore Afro-American, 21 November 1936.

"False Publicity Charged to "Professor' by Federation." Pittsburgh Courier, 17 December 1932.

"Gibbons Institute Head Still at "Farmhouse.' " Baltimore Afro-American, January 1934.

"Gibbons Institute Trustee Accused of Insincerity." Baltimore Afro-American, 23 December 1933.

Inman, Cora Grace. "Open Letter to Catholics." Baltimore Afro-American, 25 February 1933.

"Pots, Kettles, Soap and Water Needed in Catholic Controversy." Baltimore Afro-American, 18 February 1933.

Letter to the editor. Baltimore Afro-American, 24 December 1932.

"Markoe Calls D.C. Catholic Meeting a "Cry-Fest.' " Baltimore Afro-American, 21 January 1933.

"Markoe Refers to Dr. Turner as "Kingfish.' " Baltimore Afro American, 4 February 1933.

"Negro Catholics to Meet at St. Louis, Sept. 5-7." New York Age, 1 August 1931.

New York Amsterdam News, 29 July 1931.

New Jersey Monitor, 17 September 1927.

New York Age, 1 August 1931.

"Our Catholics Need Organization." Pittsburgh Courier, 21 January 1933.

"Pa. Catholics Back Turner." Baltimore Afro-American, 7 January 1933.

"Plan Organization of Negro Catholics." New York Amsterdam News, 29 July 1931.

"President Is Vindicated by National Executive Committee of Catholics." Washington Tribune, 13 January 1933.

"Race Prejudice Keeps Colored Priests Out." Baltimore Afro-American, 14 November 1936.

"Rump Catholics Are Denounced in Washington." Baltimore Afro-American, 14 January 1933.

"Would Reopen Gibbons Institute Just to Get State Funds." Baltimore Afro-American, 30 December 1933.

Unpublished Sources

Baltimore, Maryland. Josephite Fathers Archives. John T. Gillard Papers.

Gilligan, Francis J. "The Morality of the Color Line." Ph.D. dissertation, The Catholic University of America, 1928.

Washington, D.C. Moorland-Spingarn Research Center, Howard University. Thomas W. Turner Papers.

Markoe, William M. "An Interracial Role." Memoirs, Milwaukee, 1963.

New York, New York: Woodstock College Library. John LaFarge Papers.

Stanton, Edward S. "John LaFarge's Understanding of the Church, especially in the Area of Race Relations." Ph.D. dissertation, Saint Paul University, 1972.

Steins, Richard H. "The Mission of the Josephites to the Negro in America." Master's thesis, Columbia University, 1966.

Interviews

Davis, Brother Joseph M. National Office for Black Catholics, Washington, D.C. Interview, 17 December 1974.

Heithaus, Rev. Claude. St. Louis University. Interview, June 1973.

McKenna, Rev. Horace B. Washington, D.C. Interview, November 1974.

Markoe, Sister Mary Joseph. St. Louis, Missouri. Interview, June 1973.

Robinson, Mrs. Antoinette. St. Louis, Missouri. Interview, June 1973.

Turner, Dr. Thomas W. Hampton Institute. Interview, March 1973.

_____. Washington, D.C. Interview, December 1974.

Radio Programs

NPR. "Options." Interview with Dr. Thomas W. Turner, April 1974.

The Heritage of American Catholicisim

1. EDWARD R. KANTOWICZ, EDITOR
   MODERN AMERICAN CATHOLICISM, 1900-1965:
   SELECTED HISTORICAL ESSAYS
   New York 1988

2. DOLORES LIPTAK, R.S.M., EDITOR
   A CHURCH OF MANY CULTURES:
   SELECTED HISTORICAL ESSAYS ON ETHNIC AMERICAN CATHOLICISIM
   New York 1988

3. TIMOTHY J. MEAGHER, EDITOR
   URBAN AMERICAN CATHOLICISM:
   THE CULTURE AND IDENTITY OF THE AMERICAN CATHOLIC PEOPLE
   New York 1988

4. BRIAN MITCHELL, EDITOR
   BUILDING THE AMERICAN CATHOLIC CITY:
   PARISHES AND INSTITUTIONS
   New York 1988

5. MICHAEL J. PERKO, S.J., EDITOR
   ENLIGHTENING THE NEXT GENERATION:
   CATHOLICS AND THEIR SCHOOLS, 1830-1980
   New York 1988

6. WILLIAM PORTIER, EDITOR
   THE ENCULTURATION OF AMERICAN CATHOLICISM, 1820-1900:
   SELECTED HISTORICAL ESSAYS
   New York 1988

7. TIMOTHY WALCH, EDITOR
   EARLY AMERICAN CATHOLICISM, 1634-1820:
   SELECTED HISTORICAL ESSAYS
   New York 1988

8. JOSEPH M. WHITE, EDITOR
   THE AMERICAN CATHOLIC RELIGIOUS LIFE:
   SELECTED HISTORICAL ESSAYS
   New York 1988

9. ROBERT F. TRISCO
   BISHOPS AND THEIR PRIESTS IN THE UNITED STATES, 1789-1918
   New York 1988

10. Joseph Agonito
    THE BUILDING OF AN AMERICAN CATHOLIC CHURCH:
    THE EPISCOPACY OF JOHN CARROLL
    New York 1988

11. ROBERT N. BARGER
    JOHN LANCASTER SPALDING:
    CATHOLIC EDUCATOR AND SOCIAL EMISSARY
    New York 1988

12. CHRISTINE M. BOCHEN
    THE JOURNEY TO ROME:
    CONVERSION LITERATURE BY NINETEENTH-CENTURY AMERICAN CATHOLICS
    New York 1988

13. MARTIN J. BREDECK
    IMPERFECT APOSTLES:
    "THE COMMONWEAL" AND THE AMERICAN CATHOLIC LAITY, 1924-1976
    New York 1988

14. JEFFREY M. BURNS
    AMERICAN CATHOLICS AND THE FAMILY CRISIS, 1930-1962:
    THE IDEOLOGICAL AND ORGANIZATIONAL RESPONSE
    New York 1988

15. ALFRED J. EDE
   THE LAY CRUSADE FOR A CHRISTIAN AMERICA:
   A STUDY OF THE AMERICAN FEDERATION OF CATHOLIC SOCIETIES, 1900-1919
   New York 1988

16. JO RENEE FORMICOL
   THE AMERICAN CATHOLIC CHURCH AND ITS ROLE IN THE FORMULATION
   OF UNITED STATES HUMAN RIGHTS FOREIGN POLICY, 1945-1978
   New York 1988

17. THOMAS J. JONAS
   THE DIVIDED MIND:
   AMERICAN CATHOLIC EVANGELSTS IN THE 1890s
   FOREWORD BY MARTIN E. MARTY
   New York 1988

18. MARTIN J. KIRK
   THE SPIRITUALITY OF ISAAC THOMAS HECKER:
   RECONCILING THE AMERICAN CHARACTER AND THE CATHOLIC FAITH
   New York 1988

19. NORLENE M. KUNKEL
   BISHOP BERNARD J. MCQUAID AND CATHOLIC EDUCATION
   New York 1988

20. JAMES M. MCDONNELL
   ORESTES A. BROWNSON AND NINETEENTH-CENTURY CATHOLIC EDUCATION
   New York 1988

21. ELIZABETH MCKEOWN
   WAR AND WELFARE:
   AMERICAN CATHOLICS AND WORLD WAR I
   New York 1988

22. BARBARA MISNER, S. C. S. C.
   "HIGHLY RESPECTABLE AND ACCOMPLISHED LADIES:"
   CATHOLIC WOMEN RELIGIOUS IN AMERICA 1790-1850
   New York 1988

23. BENITA A. MOORE
   Escape into a Labyrinth:
   F. Scott Fitzgerald, Catholic Sensibility, and the American Way
   New York 1988

24. MARILYN WENZKE NICKELS
   Black Catholic Protest
   and the Federated Colored Catholics, 1917-1933:
   Three Perspectives on Racial Justice
   New York 1988

25. DAVID L. SALVATERRA
   American Catholicism and the Intellectual Life, 1880-1920
   New York 1988

26. HELENA SANFILIPPO, R. S. M.
   Inner Wealth and Outward Splendor:
   New England Transcendentalists View the Roman Catholic Church
   New York 1988

27. FAYETTE BREAUX VEVERKA
   "For God and Country:"
   Catholic Schooling in the 1920s
   New York 1988

28. TIMOTHY WALCH
   The Diverse Origins of American Catholic Education:
   Chicago, Milwaukee, and the Nation
   New York 1988